# Medieval Manuscripts and their Provenance

# MEDIEVAL MANUSCRIPTS AND THEIR PROVENANCE

Essays in Honour of Barbara A. Shailor

Edited by
A. S. G. Edwards

D. S. BREWER

First published 2024
D. S. Brewer, Cambridge

ISBN 978 1 84384 723 6

D. S. Brewer is an imprint of Boydell & Brewer Ltd
PO Box 9, Woodbridge, Suffolk IP12 3DF, UK
and of Boydell & Brewer Inc.
668 Mt Hope Avenue, Rochester, NY 14620–2731, USA
website: www.boydellandbrewer.com

A CIP catalogue record for this book is available
from the British Library

# Contents

# Illustrations
~

Full credit details are provided in the captions to the images in the text. The
editor, contributors and publisher are grateful to all the institutions and persons
for permission to reproduce the materials in which they hold copyright. Every
effort has been made to trace the copyright holders; apologies are offered
for any omission, and the publisher will be pleased to add any necessary
acknowledgement in subsequent editions.

# CONTRIBUTORS

~

JULIA BOFFEY is Professor Emerita of Medieval Studies in the Department of English at Queen Mary, University of London. She works on the production, transmission and reception of late medieval and early sixteenth-century literature in Britain, especially poetry, and on late medieval literary culture more generally. She has recently edited (with A. S. G. Edwards) volume 3 of *The Oxford History of Poetry in English*, on the fifteenth century, and is currently co-editing a collaborative new edition of the works of Chaucer for Cambridge University Press.

LISA FAGIN DAVIS received her PhD in Medieval Studies from Yale University in 1993. In addition to authoring numerous publications in the field of manuscript studies, she has catalogued multiple medieval manuscript collections across North America. She has taught Latin palaeography at Yale University and Rare Book School, and regularly teaches an introduction to Manuscript Studies at the Simmons University School of Library and Information Science. Davis was elected to the Comité international de paléographie latine in 2019 and has served as Executive Director of the Medieval Academy of America since 2013.

CHRISTOPHER DE HAMEL is a Fellow of Corpus Christi College, Cambridge, where he was formerly librarian. He was previously responsible for sales of medieval manuscripts at Sotheby's. His best-known book, of many, is *Meetings with Remarkable Manuscripts* (2016), winner of the Wolfson Prize for History.

CONSUELO DUTSCHKE completed her PhD at UCLA, with a dissertation on the manuscripts of Marco Polo's Travels. She has published catalogues of the medieval and Renaissance manuscripts in the Claremont Colleges (1986) and in the Huntington Library (1989). Subsequently she was involved in establishing the Digital Scriptorium, an online database of manuscripts in various North American collections.

A. S. G. EDWARDS has taught medieval and early modern literature, bibliography and textual criticism at various universities in North America and the United Kingdom. He is a Guggenheim Fellow, a Fellow of the Society of Antiquaries and a Fellow of the English Association.

ANDREW KRAEBEL is Associate Professor of English at Trinity University, a liberal arts college in San Antonio, Texas. His monograph, *Biblical Commentary and Translation in Later Medieval England: Experiments in Interpretation* (2020), won the Ecclesiastical History Society's book prize, and he is now at work on editions and translations of texts by the English mystic Richard Rolle.

MICHAEL P. KUCZYNSKI holds the Pierce Butler Chair in English in the School of Liberal Arts, Tulane University, New Orleans. He has published widely on medieval manuscripts and early printed books, especially psalters. His two-volume critical edition of a glossed Wycliffite psalter was published in 2019 by the Early English Text Society. He is completing a book-length study of the *Epistola Lentuli*, a Psalms-based medieval forgery that purports to describe the physical appearance and demeanour of Jesus Christ.

WILLIAM P. STONEMAN was until his retirement curator of early books and manuscripts at Harvard University's Houghton Library; he had previously served as Florence Fearrington Librarian of Houghton Library and as Scheide Librarian of Princeton University. His research interests include the role of private collections in building public libraries. Recent articles by him include: 'The Role of Giuseppe Martini in Building the Medieval and Renaissance Manuscript Collections now in North American Libraries,' in Edoardo Barbieri, ed., *Da Lucca a New York a Lugano: Giuseppe Martini Libraio tra Otto e Novecento*. Biblioteca di Bibliografia, Documents and Studies in Book and Library History CCVI (2017), pp. 65–80 and 'North American Collection-Building: Gathering Monastic Books from Long Ago and Far Away,' in Cristina Dondi, Dorit Raines & Richard Sharpe, eds, *How the Secularization of Religious Houses Transformed the Libraries of Europe, 16th–19th Centuries*, Bibliologia 63 (2022), pp. 467–86.

ROGER WIECK is the Melvin R. Seiden Curator and department head of medieval and Renaissance manuscripts at the Morgan Library & Museum, where he has worked since 1989. His books include *The Medieval Calendar: Locating Time in the Middle Ages* (2017) and *Miracles in Miniature: The Art of the Master of Claude de France* (2014).

# Acknowledgements

~

I wish to express my thanks to all the contributors for the promptness of their contributions and for their patience throughout the editorial processes. I would also like to thank the anonymous reader for D. S. Brewer for helpful comments. Not for the first time I have the pleasure of thanking Caroline Palmer for her support and forbearance. For particular assistance at different stages of the development of this book I am grateful to Katherine Hindley and Susan Gibbons.

# ABBREVIATIONS

~

| | |
|---|---|
| Beinecke | New Haven, CT, Beinecke Rare Books and Manuscript Library |
| BL | London, British Library |
| BNF | Paris, Bibliothèque Nationale de France |
| BodL | Oxford, Bodleian Library |
| CUL | Cambridge University Library |
| de Ricci & Wilson | Seymour de Ricci and W. J. Wilson, *Census of Medieval and Renaissance Manuscripts in the United States and Canada*, 3 vols (New York: W. H. Wilson, 1935–40) |
| ed./eds | edited by |
| EETS | Early English Text Society |
| Faye & Bond | C. U. Faye & W. H. Bond, *Supplement to the Census of Medieval and Renaissance Manuscripts in the United States and Canada* (New York: Bibliographical Society of America, 1962) |
| MS(S) | manuscript(s) |
| *ODNB* | Colin Matthew & Brian Harrison, eds, *The Oxford Dictionary of National Biography* (Oxford: Oxford University Press, 2004), continued online |
| STC | *A Short-Title Catalogue of Books Printed in England, Scotland & Ireland and of English Books Printed Abroad 1475–1640*, first compiled by A. W. Pollard & G. R. Redgrave, 2nd edn, revised and enlarged, begun by W. A. Jackson & F. S. Ferguson, completed by Katharine F. Pantzer, 3 vols (London: Bibliographical Society, 1976–91) |
| vols | volumes |

# Barbara Ann Shailor

~

## *A. S. G. Edwards*

Barbara Ann Shailor was born on 27 January 1948. She grew up in Hamden, Connecticut, before entering Wilson College in Chambersburg, Pennsylvania in 1965, where she read classics, graduating in 1969. The decision to attend this private women's college was to shape the course of her career. There she met Cora Lutz, a distinguished classicist.[1] Lutz was already engaged in cataloguing the medieval and Renaissance manuscripts of the Beinecke Library in New Haven and she hired Barbara as a summer assistant. After Lutz's retirement from Wilson College in 1969, Barbara continued to assist her until she retired from the cataloguing project in 1975.[2] Barbara then took over the cataloguing of the Beinecke manuscripts. By this time she had completed both an MA (1971) and a PhD on 'The scriptorium of San Pedro de Berlangas' (1975), both in the Classics Department at the University of Cincinnati. Cincinnati provided an environment that must have been especially congenial to her interests. It is unique among American universities in having an endowed chair in palaeography, the John Miller Burnam chair of Latin and Romance Palaeography. Barbara was supervised by the then-incumbent, Carl Trahman.[3]

---

[1] There are various accounts and obituaries of Lutz. The most relevant are Marjorie G. Wynne, 'Cora Elizabeth Lutz,' *Yale University Library Gazette*, 60 (1985), 9–10 and Deanna Delmar Evans, 'Cora Elizabeth Lutz (1906–1985) *Magistra Egregii*,' in Jane Chance, ed., *Women Medievalists and the Academy* (Madison, WI, 2005), pp. 671–82.

[2] The first volume of her *Catalogue of Medieval and Renaissance Manuscripts in the Beinecke Library* is dedicated 'For Cora E. Lutz,' and Barbara discusses Lutz's early work on the Beinecke manuscripts on p. xviii there.

[3] For some account of the University of Cincinnati chair in palaeography, see R. H. Rouse, 'Latin Paleography and Manuscript Studies in North America,' in *Un Secolo di Paleografica e Diplomatica (1887–1986)*, (Rome Gela editrice in Roma, 1988), pp. 307–27 (at 309–10, 317–18).

On the completion of her doctorate Barbara joined the classics department at Bucknell University. While engaged in other research, teaching and growing administrative responsibilities there she continued to commute to New Haven to work on the several volumes of the Beinecke catalogue, all of which were completed during her time at Bucknell.

In 1996 Barbara left Bucknell to become professor of classics and dean at Douglass College, the undergraduate women's college of Rutgers University. In 2001 she was appointed director of the Beinecke Rare Book and Manuscript Library at Yale. In July 2003 she became deputy provost for the arts at Yale, a position that she held until her retirement in December 2012. She has continued as senior lecturer in the Classics Department and as senior scholar at Yale.

While she has assumed steadily greater administrative responsibility in the academic world Barbara has produced substantial and significant scholarship. The first volume of her *Catalogue of Medieval and Renaissance Manuscripts in the Rare Book and Manuscript Library Yale University* was published in 1984. It covered manuscripts 1–250. A second volume (manuscripts 251–500) appeared in 1987 and the catalogue of the Marston manuscripts in 1992.

In all, these three volumes described nearly eight hundred manuscripts. They gave, for the first time, bibliographical control over significant parts of the largest collections of medieval and Renaissance manuscripts in the United States.[4] The manuscripts catalogued range in date from the eighth to the eighteenth centuries and are written in languages that include Latin, Greek, Austrian, Italian, Spanish, French, English (including Old and Middle), Flemish German, Armenian, Swabian and Yugoslavian. Nothing like it had been attempted before in America in such detail and with such scope.

The only undertaking comparable at that time in scale was Neil Ker's *Medieval Manuscripts in British Libraries*, the first volume of which had appeared in 1969.[5] Barbara acknowledges the example and influence of Ker's work in the first volume of her catalogue. Her entries follow Ker in their clear and consistent form: heading, including shelf mark and date, list of contents, physical description, including material(s), scribe(s) and script(s), categories of decoration and illustration, binding, provenance and bibliography. In sum, the descriptions provide a clearly navigable, detailed analysis of all relevant aspects of the structure and content of a manuscript.

---

[4]   The Mellon collection of alchemical manuscripts was catalogued separately by others. There is no published catalogue of the manuscripts in the Osborn collection.

[5]   'For the Beinecke Catalogue we have adopted an entry similar to that used by the late N. R. Ker in his multi-volume *Medieval Manuscripts in British Libraries* (p. xviii).

Barbara's catalogues were at the vanguard of a new phase in the publishing of detailed descriptions of the medieval manuscripts in some of the major American research libraries, including the Huntington Library in San Marino, California, the Newberry Library in Chicago, Harvard's Houghton Library, the Claremont Colleges and UCLA libraries in California and the Walters Library in Baltimore. A driving force behind much of this work was Richard H. Rouse (1933–2022) of the History Department at UCLA, who was a member of the Advisory Board for Barbara's catalogues and who was involved in the preparation of most of the other catalogues mentioned above. Some of this work, including Barbara's own, was supported by the National Endowment for the Humanities. Her own research for all three volumes on the Beinecke manuscripts received the first in a series of grants from the NEH in 1982 and she concludes her Introduction to the volume on the Marston manuscripts with an acknowledgement of their support.

The Beinecke catalogues formed part of the basis for Barbara's best known and most influential work, *The Medieval Book*. This originally appeared as a catalogue for an exhibition that she curated, held at the Beinecke Library in 1988, to accompany the twenty-fifth anniversary of its opening. The catalogue was subsequently revised and reprinted by the University of Toronto Press in 1990 as part of the Medieval Academy Reprints for Teaching series and has been regularly reprinted since. It has become a standard tool for the study of and teaching about medieval manuscripts.

Beyond her central achievements in her three Beinecke catalogues and *The Medieval Book* Barbara has pursued other scholarly avenues of enquiry. The work deriving from her doctoral dissertation has established her as an authority on Spanish and Visigothic manuscripts, as the list of her publications shows. For some years she has been examining the career of the notorious American breaker of manuscripts Otto Ege (1888–1951), whose activities have come to attract much interest and who is a crucial figure in the emerging discipline of fragmentology. Her interest in Ege is also related to her exploration of the fruitful implications of computer technology in linking leaves from the same manuscripts that have been broken up for commercial advantage, another growing field of academic study in which she was also a pioneer.

Barbara has also given much service to medieval studies in general and to the study of palaeography in various administrative capacities. She continues to be a member of the Advisory Board for the journal *Manuscripta*. She was elected a Fellow of the Medieval Academy in 2006 and served as its Treasurer between 2002 and 2007 and as a member of the John Nicholas Brown Prizes committee between 2014 and 2016. She has also been an active member of the Comité Internationale de la Paléographie Latine, to which she was elected in 2000, and, with Consuelo Dutschke, edited the volume of its Twentieth Colloquium published in 2022. She has held fellowships or grants from the Mellon Foundation, National Endowment for the Humanities and the American Council of Learned Societies. Barbara has been president of the Bibliographical Society of America (2018–22), a member of the Council of the Grolier Club and a trustee of the Samuel H. Kress Foundation. Currently she is president of the American Trust for the British Library and continues to regularly cross the Atlantic in its service.

Amid her myriad academic, professional and scholarly responsibilities Barbara has contrived to retain a central focus on teaching. Since administrative retirement from Yale in 2012 she has continued to teach courses at the Beinecke Library and at the Rare Book School at the University of Virginia in palaeography and aspects of manuscript studies. Many graduate students at Yale and elsewhere have profited from her expertise and her active interest in their research, which has often extended considerably beyond the classroom to provide astute mentoring and professional guidance. A number of former students who currently hold positions in the field of medieval studies have profited from her advice and direction.

It would be an inexcusable oversight in any account of Barbara's life and work to fail to mention Harry. Barbara married Harry Wallace Blair on December 26, 1981. Few distinguished political scientists can have acquired such an intimate knowledge of medieval manuscripts. In spite of the considerable demands of his own career Harry has been a diligent and noticeably alert attender at conferences with Barbara. Many who have come to know Barbara have been able to relish the unforeseen bonus of Harry's own friendship.

Such a summary of Barbara's career and achievements conveys little of the warmth and energy of her personality and the constant enthusiasm she shows for both scholarship and friendship. I first met her at a party in a bedroom in a dorm in Kalamazoo in the late 1970s at one of the frenzied annual Medieval Congresses at Western Michigan University. It was an occasion that serves as a reminder that for Barbara scholarship is inseparable from friendship and sociability. Her daunting energy and her zest for life have remained undimmed by the passage of time.

# The Publications of Barbara A. Shailor

*A. S. G. Edwards*

The list below is of Barbara Shailor's scholarly publications. It is appropriate to also note here her published contributions in the service of the Medieval Academy of America, particularly the 'Report of the Treasurer,' *Speculum*, 77 (2002), 1036–37; *Speculum*, 78 (2003), 1037–38; *Speculum*, 79 (2004), 875–76; *Speculum*, 80 (2005), 1026–27; *Speculum*, 81 (2006), 962–63; *Speculum*, 82 (2007), 800–01 and 'The John Nicholas Brown Prizes'; *Speculum*, 89 (2014), 867 (with Steven F. Kruger, Paolo Squatrati); *Speculum*, 90 (2015), 892 (with Meredith Lilich, Steven F. Kruger); *Speculum*, 91 (2016), 886 (with Meredith Lilich, David Ninenberg).

'The Scriptorium of San Pedro de Berlangas.' *Manuscripta*, 21 (1977), 23–24.

'Madrid, Academia de la Historia, Códice 76: Berlangas or Cardeña.' *Manuscripta*, 22 (1978), 19–20.

[Entries for Beinecke Library MSS 442, Marston 151, Marston 158, 237, 335, 84] in Walter Cahn & James Marrow, eds, 'Medieval and Renaissance Manuscripts at Yale: A Selection.' *Yale University Library Gazette*, 52 (1978), 179, 181–82, 184–85, 199–200, 228–29, 239–40.

'Corrections and Additions to the Catalogue of Visigothic Manuscripts.' *Scriptorium*, 32 (1978), 310–12.

'The Scriptorium of San Pedro de Cardeña.' *Bulletin of the John Rylands Library of the University of Manchester*, 61 (1979), 444–73.

'Another Fragment of Beneventan Script.' *Manuscripta*, 25 (1981), 49–50.

'Beinecke Library, Yale University: Recent Acquisitions.' *Scriptorium*, 35 (1981), 95–101.

'A New Manuscript of Nicolaus de Lyra.' *Yale University Library Gazette*, 58 (1983), 9–16.

*Catalogue of Medieval and Renaissance Manuscripts in the Beinecke Library, Volume I: Manuscripts 1–250.* Binghamton, NY: Medieval & Renaissance Texts and Studies, 1984. Pp. xxii, 420, 32 plates.

'Beinecke Library, Yale University: An Unpublished Vitae Sanctorum.' In David F. Bright & Edwin S. Ramage, eds, *Classical Texts and Their*

*Traditions: Studies in Honor of C. R. Trahman*. Chico, CA: Scholars Press, 1984, pp. 13–24. (with Dianne L. Creasy)

'The Scriptorium of San Sahagún: A Period of Transition.' In Bernard F. Reilly, ed., *Santiago, Saint-Denis, and Saint Peter. The Reception of the Roman liturgy in León-Castile in 1080*. New York: Fordham University Press, 1985, pp. 41–61.

'The Recovery of a fifteenth-century schoolmaster's book: Beinecke MS 3.' *Yale University Library Gazette*, 60 (1985), 11–31. (with Linda E. Voigts)

*Catalogue of Medieval and Renaissance Manuscripts in the Beinecke Library, Volume II: Manuscripts 251–500*. Binghamton, NY: Medieval & Renaissance Texts and Studies, 1987. Pp. xiv, 578, 64 plates.

Review of *Hill Monastic Manuscript Library, Saint John's University: Descriptive Inventories of Manuscripts Microfilmed for the Hill Monastic Manuscript Library (Austrian Libraries)*. *Library Quarterly*, 58 (1988), 398–400.

*The Medieval Book: Catalogue of an Exhibition at the Beinecke Rare Book & Manuscript Library Yale University*. New Haven, CT: Yale University Library, 1988. Subsequently published as *The Medieval Book* (Toronto: University of Toronto Press in Association with the Medieval Academy of America, 1991). Pp. 115.

*A Spanish apocalypse: the Morgan Beatus manuscript*. Introduction and commentaries by John Williams; codicological analysis by Barbara A. Shailor. New York: G. Braziller in association with the Pierpont Morgan Library, 1991. Spanish translation *El Beato de san Miguel de Escalada. Manuscrito 644 de la Pierpont Morgan Library de Nueva York*. Madrid: Editorial Casariego, 1991.

'Marginalia [on Beinecke Library MS Beinecke 255].' *Yale University Library Gazette*, 65 (1991), 190–91. (with A. S. G. Edwards)

'The Beatus of Burgos de Osma: A Palaeographical and Codicological Study.' In *Beato de Liébana del Burgo de Osma Facsimile*. Valencia: Vicent Garcia, 1992, pp. 29–52. (with José Arranz, John William, Eugenio Romero Pose, Serafín Moralejo Álvarez)

*Catalogue of Medieval and Renaissance Manuscripts in the Beinecke Library, Volume III: The Marston Collection*. Binghamton, NY: Medieval & Renaissance Texts and Studies, 1992. Pp. xxxii, 643, 64 plates.

'Art, Palaeography and Manuscripts.' In William Kibler & Grover A. Zinn, eds, *Medieval France: An Encyclopedia*. New York: Garland, 1995, pp. 691–95

'A Cataloguer's View.' In Stephen G. Nichols & Siegfried Wenzel, eds, *The Whole Book*. Ann Arbor: University of Michigan Press, 1996, pp. 153–67.

'Adventure and Art.' In Paul Needham & Michael Joseph, eds, *Adventure and Art: the first one hundred years of printing: an exhibition of books, woodcuts, and illustrated leaves printed between 1455 and 1555*. Curated by Barbara A.

Shailor, Leonard Hansen, Michael Joseph. New Brunswick, N.J.: Rutgers University Libraries, [1998], pp. 9–19.

*Apocalipsis de San Juan.* Valencia: Scriptorium, 2000–01. (With John Williams, L. G. Freeman)

[Contribution to] Bruce Ferrini, *Important Illuminated Manuscripts.* Akron, OH: Les Enluminures, 2000.

'Introduction.' Stephen Parks, ed., *The Beinecke Library of Yale University.* New Haven, CT: Beinecke Rare Book & Manuscript Library: Yale University, 2001, pp. 9–26.

Review of Rose Walker, *Views of Transition: Liturgy and Illumination in Medieval Spain. Speculum,* 77 (2002), 647–50.

'Otto Ege: His Manuscript Fragment Collection and the Opportunities Presented by Electronic Technology.' *Journal of the Rutgers University Libraries,* 60 (2003), 1–22.

Review of Millares Carlo, *Corpus de códices visigóticos. Speculum,* 78 (2003), 1346–48.

Review of John Williams, The Illustrated Beatus: A Corpus of the Illustrations of the Commentary on the Apocalypse, vols 4–5. *Manuscripta,* 47–48 (2004), 164–67.

'Otto Ege: Portfolios vs. Leaves.' *Manuscripta,* 53 (2009), 13–27.

'The Yale Gower, Beinecke Osborn MS fa. 1: Palaeographical, Codicological, Technical Challenges.' In R. F. Yeager & Ana Saez-Hidalgo, eds, *John Gower in England and Iberia: Manuscripts, Influences, Reception.* Cambridge: D. S. Brewer, 2014, pp. 77–88.

'The Monastic Scriptorium.' In Jeffrey F. Hamburger, William P. Stoneman, Anne-Marie Eze, Lisa Fagin Davis & Nancy Netzer, eds, *Beyond Words: Illuminated Manuscripts in Boston Collections.* Boston, MA: McMullen Museum of Art, Boston College, 2016, p. 25.

'Rufinus, *Summa decretorum*: Two New Twelfth-Century Fragments.' *Florilegium,* 35 (2018), 69–91. (with Zachary J. Waters)

Ed., *Scribes and the Presentation of Texts (from Antiquity to c. 1550). Proceedings of the 20th Colloquium of the Comité internationale de la paléographie latine.* Turnhout: Brepols, 2021. Pp. 602. (with Consuelo Dutschke, Kyle Conrau-Lewis, Kristen Hardman, Alexander Perla)

Appendix to Michel Huglo†, *'Musica ex numeris.'* Graeme Boone, ed., *Music in the Carolingian World: Witnesses to a Metadiscipline: Essays in Honor of Charles M. Atkinson.* Turnhout: Brepols, 2023, pp. 121–24.

# Introduction

∿

## A. S. G. Edwards

Throughout her long and distinguished career, a consistent concern in Barbara Shailor's research has been provenance. Her catalogues of the Beinecke manuscripts set new standards in their careful tracking of manuscripts from owner to owner and from sale to sale. While she has made other important contributions to this aspect of manuscript study, her interest in the reception history of medieval and renaissance manuscripts has seemed an appropriate focus for the essays in the present volume in her honour.

In the opening essay Andrew Kraebel, a medievalist who was taught by Barbara Shailor, unusually extends the implications of provenance beyond the bibliophilic to the textual. His discussion of the early circulation of versions of Richard Rolle's *Melos amoris* in the later fourteenth and fifteenth centuries demonstrates how the transmission of a work is an aspect of provenance as it moves through different scribal environments that are, in their turn, shaped by different religious communities. He notes, for example, how Rolle's *Melos* became, over time, a specifically Carthusian work. The fact testifies to the ways in which his work retained an enthusiastic readership and energetic textual tradition more than a century after Rolle's death in 1349.

Christopher de Hamel is able to connect several great medieval bibliophiles through an examination of a single fourteenth-century leaf from a manuscript of the *Somnium viridarii* that was recently sold at auction. He shows how the manuscript of which it was once a part passed from Charles V of France to John, duke of Bedford and then to Humfrey, duke of Gloucester. His analysis of the material evidence that can be gleaned from close examination of this fragment together with that afforded by informed study of extant provenance records reveals how, in expert hands, a significant provenance history can be reconstructed.

Fragments are also of crucial importance to Roger Wieck's argument in his article 'Kissing the Paten.' In it he draws on his experience as both a scholar and a collector to show how the fortuitous acquisition of fragments can serve to elucidate problems of iconography. His own recent purchase of a cutting provides the crucial link in his survey of depictions of paten kissing in funeral and memorial masses, a practice that, as he notes, was still current in the twentieth century.

Fragments are yet again the focus of Lisa Fagin Davis's study, this time in wider historical perspectives, as she considers the career of Otto F. Ege. Ege has achieved posthumous notoriety as a breaker-up of manuscripts. His selling of individual leaves, either separately or in his various portfolios, has left posterity with enormous problems of identification. Davis indicates the great potential of modern computer technology to reunite, at least virtually, what Ege had put asunder physically. Her interest in both such technology and in fragments echoes Barbara Shailor's own engagement with these still-emerging areas of modern manuscript study.

Consuelo Dutschke's account of another twentieth-century American collector, the enigmatic Mark Lansburgh, also involves fragments. Lansburgh collected them as well as complete manuscripts (and some of the manuscripts that he owned were subsequently broken up). The complexities of the processes of both his acquisition and (crucially) dispersal of these materials over nearly half a century pose considerable challenges, as Dutschke demonstrates. Her paper is a pioneering study of a complex problem in the history of modern manuscript collecting.

Two papers are concerned with the histories of individual manuscripts. Julia Boffey tracks the journey of Harvard, Houghton Library MS Eng 766, a copy of part of Robert Fabyan's *New Chronicles of England and France*, completed in the early sixteenth century. The manuscript evidently served as setting copy for Pynson's first printed edition in 1516. It was subsequently sold in London in the mid-seventeenth century. Its purchaser, Samuel Lee, then brought it to New England, where it became the first early modern manuscript to reach North America. Its ownership history in the new world is carefully traced down to its acquisition by Harvard in 1945.

Michael P. Kuczynski examines another manuscript that crossed the Atlantic, albeit much later. Washington, DC, Folger Shakespeare Library MS V.a.354 is the only copy of the early modern English Macro Plays. It is a collection of considerable significance to students of early drama. Kuczynski traces what can be established about the history of the manuscript as it passed through the hands of the antiquaries, Cox Macro and Hudson Gurney, before reaching the Folger Library in 1936. He also explores the history of scholarly engagement with the manuscript from Thomas Sharp's engraving of an illustration from it in 1825, through the involvement of two distinctly dubious figures, John Payne Collier and John Stephen Farmer, to the editorial work by two equally tireless but very different scholars, F. J. Furnivall and A. W. Pollard, with the improbable assistance of Karl Marx's daughter, Eleanor.

Two other articles are concerned with twentieth century collectors of medieval manuscripts, one in America, one in England. William P. Stoneman traces the activities of Edward Duff Balken of Pittsburgh and provides the first full record of those manuscripts that passed through his hands. This is a notable effort to rediscover an almost wholly overlooked collector who has hitherto found no place in histories of modern American manuscript ownership. Stoneman establishes Balken's identity and status as a collector, particularly through his prominent, if unidentified, presence in Maggs' important 1930 catalogue, *The Art of Writing*.

A. S. G. Edwards attempts to trace those medieval and Renaissance manuscripts owned in a brief but intense period of collecting by H. Harvey Frost. He links his acquisitions in part to the famous 1931 Quaritch catalogue of *Illuminated and Other Manuscripts* and attempts to trace the fates of other medieval manuscripts in that catalogue as well as identifying other medieval and Renaissance manuscripts that Frost obtained. The article sheds some light on the post-World War II trade in such manuscripts and their sometimes notable increases in price over time.

These essays all demonstrate the fruitful potential of the study of provenance, in its historical, art historical, textual, bibliographical and biographical aspects. And in doing so they confirm the value of Barbara Shailor's own contributions to this important field of study. All the contributors hope that these essays will serve as a proper recognition of at least some of the scholarly achievements of one of the most important medieval manuscript scholars of her time.

# 1

## Text and Provenance:
## The Early Transmission of Richard Rolle's
### *Melos Amoris*

~

*Andrew Kraebel*

Abrogare, id est delere, destruere
Almiphona, id est uox sacrata
Alare, id est spirare
Amenus, id est alliciens ad amandum
Anelare, id est anxiari
Anfractus, id est circumfraccio
Angariare, id est cogere, compellere

So begins what seems likely to have been a substantial glossary of 'uerba difficilia per diuersos doctores exposita,' now preserved uniquely in CUL MS Dd.5.64, part 2, fol. 84$^{r-v}$.[1] Most of the surviving entries in this glossary are brief, and only one requires more than a single line: 'Celeuma, id est clamor nautarum in naufragio propter celum turbatum, uel propter perturbacionem uel puritatem aeris.' The scribe provides thirteen definitions on the recto and twenty-seven more on the verso, with a catchword ('degener') indicating the entry with which the next quire should begin. That new quire, however, and anything that came after it, were apparently discarded when this late fourteenth-century booklet was bound together with the rest of the present manuscript. The glossary was not then deemed to be of interest in itself, and it survives at all only because its opening was copied on the same leaf as the end of the preceding text.

The glossary in Dd.5.64 was assembled to help readers of a work the scribe calls 'Melum R. Heremite,' better known today as the *Melos Amoris* of Richard Rolle (d. 1349), the 'Hermit of Hampole,' and arguably 'the

---

[1]  Cf. Ralph Hanna, *The English Manuscripts of Richard Rolle: A Descriptive Catalogue* (Exeter, 2010), pp. 25–27.

most prominent English spiritual figure of the later Middle Ages.'[2] In some respects, the careful assembly and subsequent scrapping of this glossary fittingly reflect the fate of *Melos* among medieval readers. Unlike other pieces in Rolle's extensive corpus, such as *Incendium Amoris* or especially *Emendatio Vitae*, *Melos* seems only ever to have appealed to a self-selecting few, those already devoted to Rolle's brand of ecstatic piety and searching for more material to elaborate on – and nurture them as they pursued – his particular ideas of the contemplative life. And not just more material, but also more advanced and more challenging. In addition to the insistent alliteration for which it is best known (hence Hanna calls it '*Kunstprosa* if there ever were such'), the mannerism of *Melos* makes for difficult reading, not on the level of its grammar so much as the suggestiveness (or imprecision) of its phrasing.[3] Perhaps by design, perhaps to meet the perceived needs of intimates and other reclusive correspondents in the hermit's lifetime, in this text one often has to know what Rolle is talking about to understand what Rolle is talking about. A glossary would help, and the sort of enthusiast who wanted to read *Melos* can easily be imagined as motivated to assemble what remains in CUL Dd.5.64 – even if very few seem ever to have been interested in reading the work at all.

Though apparent in the manuscript record, the interest of these devotees has been unfortunately obscured in recent scholarship, owing in large part to the handling of the text by its editor, E. J. F. Arnould.[4] By making this unusual text available, Arnould performed a considerable service, but the usefulness of his work is limited by his selective presentation of manuscript evidence. Reflecting what one reviewer described as undue deference to 'the authority of Bédier,' Arnould identified a single manuscript with a 'more satisfactory' form of the text, and he routinely favoured its readings even when all other witnesses provided seemingly superior variants.[5] His discussion of the manuscripts of *Melos* is likewise minimal, and his account

---

[2]   Thus Ralph Hanna, 'Richard Rolle's *Incendium Amoris*: A Prospectus for a Future Editor,' *Journal of Medieval Latin*, 26 (2016), 227–61 (at p. 227).

[3]   Ralph Hanna, 'Making Miscellaneous Manuscripts in Fifteenth-Century England: The Case of Sloane 2275,' *Journal of the Early Book Society*, 18 (2015), 1–28 (at p. 3).

[4]   E. J. F. Arnould, ed., *The Melos Amoris of Richard Rolle of Hampole* (Oxford, 1957); reprinted in Arnould, ed., *Le chant d'amour*, translated by the nuns of Wisques, with an introduction and notes by François Vandenbroucke, 2 vols (Paris, 1971). Arnould's edition is the basis for Andrew Albin's virtuosically alliterative translation: *Richard Rolle's Melody of Love* (Toronto, 2018).

[5]   Review by Edmund (then Eric) Colledge in *Medium Ævum*, 27 (1958), 203–04 (at p. 203), with the second phrase from Arnould, ed., *Melos*, p. lxxxv. Colledge's

of the work's transmission is brief and inconclusive, with a sparing and (as we will see) error-prone apparatus making further investigation difficult.

The present essay attempts to make up for some of these shortcomings, exploring the transmission of *Melos* and the provenance of its manuscripts in greater detail, and thereby recovering more fully the considerable dedication, the efforts with the text, on the part of the scribes responsible for the copies that survive today. After reviewing the evidence on which the text can be established, most of the chapter is devoted to presenting the results of my collation of a significant portion of the text, the relationships among the manuscripts that this sample reveals, and, finally, some of the major trends in the early transmission and ownership of *Melos*.

I am very pleased to be able to offer this work as an expression of gratitude to, and admiration for, Barbara Shailor. In her reflections on the need for cataloguers to 'describe ... the relationship between the structure of a codex and its texts,' and to 'speculate on the apparent principle or principles' that guided 'the audiences or individuals that produced, read and used' such codices, Professor Shailor describes an approach balancing attention to texts and to the books that bear them – all of which is utterly crucial if we are to understand 'manuscripts and their cultural context.'[6] Her conclusions are wise and still timely, and this essay demonstrates some of their wider relevance.

## Evidence

*Melos Amoris* survives completely or near-completely in eight manuscripts, while two further copies seem once to have provided full texts. All but one of these manuscripts were known to Arnould, but I have assigned them new sigla.[7] The full(ish) copies are:

---

account is echoed by Ralph Hanna, 'The Oldest Manuscript of Richard Rolle's Writings,' *Scriptorium*, 70 (2016), 105–15 (at p. 111).

[6] Barbara A. Shailor, 'A Cataloguer's View,' in Stephen Nichols & Siegfried Wenzel, eds, *The Whole Book: Cultural Perspectives on the Medieval Miscellany* (Ann Arbor, MI, 1996), pp. 153–67 (at pp. 165–67).

[7] A necessary starting point for all work on Rollean manuscripts is now A. I. Doyle & Ralph Hanna, *Hope Allen's Writings Ascribed to Richard Rolle: A Corrected List of Copies* (Turnhout, 2019). For recent descriptions and discussions, see: **B** Andrew Kraebel, 'Rolle Reassembled: Booklet Production, Single-Author Anthologies and the Making of Bodley 861,' *Speculum*, 94 (2019), 959–1005; **D** Marvin L. Colker, *Descriptive Catalogue of the Medieval and Renaissance Latin Manuscripts, Trinity College, Dublin*, 2 vols (Aldershot, 1991), I, 273–76; A. I. Doyle, 'English Carthusian Books Not Yet Linked with a Charterhouse,' in Toby Barnard et al., eds, *A Miracle of Learning: Studies in Manuscripts and Irish Learning. Essays in Honour*

| Sigla | Shelfmarks, folios and dates | Arnould's sigla |
|:---:|:---|:---:|
| B | BodL, MS Bodley 861, fols 51–81 (1409) | O$^1$ |
| D | Dublin, Trinity College, MS 159, fols 1–106 (s. xv/xvi) | D |
| H | Hereford, Cathedral Library, MS O.viii.1, fols 111–144 (*after* 1409) | H |
| J | Cambridge, St John's College, MS B.1 (23), fols 41–161 (s. xiv/xv) | C$^1$ |
| L | Lincoln, Cathedral Library, MS 209, fols 105–214$^v$ (s. xiv/xv) | Lin |
| S | BL, MS Sloane 2275, fols 1–52 (s. xv med.) | L |
| V | Uppsala, Universitetsbiblioteket, MS C.1, fols 34–80$^v$ (*after* 1421) | U |
| X | Oxford, Corpus Christi College, MS 193, fols 206$^v$–251$^v$ (s. xiv/xv) | O$^2$ |

There are two fragmentary texts:

| | | |
|:---:|:---|:---:|
| B2 | BodL, MS Bodley 647, fols i–ii$^v$, 108$^r$–109$^v$ (s. xiv med.) | — |
| L2 | Oxford, Lincoln College, MS lat. 89, fols 1–25$^v$ (s. xiv/xv) | O$^3$ |

Doyle and Hanna note at least six, and perhaps as many as eight, additional complete copies attested in records of medieval holdings, and they identify eleven further manuscripts containing excerpts from the text, in addition to the series of excerpts preserved in the compilation of Rolle's writings published by Watson as *Orationes ad honorem nominis Iesu*.[8] All of this evidence should

---

*of William O'Sullivan* (Aldershot, 1998), pp. 122–36 (at p. 129); **H** Kraebel, 'Rolle Reassembled,' pp. 982–96; **J** see below, n. 25; **L** Rodney M. Thomson, *Catalogue of the Manuscripts of Lincoln Cathedral Chapter Library* (Cambridge, 1989), pp. 169–70; **S** Hanna, 'Miscellaneous Manuscripts;' **V** Monica Hedlund, 'Katillus Thorberni, a Syon Pioneer, and his Books,' *Birgittiana*, 1 (1996), 67–87 (at pp. 82–86); **X** Thomson, *A Descriptive Catalogue of the Medieval Manuscripts of Corpus Christi College, Oxford* (Cambridge, 2011), pp. 96–97; **B2** Hanna, 'Oldest Manuscript of Rolle'; **L2** wants detailed treatment, but cf. Albin, *Melody*, pp. 346–73.

8   Nicholas Watson, ed., *Emendatio Vitae. Orationes ad honorem nominis Ihesu* (Toronto, 1995), with the compilation preserved uniquely in CUL MS Kk.6.20, fols 11–26$^v$. The other manuscripts with excerpts are: Cambridge, Emmanuel College, MS 35, fols 194–238$^v$ (Arnould's C$^2$); Douai, Bibliothèque municipale, MS 396, fols 193–96; Cambridge, Corpus Christi College, MS 194, fol. 4 (ch. 39 only); BL, MS Harley 2439, fol. 31$^{r–v}$ (ch. 39 only); Beinecke, MS Osborn fa54 (*olim* Heneage), fols 24 and

be used by a future editor, but my present efforts have been focused on the full copies of the text.

To determine the relationships among these manuscripts, I have prepared a sample, consisting of Chapters 1–5, 11 and 31, with the latter two chapters chosen because they are included in **L2** and – for Chapter 11 only – **B2**. At 5,125 words, this represents just under a tenth of the total text, roughly 56,000 words in Arnould's edition. I have collated these chapters in all of the witnesses listed above, with the exception of **H**, which can be eliminated as *descriptus*, copied directly from **B**.[9] A portion of the result is included in the Appendix, which gives an edition of Chapter 11. In the following discussion, I draw my examples from the Appendix wherever possible, and further evidence from the larger sample (cited by page/line in Arnould's edition) is generally relegated to the notes. In my examples from Chapters 1–5 and 31, when Arnould correctly reports a variant, my citation ends with an asterisk, and when he reports a variant but makes some error (typically confusing one siglum for another) my citation ends with two vertically aligned asterisks. Citations without any further annotation indicate variants not reported in his edition.

## Descent of the Text

Most clearly, my sample reveals a common exemplar standing behind **B D J**, a manuscript (**β**) that was likely in existence, based on the dating of **J**, by the end of the fourteenth century. The three surviving copies deriving from **β** share a number of simple scribal errors indicating their common dependence on this source: in the Appendix, for example, the omission of *conualescat* in l. 15 is obviously scribal,

---

25$^{r-v}$; Dublin, Trinity College MS 277, pp. 542–43 (ch. 7); CUL MS Add. 5943, fol. 174 (ch. 1 and the beginning of ch. 2); New York, Columbia University Library, MS Plimpton 270, fols 65–69 (ch. 39 only); Downside Abbey, MS 48243/Clifton 12, fols 118–24$^v$; Uppsala, Universitetsbiblioteket, MS C.193, fols 1 and 171; Trier, Stadtbibliothek, MS 685, fols 139–40 and 147$^{r-v}$. Those copies attested in records were in Bruges, Charterhouse; Bury St Edmunds; Cambridge, University Library, donated by Robert Alne of York Minster in 1440, having previously belonged to Thomas Hebbeden, dean of St Andrew, Auckland (d. 1435); Isleworth, Syon Abbey (discussed further below); Leicester Augustinians; Dominicans of King's Lynn, given by Thomas Lexham in 1382. A further attestation, in the collection of the London Carmelites, gives a title for *Melos* suggesting affinities with the excerpts in Douai, Bibliothèque municipale, MS 396; see Gabriel Liegey, 'Richard Rolle's *Carmen Prosaicum:* An Edition and Commentary,' *Mediaeval Studies*, 19 (1957), 15–36.

9    See my discussion in 'Rolle Reassembled.'

though the resulting phrase is still sensible enough.[10] In other cases, errors in
β prompted revision on the part of later scribes. Hence, in l. 6, introducing the
elaborated quotation of Ps. 67. 14, I suspect that **B** preserves an error introduced
in β, misreading an abbreviated *denique* in the phrase *denique dormiamus* and
writing *dedormiamus*, while the scribe responsible for another manuscript, a
common ancestor of **D J**, sought to correct the resulting nonsense, writing *ne
dormiamus*. (Introducing the negative conjunction, of course, fundamentally
changes the meaning of Rolle's sentence.)[11] While the only other instance of
agreement between **D** and **J** in the Appendix (24: *utique > itaque*) is not dispositive,
the larger sample includes more substantive errors supporting their descent from
this β derivative – all consistent with the grosser observation that, uniquely
among surviving copies, **D J** conclude *Melos* with a series of extra chapters, taken
from *Incendium Amoris*, and otherwise found apart from *Melos* in another Rolle
anthology, New York, Pierpont Morgan Museum and Library, MS M.872.[12] At
the same time, examples of agreement or related error in **B D**, where **J** agrees with
all or a majority of the remaining witnesses, seem to indicate that the text in **J** is
in some way conflated.[13] That is, the scribe of **J** either worked directly from the
β derivative while consulting another copy or he simply copied an exemplar that
was itself prepared from the β derivative and subsequently corrected.[14]

The scribe of **D** – Arnould's copy-text – therefore inherited an exemplar at
least two generations removed from the archetype, with some errors introduced

---

[10]   Here I give the earliest instances of **B D J** agreeing against other copies in the
sample, with the reading in other witnesses provided first and the **B D J** variant
second: *claritudinem > claritatem* (3/8‡), *amabilis >* om. (5/6‡), *auolans > uolans*
(*euolans* in **S**; 6/21‡), *anima >* om. (6/25‡), *incunctanter >* om. (6/26*), *temptant a
nobis > a nobis … temptant* (8/21), *in > ad* (9/14), *expertus est > expertus* (9/33*),
*mortalitatem > mortalem* (11/1), *furentis >* om. (*furientis* **L S**; 11/5*), *subito >* om.
(11/25*), *aurum > aurum et* (12/6), *carpunt > capiunt* (12/14‡), *gerunt gaudium >
trans.* (12/14–15), *apte >* om. (12/21‡).

[11]   Cf. Albin, *Melody*, p. 164 n. 2.

[12]   On the extra chapters, see Hanna, 'Transmission,' p. 325. Likewise, both **D** and **J**
run Chapter 2 into Chapter 3 without any break. Other examples of **D J** agreement
supporting the existence of this β derivative include (with the **D J** reading given
second): *apte > aperte* (5/11‡), *decepta > deceptos* (*decepti* **L S**; 13/11*), *linire > lenire*
(14/7*), *texerunt > texuerunt* (14/23*), as well as *clari > clares* **B** > *clare* **D J** in the
Appendix, line 3.

[13]   Examples include (**B D** given second): *modesta > modeste* (*molesta* **X**; 8/29‡),
*uolui > uolui ac* (12/24), *deuoratur > deuorabitur* (14/11‡), *descenderem ad dolorem
dampnandorum > ad dolorem dampnandorum descenderem* (93/8–9), *nam dum > nam*
(94/26), *anima > animo* (95/5).

[14]   Alternatively, the β-derived ancestor of **D J** could itself have been corrected prior to
the copying of **J** but after the copying of δ, discussed below.

in β and further variants, some as attempts at correction, introduced in the β derivative. In addition to these inherited variants, **D** shows signs of an effort to revise the β derivative and create a sensible, legible text. **D** therefore presents a high frequency of readings otherwise unattested in full copies (168 in the sample), some errors but many more representing attempts at 'smoothing' or other forms of improvement.[15] Many of these show an appreciation of Rolle's alliteration, as in the addition of *uolutabro* (2) in the Appendix, and in some cases the reviser seems to have intervened simply to perfect what he took to be an insufficiently alliterative phrase.[16] Elsewhere he clearly recognises and responds to errors introduced in β or its derivative: for example, in the Appendix, 42, where β apparently dropped *existunt*, attested in other copies, **D** makes up for the omission by supplying *sunt*. The reviser's eagerness to improve upon his exemplar could account for instances of **B J** agreeing against other copies, with **D** forming part of this majority.[17] These are rare, and perhaps therefore more likely to be a matter of convergence, of the reviser applying his editorial acumen and getting it right, than of his consulting a second manuscript. While the evidence of the full copies would suggest that this reviser was most likely the scribe of **D** himself, variants recorded by Arnould in copies containing extracts of the text, discussed below, indicate that these revisions were made earlier, in the preparation of an intervening copy (δ) – a point to which we will return.

Of the remaining manuscripts, **L S** clearly form a pair, descending from a common exemplar. Chapter 11 alone presents fourteen instances of these two copies agreeing in a reading otherwise unattested and apparently scribal, and that number swells to 122 across my larger sample. Though not in evidence in the Appendix, the sample also offers instances of **L S** sharing substantive errors with the now-fragmentary **L2**. All of these shared variants represent fairly minor mistakes, but they are consistent across the sample where **L2** survives, indicating some genetic relationship.[18] The relative dating of the manuscripts

---

[15] Some of **D**'s more straightforward scribal errors were nevertheless printed by Arnould: in the Appendix, for example, see line 9 *consolaminis > consolacionis*; 18 *assumpserit > assumpsit*; 28 *in > om.*; 41 *coinquinatum > inquinatum*, and see the transpositions in lines 14 and 50.

[16] For example, *risu implebitur > risu replebitur* (6/10*), *ut illam desideret > ut illam affectaret* (8/20*), *portis profecto appropiant > portis profecto propinquant* (11/11–12*), *quiescentes sonorum > quiescentes canorum* (12/14*). One additional case shows **D**'s improvement on an error introduced in β: *in solio solempni > in solio regnante* **B**, *in solio regnanti* **J** > *in solio solempni* **D** (16/15*).

[17] See the Appendix, lines 14 and 37. The sample includes only one other clear instance, *quid > quod* (95/26), in this case with **B J** joined by **V** (see further below).

[18] For example, *accusabit > accusabunt* (14/15), *perdentes > pendentes* (15/9✝), *et > sed* (94/2), *penetraui > perpetraui* (94/16, later corrected in **S**), *sed > om.* (95/12).

holds out the possibility that **L2** could have served as exemplar for the manuscript from which **L S** derive, but, though **L2** is a relatively good copy, it presents sufficient separative variants to rule out such direct dependence.[19] Instead, it seems more likely to have been prepared from a manuscript (λ) that also served as the exemplar for the common source of **L S.**

The two remaining complete copies, **V X**, and the fragment **B2**, likewise show some signs of common descent, though here matters quickly become complicated. **V X** both present *Melos* immediately after Rolle's *Incendium*, and my work towards an edition of *Incendium* has indicated that **V** and **X** descended from a common exemplar. This seems likely to have been a book available somewhere in the vicinity of York, reflected in **X**'s early ties to the Cluniac priory in Pontefract and, in the case of the **V**, reflecting the excursion of some Brigittine brethren from Vadstena to York in 1408–21.[20] At least some evidence exists for these manuscripts' continued reliance on a single exemplar for *Melos*, too, and especially early in the text. Hence, in Chapter 3, **V X** substitute *necessaria* for an otherwise universally attested (and surely anterior) *uitam* in the phrase 'et uitam nimirum paciencia interius inspirata equanimiter sustinet' (10/10–11⁎), presumably reflecting confusion of *n* for *u* and *cc* for *it* to yield the common abbreviation *ncca*, taking the abbreviation stroke to expand that to *necessaria* rather than indicating the need for word-final -*m*. Again, in Chapter 4, in the phrase 'sed obscurati feruidis fetoribus' (11/14), where **D** substitutes *ac* for *sed*, **V X** agree on *sed et*, while, further on in the same chapter, both read 'prefulgida' to perfect the alliteration of 'percipientibus premia … paratur fulgida' (12/7). A handful of other conjunctive variants appear in my sample, and though they are all relatively minor, taken together they support the notion of some recourse to a common exemplar on the part of these two manuscripts.[21]

---

[19] In the Appendix, line 5, the added superlinear gloss in **L2** could easily have been disregarded by a copyist, but the larger sample offers instances of more clearly separative variants: for example, such errors unique to **L2** as *titubent > titubet* (*tutubent* **L S**; 13/10), *princeps > princes* (94/11), *restiti > resistiti* (94/32), *placere > om.* (*percipere* **L S**; 96/10⁎).

[20] See Hedlund, 'Thorberni,' who places **V** in the library at Vadstena, on external evidence, in the first half of the fifteenth century, but also concludes that it was copied at Vadstena in the wake of Thorberni's travels in England (including York), which likely concluded in 1421. See, too, Vincent Gillespie, 'Dial M for Mystic: Mystical Texts in the Library of Syon Abbey and the Spirituality of the Syon Brethren,' in Marion Glasscoe, ed., *The Medieval Mystical Tradition: England, Ireland and Wales. Exeter Symposium VI* (Cambridge, 1999), pp. 241–68 (at p. 263).

[21] For example, *et²* > *om.* (13/24), *delibilis > delibis* (14/9), *uisceribus suis* **B J L2** > *uisceribus eius* **V X**, *uiscera sua* **D**, *uisceribus* **L S** (15/21).

Fig. 1.1.    Portraits of Rolle in **J**, fols 1 (*Incendium Amoris*) and 41 (*Melos Amoris*). Reproduced by permission of the Master and Fellows of St John's College, Cambridge.

These agreements between **V** and **X** are limited to the first five chapters in my sample, however, and by Chapter 31 – and perhaps already by Chapter 11 – the text in **V** reflects the influence of a second exemplar. That is, Chapter 31 includes several instances in which **V** shares otherwise-unattested readings with the β-derived **J**. These variants, again, represent relatively minor errors or fiddling with the text of the exemplar, but they are sufficiently persistent and substantive to indicate a genetic relationship, and they are supported by further cases of **V** agreeing with **B D J**.[22] The simplest explanation is that **J** served as the second exemplar for the text preserved in **V** – which, as Hedlund's work suggests, was likely produced at Vadstena from a copy brought back from the North of England.[23] (Alternatively, the Brigittine brethren could have returned to Vadstena with two copies of *Melos*, conflated there to make **V**.) The only trouble here comes from **J**'s known provenance – the note 'Liber dompni Petri de Norwico' is added above a scribal contents list on **J**'s front flyleaf, and Ker concluded that it was through this Peter's

[22]  All examples are from Chapter 31. Agreements of **J V** against all other witnesses: *ludo* > *luto* (93/23), *amicam* > om. (93/30), *dilectis* > *electis* (93/35), *illum sustinent* > *sustinent te* (94/5), *uanum* > *uacuum* (94/36), *unde nec … habundat* > *unde … non habundat* (*unde … habundat* **B**; 96/1), *fecerit in finem* > *fecerat in fine* (*fecit* **D**; 96/2). Further examples of **B D J V** agreement: *fecem* > *fetentem* (94/35), *sed* > *sic* **B D J** > *et sic* **V** (94/36‡), and see n. 17 above for another.

[23]  Hedlund, 'Thorberni.'

donation that the book came into the collection at Ely Cathedral Priory.[24] The note seems unlikely to have been added too long after the book was copied, and so it could be that Dom Peter ventured up north to assemble (or simply acquire) a small anthology of Rolle's writings on the basis of good exemplars, with the result available to the scribe of V's exemplar while he, too, was in Yorkshire.[25] Such devotion to the hermit on the part of J's earliest owner could, perhaps, be reflected in the portraits added before *Incendium* and *Melos* (see Fig. 1.1). Alternatively, another copy may stand between the β derivative and J, with this copy – also consulted to make V's exemplar – reflecting some contamination from a non-β witness.

At this point it will be useful to identify with greater precision – though still tentatively – the source of contamination in J. Throughout Chapters 1–5, J agrees with L S against other witnesses in three instances, one extremely minor but the other two potentially more revealing.[26] In Chapter 31, the only suggestive example involves the handling of the vocative phrase 'Iesu benedicte,' as it appears in B D V, with the two words transposed in X (93/9). In J L S the proper name is omitted, while in L2 it appears as an interlinear correction by the scribe: 'benedicte \scilicet Iesu/'. If the handling in L2 preserves an effort at correction in λ, then it is easy to imagine the name simply dropped in the exemplar shared by L S, and the similar omission in J may reflect consultation of a manuscript of the same type. This is all relatively meagre fare, and the instances in which J agrees with all other manuscripts against B D are far more substantial, but my sample provides no comparable examples of potential conflation from a copy more closely related to the other candidate, X.

Apart from its agreements with V, X seems to be most closely related to the fragmentary B2, identified by Hanna as the earliest surviving copy of Rolle's writings.[27] Evidence for this relationship is limited, however, in part because

---

[24] N. R. Ker, *Medieval Libraries of Great Britain: A List of Surviving Books*, 2nd ed (London, 1964), p. 260.

[25] While J is preserved in what seems to be a late fourteenth-century binding, it may then be significant that it has two runs of signatures, one for *Incendium* and a second for *Melos* and *Judica*, reflecting at least some time in which these parts of the volume could have been passed around as discrete items, and the potential that they were copied out of their present order. I am grateful to Professor Beadle for these observations. The dating of J is supported by Kathleen Scott's observations concerning its miniatures, in her opinion comparable to those of Vernon's 'Illuminator B'; see Scott, *Later Gothic Manuscripts, 1390–1420*, 2 vols (London, 1996), II, 21.

[26] The first case – *internis* > *interius* (6/23✳) – depends on the ticking of the minim to distinguish *i*. More significant are *quam* > *quem* (8/15✳), *uicturisque* > *uicturusque* (10/30✳).

[27] Hanna, 'Oldest Manuscript.'

of the severely curtailed (and, where extant, damaged) text in **B2**, but also because **B2** was evidently closer to the authorial text than other surviving copies and therefore provides still fewer readings of diagnostic value. Hence, in the Appendix, the only instance in which **B2**'s text has needed emendation appears in line 3, where I have rejected a reading attested in all copies.[28] One potentially telling detail is, however, identified by Hanna, who draws attention to a passage in Chapter 21, ' ... ut postquam populum Christi per modicum tempus racionabiliter rexerint ...', with the verb, *rexerint*, attested only in **D J**. The majority of witnesses – **L L2 S V** – read *pauerint*, while in **B X** the verb is omitted. As Hanna observes, the verb was also initially omitted in **B2**, though a later hand adds the majority reading, *pauerint*, in the outer margin.[29] Based on the foregoing discussion, *rexerint* is most likely an attempt on the part of the β derivative's scribe to repair the sense of the passage, creating alliteration with the proximate adverb, while *pauerint* sustains a more diffuse alliterative pattern across the whole sentence.[30] Indeed, since *pauerint* does seem plausibly authorial, the common omission in **B X** and initially **B2** would invite some possible conclusions regarding the descent of the text. That is, either the omission of the verb represents an error in the archetype, with *pauerint* being another scribal attempt (like *rexerint*) to plug the hole, or **B2** was itself the ancestor both of β and of the antecedent common to **X V**. I suspect this second scenario to be more likely, though, again, the evidence provided by **B2** is minimal and other scenarios are therefore certainly possible. (For example, **B2** β and the common source of **X V** could all descend independently from an ancestor missing the verb.) Of course, **V** could not have taken *pauerint* from its second, β-derived ancestor, which would almost certainly have read *rexerint*, and so, unless we posit the (possible, but perhaps more unlikely than not) influence of a third manuscript on **V**, then the best source for this reading seems to be a correction in **X V**'s antecedent (as in **B2**) after the copying of **X**.

This is admittedly a lot to hang on a single omission and correction in **B2**. The stemma provided here is, therefore, simply a hypothesis on the basis of available evidence, with the relationship of **B2** to β and the ancestor of **X V** on the one hand and the source of **J**'s non-β readings on the other being the most speculative details in the transmission. Still, in its larger contours, this diagram indicates some essential points about the descent of the text – most significantly, the apparently independent derivation of λ from the archetype, and the contamination of **J** and, more severely, **V**. The latter is represented

---

[28]  My conjecture continues the first-person plural verbs from the end of Ch. 10, which resume in the next clause.

[29]  Hanna, 'Oldest Manuscript,' 112.

[30]  For a different view, see Hanna, 'Oldest Manuscript,' 112, n. 22.

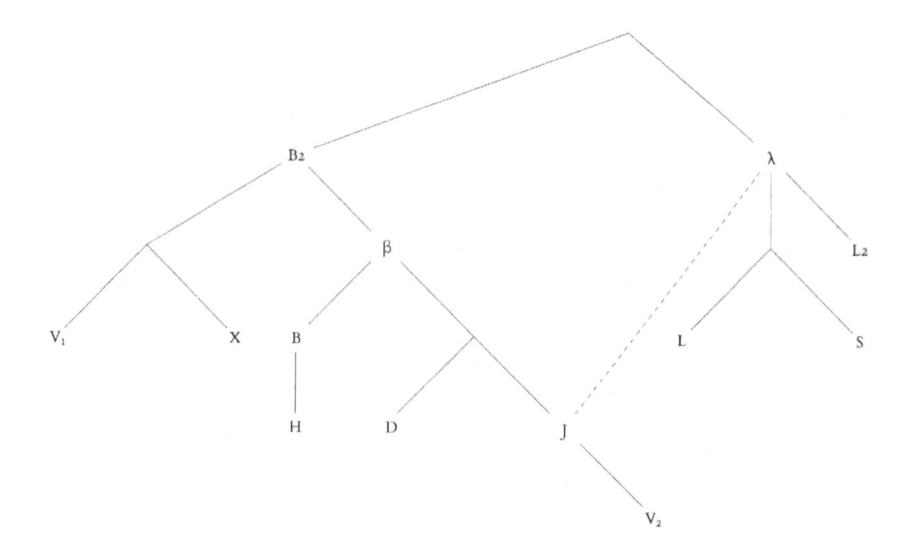

twice on the stemma, with **V1** denoting the early portion of the text and **V2** following the shift in exemplars – and note that, in both cases, a further manuscript surely stands between **V** and its surviving source.

Before turning to consider some larger patterns in the transmission of *Melos*, it should be noted that this reconstruction of the text's history points to a basic flaw in Arnould's edition. That is, Arnould mistook the clarifications and corrections preserved in **D** – its easier readings, introduced by a medieval reviser – for the authorial text.[31] In contrast, in the sample edition included in the Appendix below, **X** has been used as copy-text simply because, in the sample as a whole, it presents fewer variants in need of correction than the other manuscripts, and I have emended its text in light of all other copies. This yields twenty points at which my text of Chapter 11 differs from Arnould's, about one disagreement for every twenty-five words. Based on this work, I would suggest that a future editor of *Melos* could prepare the text from **B B2 L2 S X**, with recourse to **D J L V** reserved for resolving particularly difficult cases.

## The Transmission of *Melos*: A Carthusian Text

Whoever read *Melos* in Rolle's lifetime, the evidence of the surviving manuscripts detailed above supports the identification of two phases in the text's transmission following the death of the author. The first, in the final decades of the fourteenth century and early in the fifteenth, involved the work of a variety of interested collectors, some (perhaps Peter of Norwich, but certainly the scribe of **B**) travelling from far afield to assemble or obtain 'collected works' volumes of the

---

[31] Cf. Arnould, ed., *Melos*, p. lxxxv.

hermit's Latin. Other early collectors were apparently drawn to Rolle's works because of his status as a local saintly writer – seen most clearly in the making of **X** and, after a fashion, **V**. All of these collectors would presumably have already encountered some of Rolle's writings, and this familiarity drove them to identify and assemble fuller anthologies of his works. The conflation evident in **J** and **V**, and the correction to **B2**, suggest that these efforts could to some degree have been coordinated, that these early collectors may have benefitted from one another's work, their familiarity with different copies of the text and where to find them, or perhaps they all benefitted from knowledge about the text on the part of the owners of the books they copied.[32]

From sometime early in the fifteenth century, however, in the second major phase of its transmission, *Melos* essentially became a Carthusian text.[33] In one branch of the stemma, the once-independent copy **L** was joined to the larger Rollean anthology prepared by the scribe John Wodeburgh, and this conjunction of parts seems likely to have been done in the Kingston on Hull Charterhouse, which owned the book by *c.* 1400.[34] More extensive still is the Carthusian role in the stemma's other branch – though in this case involving some copies of extracts, and at least one book which no longer survives. Both CUL MS Add. 5943, fol. 174 (s. xv¼), which includes a brief extract from the opening of the text, and Cambridge, Emmanuel College, MS 35 (s. xv ¾), fols 195–238, which offers a wider ranging selection of passages, were very clearly owned, and perhaps also produced, by Carthusians.[35] Emmanuel 35 contains the signature of James Grenehalgh of Sheen, rusticated to Coventry after 1507/8, while the relevant portion of Add. 5943 appears to have been prepared by its original owner, Thomas Turk, after his admission to Hinton. A note on the back flyleaf of Add. 5943, in the hand of John Morton, vicar of Hinton, records that Turk gave the book to him in 1418.[36]

---

[32] Cf. Hanna, 'Oldest Manuscript', pp. 112–13.

[33] On Carthusian interest in Rolle, see Michael Sargent, 'The Transmission by the English Carthusians of Some Late Medieval Spiritual Writings,' *Journal of Ecclesiastical History*, 27 (1976), 225–40, and A. I. Doyle, 'Carthusian Participation in the Movement of Works of Richard Rolle between England and Other Parts of Europe in the 14th and 15th Centuries,' in *Kartäusermystik und -Mystiker: Dritter internationaler Kongress über die Kartäusergeschichte und -Spiritualität*, 5 vols, Analecta Cartusiana, 55 (Salzburg, 1981–82), II, 109–120.

[34] For a description of this manuscript and an account of Wodeburgh, see my forthcoming edition of Rolle's *Postille super novem lectiones mortuorum*. A second example of such Carthusian acquisition appears among the extracts listed above: Douai, Bibliothèque municipale, MS 396, acquired by Sheen early in the fifteenth century.

[35] On the collection of materials included in Emmanuel 35, see Arnould, ed., *Melos*, pp. lxxv–lxxvii; the fragment in BL, MS Add. 5943 ends at *ed. cit.*, 6/3.

[36] The note is provided by Arnould, ed., *Melos*, p. lxxxiii. On the Carthusian ownership of these books, see further Doyle & Hanna, *Allen's Writings Ascribed*, p. 73 n. 10 and

Crucially, Arnould identified the extracts in these two manuscripts as preserving variants otherwise attested only in the later full copy **D** (s. xv/xvi).[37] That is, the revisions in **D** discussed above are also in evidence in these two partial copies. Though it has not been traced with any confidence to a specific charterhouse, **D** is another Carthusian book: pointing to its inclusion of a compilation by John Walsingham (perhaps the prior of the London Charterhouse after 1477), comments by Doyle raise the possibility that **D** could have been prepared there or at Sheen, though more recently Hanna has observed that the book was almost certainly in the North of England later in the sixteenth century, and he suggests that it may therefore have been produced and kept at Hull or Mount Grace.[38] In light of the dating of these three books, it seems most likely that they all descend from the lost copy **δ**, posited above as the source for the revisions preserved in **D**, and a manuscript which, from sometime early in the fifteenth century, seems to have been circulating among the English charterhouses.

More speculatively, another glimpse of **δ** may be caught in the catalogue of Syon Abbey, across the Thames from Sheen. Syon's catalogue, prepared *c.* 1500–24, includes as volume M.27 a purported autograph of *Melos* ('et dicitur manu propria hunc scripsisse librum'), a volume in which the text is followed by Rolle's only independently circulating Latin poem, called *Canticum Amoris*.[39] As with various other claims by medieval owners to possess Rollean autographs, this one is likely inaccurate, and the cataloguer shows admirable caution in his use of *dicitur*.[40] This entry seems likely, however, to indicate the relative antiquity of the manuscript by the early sixteenth century, and, much less securely, it could reflect some understanding of the value of the text the manuscript contains – an authoritative, early witness that was circulated and copied, before being deposited in the massive collection at Syon.

As the latest copy in this cluster of Carthusian manuscripts, and perhaps the last medieval copy of *Melos*, **D** usefully illustrates that Rolle's text continued to find readers over a century after the author's death – but it also indicates

---

p. 75 n. 32. On Grenehalgh, see Michael Sargent, *James Grenehalgh as Textual Critic*, 2 vols (Salzburg, 1984), II, 478–87.

[37] Arnould, ed., *Melos*, pp. lxxxii–lxxxiv. Arnould, of course, mistakenly took these variants as preserving the anterior, authorial form of the text.

[38] Doyle, 'Books not Linked', p. 129; Doyle & Hanna, *Allen's Writings Ascribed*, p. 76 n. 40. In light of the evidence of its later provenance, adduced by Hanna, it is worth noting that Doyle found the script of **D** to be similar – though not identical – to that used in Cambridge, Trinity College, MS O.2.56, the only surviving copy of the original writings of Richard Methley, ocarth (d. 1527/8) of Mount Grace ('Books not Linked', p. 129).

[39] Vincent Gillespie & A. I. Doyle, eds, *Syon Abbey with The Libraries of the Carthusians*, Corpus of British Medieval Library Catalogues, 9 (London, 2001), p. 228.

[40] On other claims to own autographs of Rolle's works, see Kraebel, 'Rolle Reassembled,' p. 962 n. 12.

that, increasingly, such interest was to be found primarily, if not exclusively, among the inmates of charterhouses, in England and abroad.[41] To put it differently, once it was no longer sought and preserved as part of a larger effort to reassemble the author's corpus, the appeal of *Melos* was by and large limited to the elite and austere spirituality of the Carthusian Order.[42]

## Appendix: *Melos Amoris*, 11

As noted above, the text of *Melos*, 11 has been prepared on the basis of Oxford, Corpus Christi College, MS 193 (**X**), corrected against all other full or once-full copies, for the sigla of which see above, p. 16; Arnould's edition is cited as '*Arn.*' Capitalisation, punctuation and the division of the text into sentences and paragraphs are editorial, and abbreviations have been silently expanded. Biblical quotations and allusions are in italic: Ps. 54. 7 in line 1, Ps. 67. 14 in lines 6–8, Romans 14.12 in line 31, and Wisdom 17.5 in lines 46–47. All substantive variants have been noted in order to illustrate the patterns of affiliation discussed above, and to provide a sense of the frequency of errors in each witness. Orthographic variants have not been noted.

1    [fol. 212ᵛ] *Dabit michi pennas sicut columbe, et uolabo, et requiescam.* Penne profecto placabiles, non uiles, quemadmodum que uiscantur uiciosorum. Sed quia clari sumus et agiles in ascensu, properamus et pergimus ad pacificam plebem, ubi est sacietas sufficiens in sempiternum, et plenissima pulcritudo
5    puellarum et preciosi preparatus, ut reuera per racionabilem reditum ad regnum reducti cum regibus requiescamus. Denique *dormiamus inter medios cleros*, si desideramus *pennas columbe deargentate*, ut sint *posteriora dorsi eius in uirore auri.* Auolando itaque ad altitudinem admirabilis habitaculi, ignorancie error effugatur, nam increati consolaminis gustamus gaudium, et ex iusticia iudicis
10   Iesu in iubilum gerimur, quia uiperam uenenantem audacter interfecimus, euacuando omne quod uile est in uisu ueri amatoris.
     Quamobrem uenit uenustas quam uolumus, [fol. 213] et cupita caritas condescendit in cordibus canencium in conformitate cum carissimis. Quippe

---

[41]   Cf. the copy attested in the Bruges Charterhouse, noted above.

[42]   My thanks, above all, to A. S. G. Edwards, for his patience and sound editorial advice, and to Ralph Hanna, whose generous feedback improved this work as it developed. Thanks, too, to the librarians who supplied photographs of manuscripts, allowing me to do this work during pandemic lockdown, and in particular Adam Crothers (St John's College, Cambridge) and Claire Arrand (Lincoln Cathedral Chapter Library). I am likewise indebted to Andrew Albin and Katherine Zieman, who have been generous with their supplies of Rolle reproductions, and to Richard Beadle for his assessment of the St John's College manuscript.

et claritudo in consciencia confortatur in confirmacione, ut non cadat in
15  caliginem, sed clarescens magis ac magis conualescat, donec dilecta Dei
deportetur ad domum ubi non indigebit addiscere, quando omnia habentem
illuminatricem – Sapienciam scilicet eternam – cernit, que sanat sauciatos
sceleribus, et amore eius implet quos conseruat. Vnde et ex quo assumpserit
animam ad amandum, denique deinceps dulcescit in electis dulcor diuinitatis
20  mulcens merencium mentes, ne desperacione delerentur, et paulatim proficiens
in paruulis pauperibus pietate plenis prelibandam se ocium odientibus
amicabiliter ostendit, ut eciam inter tramites tempestatis tranquillitas
traducatur et turbo temporalitatis ad eternitatem tendentibus terminetur.

Istis utique arridet habundancia, implens animum e celis, et ineffabilis
25  obumbracio ardentissimi amoris, eo quod aspectum arripiunt appetitus
inuisibilis et ciuium sanctorum solaciis in laude ludifluo leuantur, languentes
in leuissimo labore luminati. Destructa demum desolacione a desideriis non
destituuntur, quia dulcedinem deceptiuam declinabant, sed pocius prediti in
paciencia et properantes ad portum sine peruersitate claritatem capere curant,
30  per quam castificati coronabuntur, quatinus inter clarificatos consedeant.
Nam uirtus ueritatis recte coram regnante *reddet racionem*, etenim expulsa
peccatorum peruersitate profecto patet intelligencie introitus, et nigredo
nociua per nuncios necabitur nobiles, ut decoretur dilecta per placentem
puritatem speciei spiritualis. Quippe quo Conditor custodiens castos in
35  eternum amoris incendium hos erigit, eo subtilius incendit et abstrahit ab
illicitis cadente concupiscencia carnali, ita quod dum sanctis celica sonat
symphonia, obscuritas interitus undique inuadat impios. Quia in indigenciam
introeunt inferorum omnes auari et diuites discedentes dolorose ducuntur,
miseriis quoque mancipantur mundani morientes.

40    Et merito non saluantur inimici et miseri, quia manent in maliciis suis usque
ad mortem, et non intrat aliquid coinquinatum in curiam Cunctipotentis, sed
omni auro amabiliores existunt qui in hanc habebunt affabilitatem, clarioresque
cristallo conspiciuntur ac sole similiter lucidiores laudantur, qui in celestibus
sunt sortiti. Inde igitur aperte ostenditur quia superbi et sceleribus subditi in
45  sua subdola securitate non subsistent, quando uiderint se tantum uilificatos
in uiciis, in luctu lapsi sine leticia, et cum *horrendam noctem* inspexerint, *quam
non poterunt illuminare siderum limpide flamme*, ac opacitas infinita omnes
occupauerit obstinatos et cuncti cupidi confusibiles comprobentur cum
carnalibus, qui captiuabantur in contagiis, ut cadant in carcerem caliginosum
50  et in chaos capiantur calamitatis, et cremabuntur continue peruersi prelati,
utique et omnes putridi peccatores.

## Variants

2. placabiles] plicabiles *L S*; uiscantur uiciosorum] uisco uiciorum uiscantur *L S*, uiscantur uiciorum *B J*, uiscantur uolutabro uiciorum *D Arn.*

3. quia clari] quia clares *B*, quia clare *J*, que clare *D Arn.*; sumus] *conjectured*, sunt *MSS and Arn.*; ascensu] quibus *add. D Arn.*

5. reuera] id est uere *add. L2 sup.*

6. denique dormiamus] dedormiamus *B*, ne dormiamus *D J Arn.*

7. pennas] penne *J*; uirore] uigore *L*, pallore *B V*

9. consolaminis] consolacionis *D Arn.*

10. interfecimus] interficimus *L S*

13. carissimis] cassimis *X*

14. in consciencia confortatur] confortatur in consciencia *D Arn.*; non] *om. B J*

15. caliginem] caligine *X*; conualescat] *om. B D J*

16. deportetur] deportatur *J*

17. Sapienciam scilicet] *transposed L S*

18. quos] quod *L S*; assumpserit] assumpsit *D Arn.*

19. animam] animum *S*; electis] dilectis *D L S Arn.*

20. merencium] merennium *X*

21. prelibandam] prelibanda *J*, prelibatam *V*, perlibandam *Arn.*; odientibus] adientibus *X*

22. inter] intra *B D Arn.*

24. utique] itaque *D J Arn.*

25. ardentissimi] ardentissini *X*; arripiunt] arripuit *J*

26. ciuium] ciuiis *D*, cuius *J*; ludifluo] ludiflua *D J V Arn.*

28. in] *om. D Arn.*

29. capere] non *add. X*

31. reddet] reddat *V*; expulsa] propulsa *L S*

33. nociua] nociuam *L*; decoretur] decore *V*; dilecta] dilictam *L*

34. speciei] spiritus *L S*; castos] custos *V*

35. erigit] erigat *L S*

35. et—**51.** peccatores] *L2 defective*

37. symphonia] symphoniam *B*; interitus] interius *L*; inuadat] inuadit *S*, madat *B*, macerat *J*; quia] *om. L S*; in] *om. D X Arn.*; indigenciam] indigencia *X*

38. introeunt—**51.** peccatores] *B2 defective*

38. inferorum] infernorum *B*; dolorose] dolore se *X*; ducuntur] dicuntur *B*, in *add. J*

40. et[1]—**41.** Cunctipotentis] *copied twice in X*

**40.**    et$^2$] *om. V*; suis] *om. L*

**41.**    coinquinatum] inquinatum *D Arn.*; curiam] curam *L*

**42.**    existunt] sunt *D Arn., om. B J*; in] *om. L S Arn.*; hanc] hac *J*; affabilitatem] stabilitatem *J*

**43.**    conspiciuntur] conspicientur *L S*; laudantur] laudabuntur *L S*

**44.**    aperte] apte *X*

**45.**    subdola] subdolosa *L S*; subsistent] subsistunt *J*

**46.**    luctu] luctum *D Arn.*; cum horrendam] tamen horridam *L S*

**47.**    flamme] flamen *X*

**48.**    obstinatos] abstinatos *X*

**50.**    in chaos capiantur] capiantur in chaos *D Arn.*

# 2

# Charles V, king of France, and Humfrey, duke of Gloucester

~

*Christopher de Hamel*

We begin with bad news. Most medieval manuscripts no longer exist. Throughout history there have usually been more occasions to destroy and lose books than to preserve them. The study of manuscripts of the Middle Ages only through those that happen to survive today can give us a very limited view of the landscape. There are two principal ways of learning about lost books from medieval Europe. One is through the careful use of inventories and catalogues. The other is by the chance survival of manuscript fragments, often recovered from use as waste material in early book bindings, a field in which the Beinecke Library leads the world. The tale offered here involves both, and it reveals the fate of several unsuspected manuscripts from the library of Charles V, king of France 1364–80, the earliest outstanding private book collector of the Middle Ages and the elder brother of the duc de Berry. This is appropriate, because Barbara Shailor wrote the principal account of the fragment of the Savoy Hours, Beinecke MS 390, owned and embellished by Charles V himself.[1]

This inquiry began in 2022 when Christie's in London offered for sale a collection of fragments formerly owned by Marvin Colker (1927–2020), of the University of Virginia. Over many decades, Professor Colker had assembled a filing cabinet of hundreds of manuscript leaves and pieces, probably for no great financial outlay. The text of lot 103 in his online sale ending on 12 December 2022 was correctly identified and dated, but no conclusions were drawn. The fragment achieved a modest three-figure sum and remains in private hands (Figure 2.1).

It is a single leaf from a later fourteenth-century manuscript of the *Somnium viridarii*, the 'Dream of the Arboretum' or 'Pleasure Garden,' usually now

[1] Barbara A. Shailor, *Catalogue of Medieval and Renaissance Manuscripts in the Beinecke Rare Book and Manuscript Library, Yale University, Volume II: MSS 251–500* (Binghamton, NY, 1987), pp. 254–57.

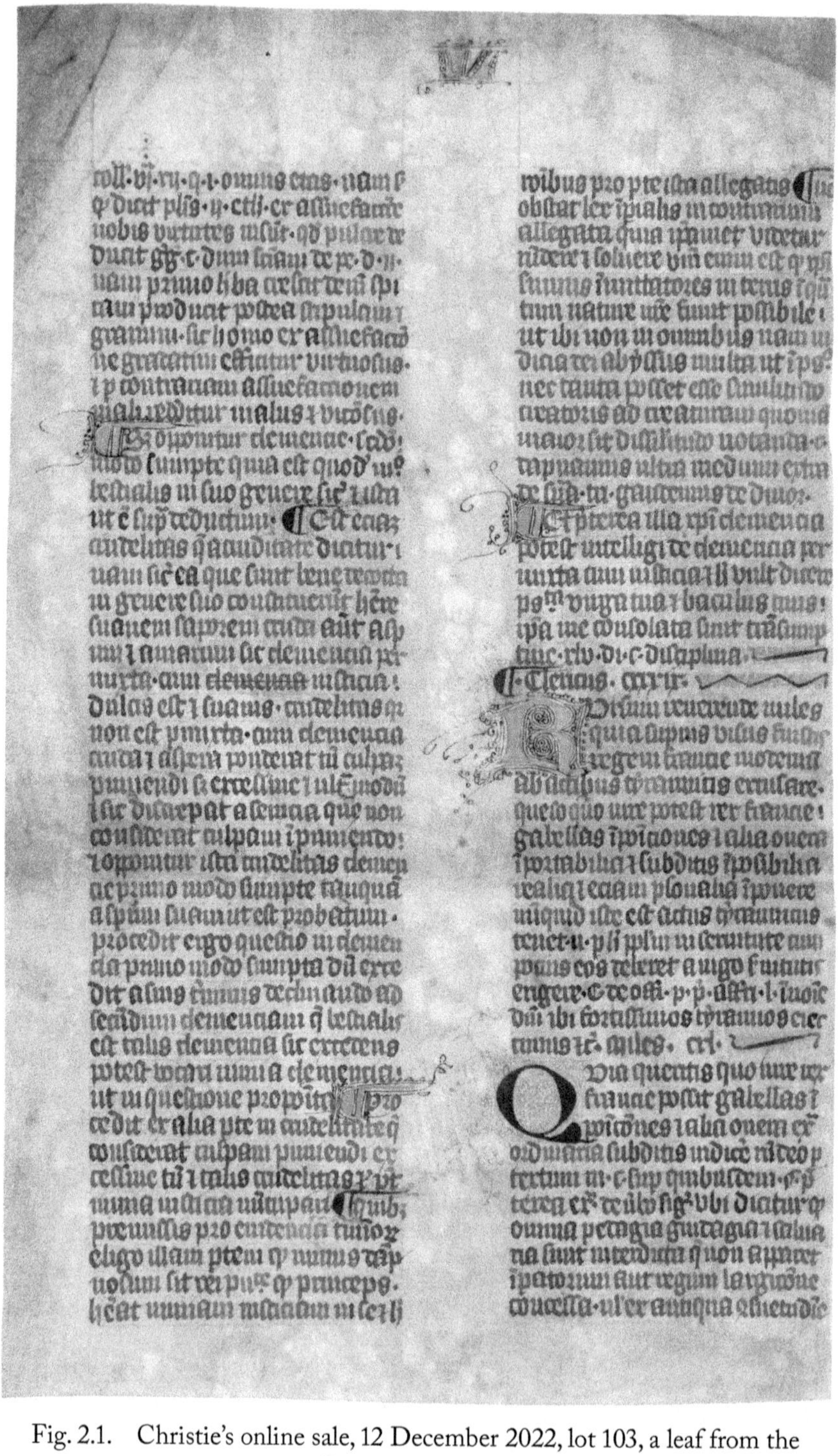

Fig. 2.1. Christie's online sale, 12 December 2022, lot 103, a leaf from the *Somnium viridarii*.

attributed to Évrart de Trémaugon, canon lawyer and royal counsellor.[2] The text was composed in Latin for Charles V, and a copy was presented to the king by the author on or soon after its completion on 16 May 1376. It describes the age-old struggle for superiority between religious and secular authority, a matter of especial topicality in France that year when the popes finally left Avignon for Rome. In the narrative, the author dreams of being in a beautiful garden where he sees Charles V caught between two quarrelling women, a noble nun, arguing for spiritual advantage, and a queen, defending temporal power. At the king's suggestion, two men are summoned instead to discuss both sides of the debate rationally, a cleric and a knight, one religious, one a layman. This was before Christine de Pizan and Barbara Shailor, and the opinions of women were regarded as unserious. The men's dialogue, concluding entirely in favour of royal supremacy over that of the church, forms the subject of the book.

For some reason, Charles V did not like the manuscript, or maybe he liked it very much but struggled with the Latin, and he sent it back to the author to have it translated and re-written out in French. This took two years, itself an interesting fact, and a new and slightly shorter vernacular version, the *Songe du vergier*, was brought to the king in 1378, as we know because Charles inscribed and dated it on receipt. That copy survives in BL, MS Royal 19.C.IV, now regarded as one of the major French royal manuscripts of its time, illuminated by the Master of the Bible of Jean de Sy (Figure 2.2).[3] It eventually became the exemplar for later manuscripts of the *Songe du vergier*, including one of the very early fifteenth century now in the Bodleian Library in Oxford.[4] As far as is known, the original and rejected Latin version was never used or circulated at all until the late 1420s (an important point to which we will come in a few moments). If no other fourteenth-century manuscript of the Latin *Somnium* was made, the obvious supposition must be that the Colker leaf is from the long-lost royal dedication copy of 1376.

[2]  For the text and probable author, see Marion Schnerb-Lièvre, ed., *Somnium Virdarii*, 2 vols (Paris, 1993–95), and the introduction to her *Le songe du vergier, édité d'après le manuscrit royal 19 C IV de la British Library* (Paris, 1982).

[3]  BL, MS Royal 19.C.IV is digitised online; the erased inscription of Charles V is on fol. 247ᵛ. Accounts of the manuscript's illumination include François Avril, *Manuscript Painting at the Court of France, The Fourteenth Century (1310–1380)* (London, 1978), p. 101 and pl. 31; *Paris 1400, Les arts sous Charles VI* (Paris, 2004), p. 51, no. 11, by Marie-Hélène Tesnière; and Scot McKendrick, John Lowden & Kathleen Doyle, eds, *Royal Manuscripts, The Genius of Illumination* (London, 2011), pp. 392–93, no. 139, by Joanna Frońska.

[4]  BodL, MS e. Musaeo 43 (SC 3685); Otto Pächt & J. J. G. Alexander, *Illuminated Manuscripts in the Bodleian Library Oxford*, I (Oxford, 1966), no. 638; about thirty-five manuscripts of the text are known.

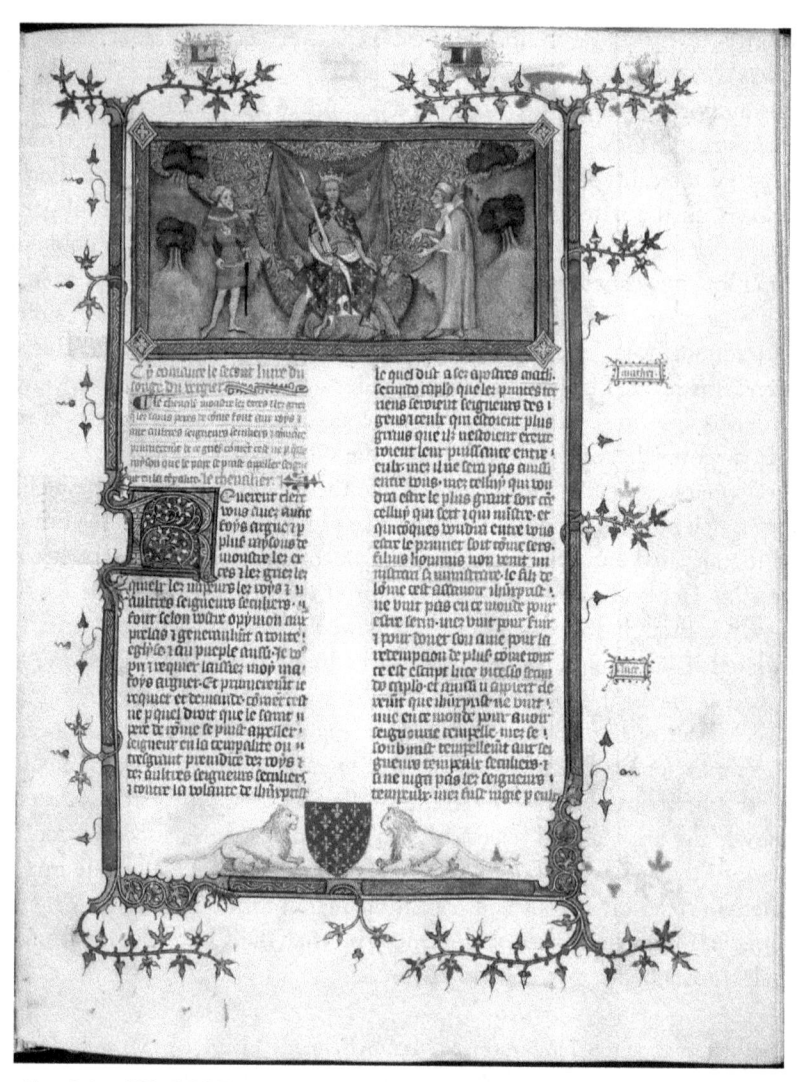

Fig. 2.2.   BL, MS Royal 19.C.IV, fol. 154, the royal dedication copy of the *Songe du vergier*. Reproduced with the permission of the British Library.

By the happy opportunity of being able to place a full-size photocopy of the new leaf over the original of the king's French *Songe du vergier* in the British Library, one can see that the two manuscripts were made as absolute twins. The ruling pattern and dimensions of the two columns of 44 lines in each manuscript are identical to the exact fraction of a millimetre. More important still, the script and illumination and pen flourishing are all in the same hands.[5] There is really

---

[5]   The written area in both manuscripts measures 205 x 130 mm. but the wide margins are mostly cropped from the leaf. The scribe fills short lines with a mark like a

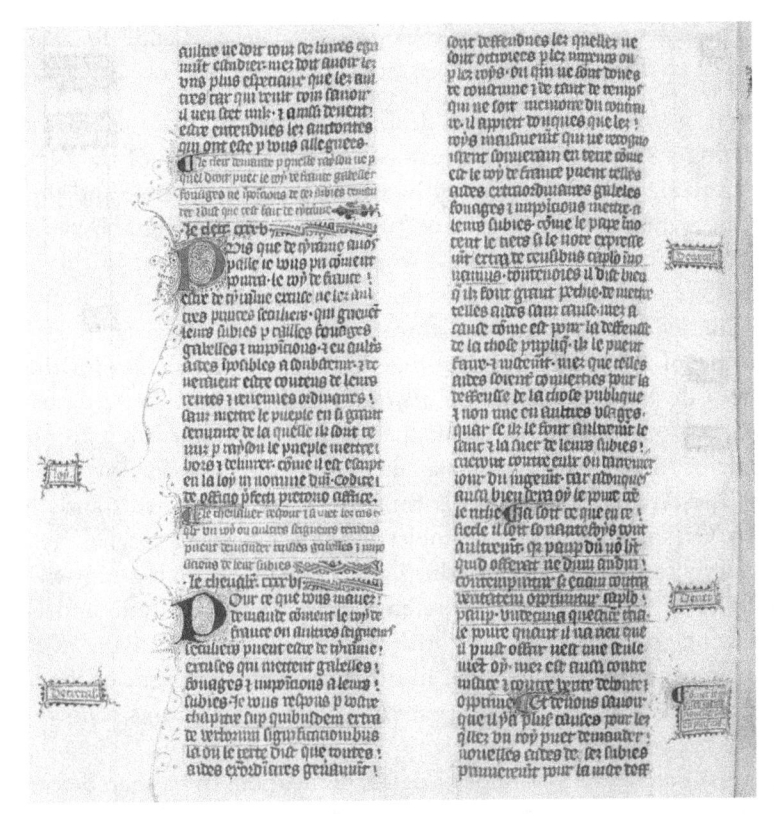

Fig. 2.3.   BL, MS Royal 19.C.IV, fol. 79ᵛ (margins cropped),
the French translation of the page illustrated in Latin in Fig. 2.1.
Reproduced with the permission of the British Library.

no margin for ambiguity in this, even though the scribe was writing a different language (Figure 2.3).

Both manuscripts were listed in the inventory of the royal library at the time of the king's death in 1380, the French first, then its Latin prototype – 'le latin du francois dudit livre' – and in more detail in the inventory of 1411 among the books of the dedicatee's son, Charles VI, king of France 1380–1422. The Latin text was in a silk chemise binding with silver-gilt clasps:

Item, un autre livre couvert de soye a queue, qui est le latin du francois du livre, appelle le songe du vergier, qui est dun advis, comment le pape ne doit avoir congnoissance en ce qui touche le temporel ne la justice du Roy,

slightly backward sloping exclamation mark; generally, very bright red is used for headings and text excisions (for example, fol. 112ᵛ of the manuscript); initials and paragraph marks alternate between deep blue with pale red penwork and unusual pale Pompeian red (maybe Armenian bole) with dark blue penwork.

escript de lettre formee a deux coulombes, commencant on ii^e fo. *dilexisti nunc* Et un dernier *Revertatur*, A ij fermoires dargent dorez[6]

The first words of the second leaf, the standard medieval method of identifying a specific copy of a manuscript since the time of the Sorbonne library catalogues of the thirteenth century, involve a minor and probably hasty misreading of 'direxisti nunc,' which occurs in paragraph xvii of the text's prologue.[7] Remember these words, for they will recur in this article. Charles V's practice of commissioning French translations of Latin texts in his library is widely attested throughout his inventory, such as the *De civitate dei* of Augustine in Latin together with its translation for the king by Raoul de Presles; Cassian's *Collationes* in Latin and its accompanying French version by Jean Goulain; the Alphonsine Tables of astronomical movements 'translatees en francais du commandement du Roy Charles le quint'; and Aristotle's *Ethics* in Latin with its commissioned translation by Nicolas Oresme. These last examples, like the *Songe du vergier*, are listed in the inventories as being inscribed and signed by the king himself.[8] It is easy to guess where the king's preferences lay. Both the Latin and French manuscripts of the *Somnium viridarii* and the accompanying *Songe du vergier* are recorded still together in the subsequent catalogue of the library of Charles VI in 1413 and then again in 1424 with valuations, following the death of the younger king.

By that date, Paris was under English occupation. In or soon before June 1425 a very large part of the royal library of the Louvre was 'bought,' doubtless no voluntary sale, by John, duke of Bedford (1389–1435), brother of Henry V and regent of France. The manuscripts remained in Paris until late 1429 when Bedford relinquished the captaincy of Paris and withdrew with his purchases to the castle in Rouen.[9] The books would have been shipped down the Seine. We know that the *Somnium viridarii* and the *Songe du vergier* were together at that moment because both were then released for copying, the Latin for the

---

[6]   Léopold Delisle, *Recherches sur la librairie de Charles V, roi de France, 1337–1380*, 2 vols (Paris, 1907), II, pp. 74*–75*, no. 435, checked against BNF, MS fr. 2700, fol. 63, digitised on Gallica; the entry from 1380 is on fol. 12.

[7]   As noted by Schnarb-Lièvre, *Somnium*, p. i, n. 3 (text, p. 6); *dilexisti* does not occur.

[8]   Delisle, pp. 51*–52*, nos. 294–97; p. 147*, nos. 898–99; pp. 99*–100*, nos. 592–95; and pp. 81*–82*, nos. 481–82. These examples are all old texts, for which the king commissioned translations; I am not aware of other contemporaneous Latin and French texts made as matching pairs.

[9]   Jenny Stratford, *The Bedford Inventories: The Worldly Goods of John, Duke of Bedford, Regent of France (1389–1435)* (London, 1993), pp. 95–96.

Fig. 2.4.   Cambridge, MA, Harvard University, Houghton Library, MS Typ 127, fol. 1, the *Somnium viridarii* copied in Rouen, *c.* 1430.

first time. At least four closely related copies of the *Somnium* were made with distinctively Rouen illumination, one of which is in the Houghton Library at Harvard (Figure 2.4).[10] All have – or were intended to have (for one is unfinished) – an opening miniature filling two thirds of the opening page, showing the principal protagonists in the royal arboretum, similar to the full-page frontispiece of Charles V's French *Songe du vergier*.

The question asked by Jenny Stratford, who first published this group and identified Bedford's household in Rouen as the point of textual dissemination, is whether the lost Latin original had an opening miniature at all or whether the Rouen artists invented it by comparison with its accompanying French-language companion. It is true that the inventories of Charles V and Charles VI do not mention illumination in the Latin *Somnium*, whereas the *Songe* was described as 'bien historie et enlumine.' However, we can now answer the question by use of the Colker leaf. By my counting, the scribe writes 908 words on the leaf, or 454 a page. The number of words from the start of the *Somnium* to its original second leaf at 'direxisti' is 566. If the verso of fol. 1 had the same average of about 454 words, the opening page contained only some 112 words plus the 25-word heading, and there was undoubtedly, therefore, a miniature occupying two thirds of the page. In 1424, the Latin volume had been valued at eight *livres parisiens*, a large sum when many books there were listed at a few shillings, but the French copy at twelve *livres*.[11] The difference would be that the *Songe* also has a spectacular single-sheet frontispiece, not in the *Somnium* or any of its subsequent copies.

From Rouen, the books bought by the duke of Bedford were eventually transported back to London. In 1427 he gave a Livy from the former library of the Louvre to his younger brother, Humfrey, duke of Gloucester (1390–1447), with a donation inscription describing it as 'envoye des parties de France,' which suggests it had already been to England. It later belonged to the dukes

10 Jenny Stratford, 'The Illustration of the *Songe du Vergier* and Some Fifteenth-Century Manuscripts,' in G. Croenen & P. Ainsworth, eds, *Patrons, Authors and Workshops, Books and Book Production in Paris around 1400* (Louvain, 2006), pp. 473–88. Stratford dates all seven Latin copies of the *Somnium* to 1429 or later, including Paris, Bibliothèque Mazarine, MS 3522, which Schnarb-Lièvre had wrongly supposed was earlier. The Harvard manuscript is Cambridge, MA, Harvard University, Houghton Library, MS Typ. 127 (see especially Anne D. Hedeman in Jeffrey F. Hamburger, William P. Stoneman, Anne-Marie Eze, Lisa Fagin Davis & Nancy Netzer, eds, *Beyond Words, Illuminated Manuscripts in Boston Collections* (Boston, 2016), p. 217, no. 180).

11 Louis Douët d'Arcq, ed., *Inventaire de la bibliothèque du roi Charles VI, fait au Louvre en 1423 par l'ordre du régent duc de Bedford* (Paris, 1867), pp. 37–38, no. 127, and p. 49, no. 165; also Delisle, pp. 74*–75*.

of Burgundy and is now in Paris. Its second leaf reading corresponds to that listed in the library of Charles V.[12]

On Bedford's death in 1435, what was still described as 'þe grete librarie þat cam owte of France' was left in the hands of his uncle Cardinal Beaufort. It was probably then that the *Songe du vergier* in French was also acquired by Duke Humfrey, who contested Bedford's entire estate as his closest legitimate heir. He added his own flamboyant autograph inscription at the end of the manuscript, imitating the wording of Charles V immediately above.[13] If the two versions of the same text had remained together as an exactly matching pair since the 1380s, it is reasonable to wonder whether the Latin *Somnium viridarii* would also have passed at the same time to Humfrey.

One thrill of studying manuscripts is that sometimes hunches or ideas are vindicated very satisfyingly. On 25 February 1442, Duke Humfrey made the third of his three famous bequests to Oxford University, to endow the foundation collection in the fifteenth-century library room now incorporated in the duke's name into the buildings of the Bodleian. No. 31 in the modern numbering of the books listed in the duke's indenture of gift that day is 'Item sompnum viridarium 2° fo. *direxisti*,' correctly reading the opening word of the second leaf in the manuscript itself.[14] It is the first evidence that any book from the French royal library came with Duke Humfrey's donation to Oxford, and it confers a quadruple medieval royal provenance on the modest leaf once owned by Professor Colker – two kings of France and two English princes. Perhaps Humfrey retained the French version himself, deeming that the Latin, too obscure for Charles V, was suitable for a university.

[12] Stratford, *Inventories*, pp. 226 and 356. The Livy is Paris, Bibliothèque de Ste-Geneviève, MS fr. 777; see Alfonso Sammut, *Unfredo duca di Gloucester e gli umanisti italiani* (Padua, 1980), p. 122, no. 35, and Stratford, *Inventories*, p. 96; its second leaf 'ner iour davoir' corresponds to Delisle, p. 161*, no. 981.

[13] Jenny Stratford, 'The Manuscripts of John, Duke of Bedford: Library and Chapel,' in Daniel Williams, ed., *England in the Fifteenth Century, Proceedings of the 1986 Harlaxton Symposium* (Woodbridge, 1987), pp. 329–50, especially pp. 340–41; David Rundle, 'Habits of Manuscript-Collecting, The Dispersals of the Library of Humfrey, Duke of Gloucester,' in James Raven, ed., *Lost Libraries, The Destruction of Great Book Collections since Antiquity* (Basingstoke, 2004), pp. 106–24, especially p. 109; Rundle, 'Good Duke Humfrey, Bounder, Cad and Bibliophile,' *Bodleian Library Record*, 27 (2014), 36–53, includes a list of the duke's extant manuscripts, pp. 46–50, of which this is p. 48, no. 18.

[14] Rodney M. Thomson with James G. Clark, *The University and College Libraries of Oxford*, Corpus of British Medieval Library Catalogues, 16 (London, 2015), p. 37, no. 31.

Duke Humfrey died in probably suspicious circumstances while under arrest in 1447 and his possessions were forfeit to the crown and largely frittered or given away. His ownership inscriptions in manuscripts were carefully erased, as were the signatures of himself and Charles V in the French copy of the *Songe du vergier*. That manuscript is assumed to have been retained by Henry VI and still kept by Edward IV, and it was first listed in the library of Henry VIII in 1542.[15] There were other books in the English royal collection which might have come through Duke Humfrey from the Louvre, but the Tudor inventories do not record the second leaves.[16]

There is, however, one more to announce. Petitioners for books from the sequestered library of Duke Humfrey included Oxford University again, unsuccessfully claiming that further volumes had been promised by the late owner, and King's College in Cambridge, which deftly secured an unknown number of manuscripts from the duke's estate, probably in 1447. Henry VI had founded the college and had ultimate control of his uncle's books. The problem is in identifying what came from Duke Humfrey, since the earliest inventory of King's College ten years later does not list names of donors, although it must include books once his. Two have been identified only because they survive, both fifteenth-century humanistic texts.[17] The inventory does, however, record the first words of all the manuscripts' second leaves. The last two items on the lowest shelf of press H at King's College in the late 1450s, which we might assume by their position to have been of large size, were:

Prima pars biblie cuius 2$^m$ fo. incipit *principio in quo posuit hominem*

Secunda pars biblie cuius 2$^m$ fo. incipit *dent semitas vite*.[18]

---

[15] Jenny Stratford, 'The early royal collections and the royal library to 1661,' in Lotte Hellinga & J. B. Trapp, eds, *The Cambridge History of the Book in Britain, III, 1400–1557* (Cambridge, 1999), pp. 255–66, especially p. 266; James P. Carley, ed., *The Libraries of King Henry VIII*, Corpus of British Medieval Library Catalogues, 7 (London, 2000), pp. 69–70, no. 260.

[16] BL, MS Royal 14.E.III, for example, *La sainte Graal*, belonged to Charles V and Henry VIII, but it bears no surviving evidence of having passed through intermediary possession of Duke Humfrey (Carley, p. 24, no. 93; its second leaf corresponds to Delisle, p. 182*, no. 1113).

[17] A. N. L. Munby, 'Notes on King's College Library in the Fifteenth Century,' *Transactions of the Cambridge Bibliographical Society*, 3 (1951), 280–86, reprinted in Nicolas Barker, ed., A. N. L. Munby, *Essays and Papers* (London, 1978), pp. 27–36, especially pp. 30–31, and Peter D. Clarke with Roger Lovatt, *The University and College Libraries of Cambridge*, Corpus of British Medieval Library Catalogues, 10 (London, 2002), pp. 282–85.

[18] Clarke with Lovatt, p. 296, nos. 94–95.

Now compare the big two-volume Latin Bible of Charles V of France in trimmed white leather chemise bindings with metal clasps and catches:

> Item, un grant livre couvert de cuir blanc a bouillons, qui fait la moitie de la bible de genesis, jusques a Job, a queue qui a este couppee, a deux fermoirs & bouillons de laton, escript en latin de lettre grosse de forme, a deux coulombes. Commencant on ij$^e$ fo. *stio & cotidiana* & on dernier *funde quasi*.
>
> Item, lautre moitie, couverte de cuir blanc, qui se commence des paraboles salmon jusques a lapocalipce, escript de lettre semblable en latin, a deux coulombes. Commencant on ij$^e$ fo. *dent semitas*, et on dernier *Jam non est*. A deux fermoirs & cloux semblables.[19]

Not all two-volume Bibles divide at the same texts. The identical opening words cited for the second leaf of volume II are Proverbs 2:19, not merely at the same verse but in the same syllable within a word, '[nec apprehen]dent semitas vitae,' and identification is beyond reasonable doubt. The inventory of the Louvre library takes the second leaf of the Bible's first volume from Jerome's general prologue, '[Quidquid enim aliis exercit]atio et quotidiana [in lege],' slightly misreading '*stio*' for '*atio*,' as the same cataloguer did in writing '*dilexisti*' for '*direxisti*' in the *Somnium Viridarii*, whereas the medieval librarian at King's College ignored the prologue and counted his second leaf from the Bible itself, for the words are from Genesis 2:8. It is more or less certain that this manuscript, too, must have come out of France through the duke of Bedford and to King's from Duke Humfrey. It is not nothing to know that King's College Chapel, probably the finest late medieval building in England, could, if they wished, have used a Bible from the owner of the Sainte-Chapelle. The manuscript was no longer recorded as present by the time of the next inventory of the library in 1557.

The books which Duke Humfrey gave to Oxford also disappeared so thoroughly at the Reformation that the library was later reported to have been burnt.[20] No part of any of Duke Humfrey's books has ever been proposed among more than two thousand recorded manuscript fragments reused in

---

[19]  Delisle, pp. 4*–5*, no. 11, also checked against BNF, MS fr. 2700, fol. 96 (on Gallica). The two volumes were listed in the inventories of 1380, 1411, 1413 and 1424, when they were valued at 3 *livres*. It is more likely than not that the manuscript was thirteenth-century.

[20]  Rundle, 'Habits,' especially pp. 115–16, citing Anthony à Wood, who said that the library was burnt.

Oxford book bindings of the sixteenth century,[21] which does suggest a process of disposal different from the route by which many college manuscripts were jettisoned. The bookcases were sold in 1556. It suited Thomas Bodley in 1598 to emphasise that not a single item remained from his predecessor's bequest. Although slightly over a dozen of Duke Humfrey's donations to Oxford have now been identified elsewhere, all may have been thefts or strays from before the fury of the Reformation. Quite possibly the *Somnium viridarii* was another, not necessarily cut up immediately. The leaf was trimmed and used sideways as a wrapper around the outside of a book almost six inches high (150 mm.) but perhaps as wide as five-and-a-half inches across (140 mm.), such as a small rectangular volume of engravings or music. There is a darker stain on what was the binding's narrow spine, evidently secured by simple tacketing stitches. This kind of temporary parchment wrapper was especially characteristic of the later sixteenth or even early seventeenth century. The leaf, detached and flattened, was afterwards part of a collection of specimen manuscript leaves assembled by or for J. T. Adams (1849–1931), classicist and manufacturer of Adams's Furniture Polish, mostly recovered from English bindings. They were sold in three large lots at Sotheby's in 1997,[22] this leaf being bought unidentified by the booksellers Maggs Bros., from whom Professor Colker acquired it.

---

[21]   N. R. Ker, *Fragments of Medieval Manuscripts used as Pastedowns in Oxford Bindings* (Oxford, 1954).

[22]   2 December 1997, lots 6–8; lot 8 is now BL, MS Add. 73525.

# 3

## KISSING THE PATEN

~

*Roger S. Wieck*

A subset of collectors – smaller today, perhaps, than in times past – is the scholar–collector. Such a person might acquire in their area of expertise as a means of learning, or as a vehicle for enjoyment. The Scotch antiquary James Dennistoun (1803–55), for example, went abroad in 1825 and 1826 and, beginning in 1836, stayed in Italy for twelve years collecting material – including illuminated single leaves – for a projected study on the history of Italian medieval art. Although that study was never completed, in 1851 he did publish the three-volume *Memoirs of the Dukes of Urbino, Illustrating the Arms, Arts, & Literature of Italy, 1440–1630*, a work that highlighted his discovery of the art of Piero della Francesca. While most of Dennistoun's art collection was auctioned off after his death, his (largely intact) album of miniatures passed to his granddaughter, Isabella Caroline Henson, née Dennistoun (1869–1949), who sold what she called 'Uncle Denny's scraps' to art historian Kenneth Clark (1903–83) around 1930.[1]

While I do not consider myself a collector of medieval illumination, I sometimes buy the odd leaf or cutting that puzzles me or whose subject particularly appeals.[2] This article tells the story of how one such acquisition

[1] On Dennistoun, see my article '*Folia Fugitiva*: The Pursuit of the Illuminated Manuscript Leaf,' *Journal of the Walters Art Gallery*, 54 (1996), 233–54 (at 240); Sandra Hindman, Michael Camille, Nina Rowe & Rowan Watson, *Manuscript Illumination in the Modern Age: Recovery and Reconstruction* (Evanston, IL, 2001), pp. 78–82, 86–89, 210; Christopher de Hamel, with an Introduction by James H. Marrow and Catalogue by Matthew J. Westerby, *The Medieval World at Our Fingertips: Manuscript Illuminations from the Collection of Sandra Hindman* (London, 2018), pp. 66–73. J. J. G. Alexander, 'Re-uniting Cuttings by Antonio Maria da Villafora, Collected by James Dennistoun in Padua in 1839, with their Parent Manuscript,' *The Art of the Renaissance Book: Tributes in Honor of Lilian Armstrong*, Ilaria Andreoli & Helena Katalin Szépe, eds (Turnhout, 2023), pp. 371–87. After Clark's death, Dennistoun's album was broken up and the cuttings auctioned piecemeal in London, Sotheby's, 3 July 1984 (some items had been sold previously at Sotheby's, 18 June 1962). The Morgan owns three Italian cuttings from the album: MSS M.1069.1–2 and M.1072, for which see the Morgan's online catalogue, CORSAIR.

[2] For two curious fragments I acquired and published, see my articles: 'Inventive Efficiency from the Master of the Ghent Privileges, or, A Little Bit of Hell Goes

inspired me and helped congeal my thoughts on a certain medieval ritual that, while once widespread, was, however, infrequently depicted and is thus little understood today.[3]

~

The subject of an exhibition I curated in 1988 at Baltimore's Walters Art Gallery (now Museum), 'Time Sanctified: The Book of Hours,' derived from my realization that of the roughly six hundred Western manuscripts at the Walters, about half were Books of Hours. The existence at the time of only a single slender monograph in English on this important genre of manuscript also inspired me to write an accompanying catalogue that might fill what I perceived as a lacuna in the field.[4] I envisioned a handbook on Books of Hours that might appeal to students and collectors.[5]

While selecting those *horae* that would best represent the rich iconography of the Office of the Dead, I became fascinated with the wide range of images illustrating various moments of the medieval funeral, episodes that began on the deathbed and ended in the grave. In between, Books of Hours also depicted such events as the procession with the corpse from home to church, the recitation or singing of the Office of the Dead over the bier in church, the funeral Mass ending with final absolution, the procession with the corpse from church to churchyard, and the final blessing of the body prior to burial. While selecting which funeral Masses to include, I encountered one in a French Hours from the 1450s that appealed, but that also perplexed me (Figure 3.1). Its central miniature depicted a funeral Mass, while its borders contained ancillary events. While I could be sure that the large miniature did indeed illustrate a Mass – the chief celebrant was wearing a chasuble – I could not pinpoint the particular moment of the Mass depicted. The celebrant, flanked by two assisting deacons (wearing dalmatics), was proffering a disk to a mourner standing before them. The

a Long Way,' Peter Rolfe Monks & D. D. R. Owen, eds, *Medieval Codicology, Iconography, Literature, and Translation: Studies for Keith Val Sinclair* (Leiden, 1994), pp. 134–42; and 'Trial by *Fleur*: The Earliest Work by the Master of Walters 219,' Kathryn A. Smith & Carol H. Krinsky, eds, *Tributes to Lucy Freeman Sandler: Studies in Illuminated Manuscripts* (London, 2007), pp. 315–29.

3   Special thanks to Colleen Barrett, Janny Chiu, Gregory Clark, Eugenio Donadoni, Mara Hofmann, Deirdre Jackson, Roger de Kesel, Peter Kidd, and Christine Sciacca for their assistance with this article.

4   Janet Backhouse, *Books of Hours* (London, 1985).

5   *Time Sanctified: The Book of Hours in Medieval Art and Life* (New York, 1988; published simultaneously in London as *The Book of Hours in Medieval Art and Life*; 2nd revised American edition, New York, 2001).

disk was not white (so it could not be a communion wafer) but gold. Was this a paten? If so, what was the priest doing, standing with his back to the altar – unusual in itself – and holding the sacred vessel before a lay mourner at close range? I wanted to include the manuscript in the exhibition because the miniature and its borders offered such rich end-of-life imagery but, unable to determine what exactly was happening in the Mass, I hid my ignorance and left the book out.

A few years later, in the mid-1990s, I was charged by the Pierpont Morgan Library (where I was then working) to reprise the theme of my 1988 show, but with Books of Hours exclusively drawn from the Morgan's own rich holdings. The result was the 1997 exhibition, 'Medieval Bestseller: The Book of Hours,' and my accompanying publication.[6] Once again, for the Office of the Dead, I took special pleasure in lining up a series of *horae* that illustrated the medieval funeral almost like the storybook of a movie. Again, I encountered an image of a funeral Mass in which the priest held what appeared to be a paten while facing mourners (Figure 3.2). And once again, I hid my ignorance and left the book out.

Not long after that show I chanced upon a miniature from a French Hours *c.* 1425 at the Morgan that served to finally enlighten me on what was happening in those two funeral Masses. The picture, for the Office of the Dead, showed a priest, having turned from the altar during Mass (as evidenced by his chasuble and the chalice with a host sitting on the altar), presenting a paten to a line of mourners, the first one of whom seems to kiss the proffered vessel (Figure 3.3). Subsequent spelunking into Joseph Jungmann's two-volume study, *The Mass of the Roman Rite*, confirmed what I thought I was seeing; in discussion of Offertory processions, he writes that, 'In many places, instead of the maniple or the stole, the offerer (after handing over his gift) kissed the hand of the celebrant, or, in other places, the corporal or even an extended paten.'[7]

6   *Painted Prayers: The Book of Hours in Medieval and Renaissance Art* (New York, 1997).

7   Joseph A. Jungmann, *The Mass of the Roman Rite: Its Origins and Development (Missarum Sollemnia)*, 2 vols (New York, 1951–55), 2, p. 18. I later stumbled across an image of kissing the paten, the iconography of which is so similar to that in Morgan MS M.865 that it, too, could have clued me in; it is from a Bourges or Paris Hours *c.* 1410 and also marks the Office of the Dead: Los Angeles, J. Paul Getty Museum, MS 36, fol. 96[v] (http://www.getty.edu/art/collection/objects/1696/unknown-maker-mass-for-the-dead-french-about-1410/).    A sixteenth-century witness to the practice of kissing the paten was John Calvin. In his Commentary on Romans 16:16, he condemns it: 'Hence has arisen that practice among the Papists at this day, of kissing the paten, and of bestowing an offering: the former of which is nothing but superstition without any benefit,

Fig. 3.1. *Funeral Mass: Presenting the Paten at the Offertory*, border: *Deathbed Communion, Procession from Home to Church, Angels Bear the Offertory Gifts to God*, and *Burial*, by the Master of the Harley Froissart, Book of Hours, France, Paris? 1450s (Baltimore, MD, The Walters Art Museum, MS W.275, fol. 108).

Two years after 'Medieval Bestseller,' I atoned for my earlier sins of omission by including both the Walters miniature and the Morgan one that had helped edify me in an article, 'The Death Desired.' While my generous editors allowed me to include an extended sequence of twenty-eight images illustrating sequential moments of the medieval funeral, I discussed the kissing of the paten in a single, short sentence.[8] The ritual, which, when mentioned at all, is often misidentified or misinterpreted, has continued to intrigue me – even if, or perhaps because, its depiction is rather rare.[9]

Returning to the Walters miniature, we can observe that there is not (yet) any kissing – the lack of which was the original cause of my confusion (see Figure 3.1). A mourner, offering a silver vessel in his left hand, approaches the priest who, holding the paten, tilts it slightly upward for the mourner's expected kiss. The deacon on the left, meanwhile, extends his hand in what appears to be a gesture of accepting the proffered vessel.[10]

Nor is there any kissing in the Morgan miniature that had also perplexed me (see Figure 3.2). The priest, his back to an altar upon which a draped chalice rests, faces forward and holds the paten toward a group of mourners who, large candles in hands, assemble around the bier. (Smaller candles feature in another image to be discussed below; see Figure 3.7). Next to the priest stands an acolyte holding a large empty situla to receive offerings of coins.[11]

---

the other serves no other purpose but to satisfy the avariciousness of the priests, if indeed it can be satisfied.' https://www.studylight.org/commentaries/eng/cal/romans-16.html.

[8] 'The Death Desired: Books of Hours and the Medieval Funeral,' Edelgard E. DuBruck & Barbara I. Gusisk, eds, *Death and Dying in the Middle Ages* (New York, 1999), pp. 431–76 (at 438–39, figs. 14, 15).

[9] In the spring of 2008 Barbara Shailor invited me to Yale University to deliver a lecture on the Sacred Bleeding Host of Dijon. I would like to think that she would find the Eucharistic subject of this tribute, research I could imagine telling her over cocktails, amusing.

[10] For Walters MS W.275, see Lilian M. C. Randall, *Medieval and Renaissance Manuscripts in the Walters Art Gallery. Volume II: France, 1430–1540*, 2 vols (Baltimore, 1992), 1, pp. 132–39, no. 128; on p. 135 she describes the miniature as 'three clerics behind bier receive paten from mourner with cruet at right,' correctly recognizing the paten but somewhat misidentifying the action.

[11] For Morgan MS M.1004, see the Morgan's online catalogue, CORSAIR. Similar iconography – priest holding paten, procession nearing, and acolyte holding a basin – characterizes the miniature for the Office of the Dead in a Lyons Hours *c.* 1430 attributed to the Master of the Vienna *Roman de la Rose* (Jean Hortart?). I had the pleasure of studying the unpublished manuscript, which does not appear in Mireia Castaño, *Le Maitre du Roman de la rose de Vienne* (Milan, 2022), in spring 1997: Lexington, KY, University of Kentucky, Margaret I. King Library,

Fig. 3.2. *Funeral Mass: Presenting the Paten at the Offertory*, by a follower of the Boucicaut Master, Book of Hours, France, Paris, *c.* 1420–25 (New York, NY, Morgan Library & Museum, MS M.1004, fol. 99ᵛ).

Fig. 3.3.  *Funeral Mass: Kissing the Paten at the Offertory*, by an artist influenced by the Limbourg brothers, Book of Hours, France, Brittany? *c.* 1425 (New York, NY, Morgan Library & Museum, MS M.865, fol. 130, detail).

The enlightening Morgan miniature that shows the paten actually being kissed has another interesting detail (Figure 3.3).[12] The order of the members of the procession reveals that there was a strict hierarchy to be maintained

---

MS Latin Kentucky VI, fol. 84, online at: https://exploreuk.uky.edu/catalog/xt7z8w383z8v#page/169/mode/1up.

[12] For Morgan MS M.865, see the Morgan's online catalogue, CORSAIR.

Fig. 3.4. *Funeral Mass: Kissing the Paten at the Offertory*, by the master of Morgan 293, cutting from a Book of Hours, France, Besançon, 1430s (New York, NY, Roger Wieck collection).

in these Offertory processions. As illustrated here, official mourners first, lay folk second.[13]

In 2019 a cutting appeared on the art market containing one of the clearest representations of the ritual of the lay kissing of the paten (Figure 3.4). In the foreground, members of the choir, open-mouthed, sing the Offertory hymn while three acolytes assemble around the bier with candles and a processional cross. At the altar, an eager mourner is about to kiss the paten. With eyes intensely fixed on the celebrant, he discreetly palms an unseen coin into the extended hand of the deacon, who will add it to the others already donated into the gold basin that he holds. On the paten, a clearly delineated inner circle probably represents its 'foot,' an indication that the priest is offering to these lay mourners the paten's convex side, that is, its bottom, the side that does not come in contact with the Eucharist. (See the quotation from McGarvey and Burnett below.) My serendipitous acquisition of this cutting inspired me to gather my thoughts and images in order to write the present essay on these rare depictions of the lay kissing of the paten.[14]

---

[13] Thomas Frederick Simmons, ed., *The Lay Folks Mass Book, or, The Manner of Hearing Mass, with Rubrics and Devotions for the People, in Four Texts, and Offices in English According to the Use of York, from Manuscripts of the Xth to the XVth Century, with Appendix, Notes, and Glossary*, EETS, original series 71 (London, 1879), p. 236. (The passage about processional hierarchy is quoted near the end of this article.)

[14] The cutting was offered at auction in London, Christie's, 9 December 2020, lot 25, but failed to sell; I was lucky when its owner accepted my private-treaty offer. Because of its style (not its subject matter), I referred briefly to the cutting in my article, 'The Sacred Bleeding Host of Dijon in Books of Hours,' Mara Hofmann & Caroline Zöhl, eds, *Quand la peinture était dan les livres: Mélanges en l'honneur de François Avril à l'occasion de la remise du titre de Docteur Honoris Causa de la Freie Universität Berlin* (Turnhout, 2007), pp. 393–404 (at 401 n. 10). About the cutting, both Joachim M. Plotzek, *Andachtsbücher des Mittelalters aus Privatbesitz* (Cologne, 1987), p. 109, no. 19, illus.; and Jörn Günther Antiquariat, *Collecting Miniatures* (2006; Brochure 9), no. 32, illus., describe the scene as mourners kissing the paten before receiving communion (mistaking the coins in the acolyte's basin for Eucharistic wafers). Gregory T. Clark refers to the artist of the cutting as the 'Besançon master of Morgan 293 and Latin 1186' in 'Beyond Saints: Variant Litany Readings and the Localization of Late Medieval Manuscript Books of Hours – The D'Orge Hours,' *Books of Hours Reconsidered*, Sandra Hindman & James H. Marrow, eds (London, 2013), pp. 213–33, *passim*. François Avril, citing this cutting (as a funeral service), refers to the illuminator as that of Morgan 293 and a Book of Hours in Louisville, Speed Art Museum, 2008.4; see 'Untersuchung zu Inhalt und künstlerischer Herkunft der Handschrift,' *Das Stundenbuch der Maria Stuart: Ms. Lat. Q.v.I.112 der Russischen Nationalbibliothek. Kommentarband zur Faksimileausgabe* (Berlin, 2015), pp. 57–90 (at 75–78, 89 n. 41). Mireia Castaño's identification of the artist with a certain Jean Antoyne, and her attribution of the present cutting to Hand B of Vienna, ÖNb series nova 2615, are not credible; see *Le Maître du Roman de la rose de Vienne* (Milan, 2022), pp. 64–67, 144, and pp. 33–34. The bottom of the paten is the side clearly being

Fig. 3.5. *Funeral Mass: Presenting the Paten at the Offertory*, by the Master of Morgan 366, Book of Hours, France, Tours, *c*. 1470 (New York, NY, Morgan Library & Museum, MS M.366, fol. 105, detail).

Yet another Morgan Book of Hours underscores the importance of the Offertory donations (Figure 3.5). In this *c.* 1470 codex, the mourners kissing the paten will, at the moment of osculation, be flanked by a pair of acolytes – something new here – both of whom bear basins to receive coins.[15]

The images discussed so far all depict kissing the paten at funeral Masses, that is, Masses with the corpse of the deceased present (normally in a pall-covered coffin); these Masses usually took place in the morning, immediately prior to burial.[16] Other images reveal that the ceremony also took place at memorial Masses. These are Masses of commemoration whose numbers and dates might have been stipulated by the deceased in their will for the benefit of their soul. In a Morgan Hours *c.* 1430, the image for the Office of the Dead shows a Mass in which the celebrant holds the paten while facing the congregation (Figure 3.6). There is, however, no pall-covered coffin; instead a tall stone tomb, complete with statues or reliefs carved at its sides, stands in the nave, possibly where the bier once stood. Considering its prominent role in the miniature, this tomb is no doubt meant to signify that it contains the body of a person of some significance. Mourners, including one in armor, enter the church waving heraldic banners – even bringing their horses! The celebrant himself is a bishop: he wears a miter and keeps a crozier nearby (tended by a deacon). While holding the paten, the bishop looks up toward the church's vaults from which hangs (at the upper left in the miniature) a helmet – probably that of the deceased.[17]

The Office of the Dead miniature in an Hours from the 1520s at the Victoria & Albert Museum also shows a memorial Mass (Figure 3.7). While no tomb stands on the spot where the deceased once lay, that place is marked

---

offered for kissing in a miniature by Jean Bourdichon of a priest presenting the sacred vessel in the early sixteenth-century Hours of Frederick III of Aragon: BNF, MS latin 10532, p. 100; the miniature illustrates a Requiem Mass, one of an interesting series of five votive Masses, each marked by an image of a particular and identifiable moment within the Mass, online at: https://gallica.bnf.fr/ark:/12148/btv1b8427228j/f104.item.r=Jean%20Bourdichon%20frederic%20d'aragon#. A facsimile of the manuscript, with a commentary by Teresa D'Urso, *Libro de Horas de Frederico III de Aragón*, is in preparation by CM Editores of Salamanca.

[15]  For Morgan MS M.366, see the Morgan's online catalogue, CORSAIR.

[16]  The only other example of kissing the paten at a funeral Mass that I know is in an Hours illuminated by the Master of the Harvard Hannibal *c.* 1420: Paris, Musée national du Moyen Âge/Thermes de Cluny, Cl. 1252, fol. 110; see Dominique Vanwijnsberghe, 'Le livre d'heures et la mort,' Paris, Bibliothèque Mazarine and Bibliothèque Sainte-Geneviève, *Le livre & la mort, XIVe–XVIIIe siècle* (Paris, 2019), pp. 27–51(at 39), ill. 7; he is the rare scholar to identify the ritual correctly.

[17]  For Morgan MS M.64, see the Morgan's online catalogue, CORSAIR.

Fig. 3.6. *Memorial Mass: Presenting the Paten at the Offertory*, Book of Hours, France, Lyons, *c.* 1430 (New York, NY, Morgan Library & Museum, MS M.64, fol. 91, detail).

Fig. 3.7. *Memorial Mass: Kissing the Paten at the Offertory,* by Simon Bening, Book of Hours (fragment), Belgium, Bruges, 1520s (London, Victoria & Albert Museum, National Art Library, MS L/1981/39, fol. 21ᵛ).

Fig. 3.8. *Mass of the Virgin: Kissing the Paten at the Offertory*, by the Mazarine Master (borders by the Egerton Master), Book of Hours, France, Paris, *c.* 1415–20 (Florence, Collection Prince Filippo IX Corsini, s. n., fol. 204ᵛ, detail).

by a luxurious pink and gold pall stretched out on the floor and surrounded by four candlesticks and a situla with aspergillum. As the mourners line up for the Offertory procession to kiss the paten, they are given lit tapers, which, it would appear, they surrender to an acolyte once they have made their donations (his head and fist full of tapers are visible to the right of the priest). The talented illuminator of this miniature was Simon Bening, so it is not a surprise to see further enriching details. On the altar, for example, are a missal, draped chalice, framed altar card, and large altarpiece depicting, appropriately, the Raising of Lazarus in grisaille.[18]

Finally, a miniature and its accompanying text in a Book of Hours *c.* 1415–20 in the Corsini Collection in Florence reveals that kissing the paten in the Middle Ages took place at other Masses than just those relating to death (Figure 3.8). The miniature shows the celebrant, in chasuble and almuce, extending the paten (clearly its bottom side) to a worshipper who, genuflecting, kisses it while placing a coin in the basin held by an acolyte. Behind him another congregant, coin in hand, awaits his turn. The text is not the Office of the Dead but the Mass of the Virgin, beginning with the Introit, 'Salve sancta

---

[18] The Raising of Lazarus is fitting because images of this miracle often illustrate the Office of the Dead in Books of Hours. For the Victoria & Albert Museum manuscript, see Christopher de Hamel, *The Posthumous Papers of the Manuscripts Club* (London, 2022), p. 151, where, reproducing the miniature, he says that the people are 'receiving holy communion'; and Rowan Watson, *Western Illuminated Manuscripts: A Catalogue of Works in the National Art Library from the Eleventh to the Early Twentieth Century, with a Complete Account of the George Reid Collection*, 3 vols (London, 2011), 2, pp. 735–41, no. 139, illus., where the author says that the 'priest is offering a pax tablet for the laity to kiss.' Watson correctly points out that the composition is nearly identical to an earlier version (by Gerard Horenbout) in the famous 'Rothschild Prayer Book,' fol. 28ᵛ; the miniature illustrates the Monday Mass of the Dead, one of a series of seven votive Masses for the days of the week, each marked (as in the Hours of Frederick of Aragon mention in note 14) by a miniature illustrating a particular moment within the Mass. Once owned by Vienna's ÖNb (as Codex Vindobonensis series nova 2844), the Prayer Book (actually a Book of Hours) is now part of the Kerry Stokes Collection in Perth, Australia (LIB.2014.017); see Kay Sutton, *Revealing the Rothschild Prayer Book, c.1505–1510, from the Kerry Stokes Collection* (West Perth, 2015). For a facsimile, see Ernst Trenkler, *Rothschild-Gebetbuch: Vollständige Faksimile-Ausgabe im Originalformat des Codex Vindobonensis Series Nova 2844 der Österreichischen Nationalbibliothek* (Graz, 1979), where the author misidentifies the paten as a monstrance. In the miniature of the Funeral Mass for the Office of the Dead in the Spinola Hours *c.* 1510–20 in Los Angeles, J. Paul Getty Museum, MS Ludwig IX 18, fol. 185, Horenbout depicts the distribution of small candles to a group of mourners with the chief celebrant facing the congregation; this distribution could be signaling the start of the Offertory procession, a procession that would climax, as we now know, in the mourners' kissing the paten. Images from the Spinola Hours are on the Getty's website.

Fig. 3.9.
*Mass: Kissing
the Paten at the
Kiss of Peace,*
by the Pseudo-
Jacquemart,
*Petites Heures*
of Jean, duc de
Berry, France,
Paris, 1375–90
(Paris, BNF, MS
latin 18014, fol.
173ᵛ, detail).

parens' (Hail, holy parent). The altar, upon which rest a missal and a chalice, is dominated by a large statue of the Virgin and Child.[19]

The famous *Petites Heures* of Jean, duc de Berry (the first in a long series of Books of Hours he would commission), contains a suite of miniatures illustrating prayers to be said at various moments in the course of a Mass.[20] One of these

[19]  For the Corsini Hours, see Millard Meiss, *French Painting in the Time of Jean de Berry: The Boucicaut Master* (New York, 1968), pp. 29, 33, 69, 86–87, 128, 135, figs. 128, 167–70, 278–82; Meiss misidentifies the osculation (fig. 169) as the kissing of the pax. The manuscript has an Office of the Dead, illustrated with clerics singing the Office of the Dead over the bier (fig. 167), and a requiem Mass, illustrated with a funeral Mass (fig. 170). Gabriele Bartz, *Der Boucicaut-Meister: Ein unbekanntes Stundenbuch* (Heribert Tenschert Katalog XLII, Ramsen, 1999), pp. 69, 70–71, 72, 119, figs. 8, 30, attributes the miniatures in the Corsini Hours to the Mazarine Master. Mara Hofmann follows Bartz' attribution in her description of the Corsini Hours in *Sotheby's Italia Fiftieth Anniversary: The Exhibition* (Milan, 2018), pp. 16–22, where she also reprises Meiss's misidentification of the paten as a pax. For the Mass of the Virgin, see J. Wickham Legg, ed., *The Sarum Missal, Edited from Three Early Manuscripts* (Oxford, 1969), pp. 389–91, or Robert Lippe, ed., *Missale Romanum: Mediolani, 1474*, 2 vols (London, 1899–1907), 1, pp. 456–58.

[20]  Jean de Berry was inspired to commission his *Petites Heures* by the lavish 'Savoy Hours,' which was then in the possession of his brother King Charles V (who added miniatures, a jewelled cover, and a jewelled bookmark). While the bulk of the

Fig. 3.10.
*Mass: Kissing the Celebrant's Hand at the Offertory,* by the Pseudo-Jacquemart, *Petites Heures* of Jean, duc de Berry, France, Paris, 1375–90 (Paris, BNF MS latin 18014, fol. 171, detail).

images illustrates Jean's kissing a paten (Figure 3.9). The text, however, reveals that the moment is not the Offertory but the Kiss of Peace. The paten here is standing in for a traditional pax. The Offertory prayer in the book is illustrated with a scene of Jean's kissing not the paten but the hand of the celebrant (Figure 3.10). While doing so, he slips a coin into the acolyte's basin.[21]

---

manuscript was destroyed in the 1904 fire at Turin's Biblioteca Nazionale, a fragment survives in Beinecke, MS 390. The Savoy Hours fragment was included by Barbara Shailor in her 1988 Beinecke exhibition, 'The Medieval Book,' and in its influential catalogue; see Shailor, *The Medieval Book: Catalogue of an Exhibition at the Beinecke Rare Book & Manuscript Library, Yale University* (New Haven, 1988), p. 46, no. 46, illus. p. 47 and on the cover. For a facsimile of the surviving New Haven fragment of the Savoy Hours, see Roger S. Wieck & Raymond Clemens, *Die Savoy Hours/The Savoy Hours/Les Heures de Savoie: New Haven, Yale University, Beinecke Rare Book and Manuscript Library, MS 390* (Luzern, 2017). A digital facsimile on the Beinecke's website can be found here: https://collections.library.yale.edu/catalog/2002815.

21    For a facsimile of the *Petites Heures*, see François Avril et al., *Les Petites Heures du Duc de Berry: Kommentar zu Ms. lat. 18014 der Bibliothèque nationale, Paris* (Luzern, 1988–89). A digital facsimile on the BNF's Gallica website can be found here: https://gallica.bnf.fr/ark:/12148/btv1b8449684q/f1.item. Another image of the kissing of the celebrant's hand during the presentation of gifts during the Offertory procession is found in a late thirteenth-century Castilian manuscript of the first part (*Primera Partida*) of the Law Code of King Alfonso X of Spain: BL, MS Add. 20787, fol. 105[v]; the image marks the start of Titulo XX, on tithes. For this codex, see the BL's online catalogue of illuminated manuscripts; the miniature is described and reproduced in

Fig. 3.11. *Mass: Kissing the Celebrant's Stole at the Offertory*, by the
Master of the Privileges, *Leges Palatinae*, Spain, Majorca, 1337
(Brussels, Bibliothèque Royale, MS 9169, fol. 20ᵛ, detail).

As we learned from Jungmann (quoted above), the congregation, when making their donations at the Offertory procession, could kiss the paten, the hand of the celebrant, the corporal, the priest's maniple, or his stole. An illustration of the last – kissing the celebrant's stole – can be found in the famous manuscript of the *Leges palatinae*, commissioned by King James III of Majorca in 1337 (Figure 3.11). The second chapter of the *Rules of the Palace* deals with the duties of the chamberlain (*camerlingue*). It is marked by a large miniature showing the king with a small retinue, including his chamberlain kneeling directly behind him, at Mass. Having walked up to the priest, James kneels and kisses the red stole that the priest extends to him from beneath the folds of his chasuble. At the priest's side, an acolyte kneels with a large basin to collect the offerings.[22]

---

Percy Dearmer, *Fifty Pictures of Gothic Altars* (London, 1910), pp. 34–35, pl. V. Priests' hands are also kissed by lay folk while making offerings in three miniatures in the late thirteenth-century *Cantigas de Santa Maria*, the authorship of some of which is also associated with Alfonso X: Florence, Biblioteca Nazionale MS B.R.20, fols 4 and 72; and San Lorenzo de El Escorial, Biblioteca de El Escorial, MS T.I.1, fol. 229$^v$. A cloth relic, possibly the hem or girdle of the Virgin, is also kissed during lay offerings in two miniatures in the El Escorial *Cantigas*, fols 126 and 170$^v$. For this kissing in the *Cantigas*, see Kirstin Kennedy, 'Seeing Is Believing: The Miniatures in the *Cantigas de Santa Maria* and Medieval Devotional Practices,' *Portuguese Studies*, 31 (2015), 169–82 (at 178, 180–81). The two *Cantigas* codices are online at: https://archive.org/details/b.-r.-20/page/n30/mode/thumb and https://rbdigital.realbiblioteca.es/s/rbme/item/11337#?c=&m=&s=&cv=&xywh=-3673%2C-313%2C11089%2C6240.

[22] For a facsimile of the *Leges palatinae*, see Joan Domenge i Mesquida, *James III, King of Majorca: Leges Palatinae* (Bloomington, 1994). In reference to the miniature on fol. 20$^v$, Johann Konrad Eberlein, 'Überlegungen zur bildlichen Ausstattung des Codex Brüssel Ms. 9169,' in Gisela Drossbach & Gottfried Kerscher, eds, *Utilidad y decor: Zeremoniell und symbolische Kommunikation in den 'Leges Palatinae' König Jacobs III. von Mallorca (1337)* (Wiesbaden, 2013), pp. 137–38 (of 135–46), mistakenly says the king kisses the priest's maniple (an impossibility here since priests wear their maniples on their left wrists); Françoise Lainé, 'Le roi dans l'illustration des "Cantigas de Santa María" (fin XIIIe s) et des "Leges Palatinae",' *Utilidad y décor* ... pp. 191–204 (at 199), mistakenly says James kisses the priest's hand. Cyril E. Pocknee, *The Christian Altar in History and Today* (London, 1963), p. 73, and Susanne Wittekind, 'Die "Leges Palatinae" als illuminierte Rechtshandschrift,' in *Utilidad y décor*, pp. 147–71 (at 152–53), correctly identify the object of the king's osculation as the celebrant's red stole. Another image of kissing the stole is found in Leonhard Beck's woodcut of the 'Funeral Mass for the Old White King' from Emperor Maximilian I's early sixteenth-century ambitious but never-published book project, the *Weisskunig*, see Walter L. Strauss, ed., *The Illustrated Bartsch* (New York, 1978–), 11, p. 155, no. 80 (224)–212. A genuine representation of a layman kissing a priest's maniple is to be found, as Dominique Vanwijnsberghe kindly pointed out to me, in one of five scenes illustrating high points within the Mass in the border of the 'Te igitur' page of the so-called 'Missal of Pius V' produced in Flanders *c.* 1450 and illuminated within the circle of Jean Le Tavernier: Mondovi, Achivio capitolare, MS

Fig. 3.12a. *Annunciation*, border: *Offering of Joachim and Anne Rejected*, *Joachim and Anne Meeting at the Golden Gate*, *Birth of the Virgin*, and *Presentation of the Virgin in the Temple*, by François le Barbier *fils*, Book of Hours, France, Paris, 1485–90 (New York, NY, Morgan Library & Museum, MS M.231, fol. 31).

Fig. 3.12b.   *Offering of Joachim and Anne Rejected*, by François le Barbier *fils*,
Book of Hours, France, Paris, 1485–90 (New York, NY, Morgan Library &
Museum, MS M.231, fol. 31, detail).

With educated eyes we can now properly interpret a vignette whose unusual
details might previously have eluded us. The illuminator François le Barbier
*fils* enjoyed enlivening the pages of his Books of Hours by adding ancillary
scenes to borders framing important miniatures. In a Morgan *horae* from the
late 1480s, he surrounded the main miniature of the Annunciation, marking
Matins of the Hours of the Virgin, with four vignettes depicting significant
events from the early life of Mary (Figure 3.12a). These vignettes depict the
Rejection of the Offering of Joachim and Anne, Joachim and Anne Meeting
at the Golden Gate, Birth of the Virgin, and Presentation of the Virgin in the
Temple. The first of these events – the rejection by the temple's high priest of the
offering of Mary's future parents – is illustrated in such a way that we might not

s. n., fol. 152; see Brussels, Palais des Beaux-arts, *Le siècle d'or de la miniature flamande:
Le mécénat de Philippe le Bon. Exposition organisée à l'occasion du 400e anniversaire de la
fondation de la Bibliothèque royale de Philippe II à Bruxelles, le 12 avril 1559* (Brussels,
1959), p. 43, no. 39. The high points illustrated in the vignettes are the procession at the
start of Mass of priest and acolyte to the altar; prayers at the foot of the altar; an acolyte
reading (the Gospel lesson); the kissing of the maniple (at the Offertory procession);
and the elevation.

immediately recognize it. In an unusual manner, the artist has 'Christianized' the Old Testament scene (Figure 3.12b). He depicts the Jewish high priest as a Catholic celebrant at Mass, dressed in a chasuble. At the Offertory, he faces the people, his back to the altar and acolyte at his side, and offers the paten to be kissed. Approaching the altar is Joachim holding his offering, a lamb, with his wife, Anne, behind him. Rejecting their gift because of their childless marriage, the priest fends Joachim off with a raised hand and, turning his head away in disgust, pulls back the paten that Joachim sought to kiss.[23]

≈

In addition to Jungmann, other liturgists have enlightening observations to make about the lay kissing of the paten. Thomas Frederick Simmons informs us that at the Offertory, up to the Reformation:

> The offerings were placed in the hand of the celebrant, or in the paten held by the deacon, or in a bason, held by the clerk or by laymen of estate standing on the left side of the priest. The offerers went up, first men and then women, in the order of precedence, according to their 'degree' – two and two, if mourners at funerals, members of gilds in procession, etc. – and after kissing the paten in the hands of the deacon, or the hand of the celebrant, and, if a bishop, receiving his blessing, they returned to their places.[24]

Simmons also notes that the practice was forbidden by Pope Pius V (r. 1566–72) and by the Third Provincial Council of Milan, held under Cardinal Carlo Borromeo in 1574 (prohibitions also noted by Jungmann).[25] The author observes, however, that on high feast days in Rouen, in the cathedral and parish churches, the forbidden practice continued until at least the eighteenth century.[26]

William McGarvey and Charles P.A. Burnett tell us that:

---

[23]  For Morgan MS M.231, see the Morgan's online catalogue, CORSAIR.

[24]  Simmons, ed., *The Lay Folks Mass Book*, p. 236.

[25]  J. Donovan, trans., *The Catechism of the Council of Trent, Published by Command of Pope Pius the Fifth* (New York, 1829), p. 172; see the section titled, 'The laity prohibited to touch the sacred vessels, etc.'

[26]  For the practice at Rouen, Simmons cites Jean-Baptiste Le Brun des Marettes, *Voyages liturgiques de France, ou, Recherches faites en diverses villes du royaume, contenant plusiers particularitez touchant les rits et les usages des églises: avec des découvertes sur l'antiquité ecclésiastique & payenne* (Paris, 1718), p. 366. George Every, *The Mass* (Dublin, 1978), p. 144, reproduces a seventeenth-century print that depicts a man, tall candle in hand, bending to kiss the paten held by the celebrant during a funeral Mass; next to the priest a deacon holds a basin for offered coins. Unfortunately, the author does not cite the print's source, and I have been unable to trace it.

…while the choir sing the Offertory, the Celebrant having made an inclination to the altar, presents the paten to the deacon, sub-deacon and acolytes to be kissed by them. The acolytes carry, one a holy-water vessel and sprinkler, the other the basin or vase in which the offerings are to be received. Then the Celebrant standing erect, between the deacon and sub-deacon, upon the lowest step of the altar, or at the balustrade of the sanctuary, receives the offerings, and to those who approach he then presents the paten to be kissed. To the priests, deacons, and sub-deacons, he presents the concave part; to others he presents the convex; wiping the paten each time with the purificator, and saying, 'Pax tibi.' They who kiss the paten bow and reply, 'Et cum spiritu tuo,' and bow again after kissing the paten.[27]

McGarvey and Burnett note that the practice, although officially prohibited, continued in various places in France until the middle of the nineteenth century.

Writing in the middle of the twentieth century, Jungmann and Croegaert remark that the prohibited osculation continued until the present day (that is, the 1950s) at funeral Masses.[28] Finally, there is a documented lay kissing of the paten from as late as 1965. As indicated by a photograph published on their website, members of the Confraternity of St Vincent in the small French town of Ménétréol-sous-Sancerre kissed the paten after making their offerings during the Mass celebrated that year for their patron saint in the town's church of St Hilaire.[29]

The images of Offertory kissing reproduced or cited in this essay – two dozen, but all I know of – are few in number. But they document a liturgical

---

[27] William McGarvey & Charles P. A. Burnett, *The Ceremonies of the Mass, Arranged Conformably to the Rubrics of the Book of Common Prayer* (London, 1905), pp. 199–200.

[28] Joseph A. Jungmann, *The Mass of the Roman Rite: Its Origins and Development (Missarum Sollemnia)*, 2 vols (New York, 1951–55), 2, p. 18, who specifies funeral Masses in Belgium. A. Croegaert, *The Mass: A Liturgical Commentary*, 2 vols (Westminster, 1958–59), 2, p. 78, writes, 'The ancient offertory procession still survives in some countries on certain occasions. At funeral Masses, after the celebrant has read the offertory (*offertorium*) the faithful with candles in their hands make their way to the altar; they "are going to the offertory." They kiss the offering-dish, the paten, to show that they want peacefully and lovingly to share in the priest's oblation; then they make a pecuniary 'oblation' which replaces the ancient oblation of natural products.'

[29] For the 1965 photographs of the ceremony, see https://memoires-pour-demain. pagesperso-orange.fr/saint%20vincent/celebration.html. In another online example, this time literary, the protagonist in Patricia Lacroix's story, 'Un relent de vieux velours humide,' published in 2003 on the Belgian website La Libre, kisses the paten while attending her grandfather's funeral: https://www.lalibre.be/culture/livres-bd/un-relent-de-vieux-velours-humide-51b8807ce4b0de6db9a9556d.

practice, once widespread, whereby lay people had direct and intimate contact with a sacred Eucharistic vessel, a priestly garment, or, indeed, the hand of the celebrant himself. While the custom of lay contact with sacred vessels was prohibited by the Church following the sixteenth-century Council of Trent, the custom of kissing the paten nevertheless continued, albeit rarely and not universally, past the middle of the twentieth century. It would seem, however, that reforms initiated by Vatican II, whose concluding session met in December 1965, may have finally eradicated a ritual tradition that was by then hundreds of years old. That paten in Ménétréol-sous-Sancerre may be the last one that lay folk ever kiss.

# 4

## *THE NEW CHRONICLES OF ENGLAND AND FRANCE* IN NEW ENGLAND

~

*Julia Boffey*

The increasing ease with which it is possible to consult digital facsimiles of medieval manuscripts can occasionally obscure the extraordinary journeys which some of these books have made, and the variety of routes that they have taken to reach their present locations. It is true that some manuscripts, such as those serving institutional or family purposes, have stayed close to home and still reside in the locations where they were first read. But more often than not the work of reconstructing a manuscript's history leads a considerable distance from its place of origin, and through the hands of a succession of owners and readers who may have used it for a succession of different purposes. A manuscript's reception and influence can thus change considerably over time.

The particular concern of this essay is the arrival of a Middle English manuscript in North America in the seventeenth century, at a point well before the more comprehensively documented activities of important late-nineteenth and early twentieth-century American collectors like J. P. Morgan and Henry E. Huntington. The manuscript in question, a late Middle English chronicle copied in the very early sixteenth century, may very well have the distinction of being the first Middle English manuscript to reach North America; it was brought to attention in a paper that grew from conference sessions organized by Barbara Shailor on the travels of manuscripts.[1] A copy of part of Robert Fabyan's *New Chronicles of England and France*, it is now in the Houghton

---

[1]   Richard A. Linenthal, "'The Collectors Are Far More Particular Than You Think'": Selling Manuscripts to America,' *Manuscripta*, 51 (2007), 131–42 (at 132). A brief anonymous account of the manuscript, entitled 'Neglect of Manuscripts in America,' was published in *The Springfield Sunday Republican*, 11 September 1910. The manuscript's early arrival in North America is also noted by Scott Gwara, 'Peddling Wonderment, Selling Privilege: Launching the Market for Medieval Books in Antebellum New York,' *Perspectives Médiévales*, 41 (2020), 1–35 (p. 6), and 'Collections, Compilations, and Convolutes of Medieval and Renaissance

Library at Harvard as MS Eng 766.[2] Its early history and travels not only offer significant insights into the reception and fluctuating appeal of Fabyan's work but also constitute an intriguing narrative of the various kinds of value that a book might hold for its successive owners.

The *New Chronicles of England and France*, completed by the Londoner Robert Fabyan in 1504, is formed of parallel accounts of English and French history, from early times (the legendary arrival in countries of western Europe of the Trojan heroes Brutus and Francus) to the accession of Henry VII of England in 1485 and the end of the reign of Charles VIII of France in 1495.[3] Compiled from a great variety of sources that must have included a *Brut* chronicle, a *Polychronicon*, one or more London chronicles, and various accounts of French history, it survives in a two-part manuscript (now Holkham Hall MS 671 and BL MS Cotton Nero C XI) which was evidently copied and decorated by Fabyan himself. At some point fairly soon after the completion of Fabyan's own copy a second two-part copy was made, perhaps for reference purposes or for retention in a London institutional library.[4] The two parts of this copy became separated at what must have been a relatively early stage in their history; part I is now York Minster Library MS XVI. Q. 9 and part II is Cambridge, MA, Harvard University, Houghton Library MS Eng 766.

One of the notable features of both the York and Houghton manuscripts is that they contain a series of marginal marks probably made in preparation for Richard Pynson's printing of the *New Chronicles of England and France* in 1516 (STC 10659). This evidence that the manuscript served as setting copy would seem to indicate that both parts of this copy of the *New Chronicles* were in use in London, in Pynson's printshop, after Fabyan's own death in 1513. The copy represented by the York and Houghton manuscripts may possibly

---

Manuscript Fragments in North America before ca. 1900,' *Fragmentology*, 3 (2020), 73–139 (p. 132).

[2]   It is noted in de Ricci & Wilson, I, 954, and Faye & Bond, p. 227. A summary description of the manuscript and its contents is in Linda Ehrsam Voigts, 'A Handlist of Middle English in Harvard Manuscripts,' *Harvard Library Bulletin*, 33 (1985), 32–37; for the chronicle itself, see Henry Ellis, ed., *The New Chronicles of England and France, in Two Parts: by Robert Fabyan* (London, 1811).

[3]   Accounts of Fabyan and his activities are in Julia Boffey, *Manuscript and Print in London, c. 1475–1530* (London, 2012), pp. 162–207, and Matthew Payne, 'The Books of Robert Fabyan (*c.* 1450–1513),' unpublished PhD thesis, Queen Mary University of London, 2021.

[4]   The break between volumes comes at the same point in the two copies, at the end of the reign of Philip II of France. The second volume, starting with the reign of Richard I of England at 1189, begins to make use of the content of London chronicles, which customarily began at this date.

have been commissioned specifically for the purposes of a printer, made at the request of Pynson, or of Fabyan's family and friends, in the years following the author's death. Both parts of this copy are less carefully finished than Fabyan's holograph manuscripts, lacking the careful ornamentation and illustrations that Fabyan supplied. They are constructed of very large gatherings, some of over forty leaves, and were produced by a number of scribes who although writing practised hands seem to have worked fairly quickly. At least the second part of the copy (now Houghton MS Eng 766) was apparently quickly put into what appears to be a tacketed leather binding which it still retains. (The first volume may have been treated in the same way but subsequent rebinding has obscured its earlier treatment.) Such bindings were strong and inexpensive, and often used for books that would be in regular use.[5]

In the course of the sixteenth century, the two parts of this marked-up copy must have become separated. Neither part retains significant marginal annotation by hands other than those of the original scribes, and their whereabouts for the century or so after their production is not clear. Ownership inscriptions suggest that Part I, now York Minster Library MS XVI. Q. 9, must have made its way to the north of England by the end of the sixteenth century, and possibly remained there until acquired by York Minster Library in the eighteenth century.[6] The later sixteenth-century life of Houghton MS Eng 766 is undocumented, and the earliest indication of ownership is on fol. 1: 'Samuel Lee bought / 1656 Jun. 26 [from / ..] M Bourne in / Bethlehem,' with a noted cost that appears to be one shilling. Probably related to this inscription is a pencilled 'July 1656' on the unfoliated first recto of the introductory table of contents.

The record of this transaction serves as a neat hinge between two milieux significant in the manuscript's history: first the city of London, and then, more unexpectedly, New England. The *New Chronicles'* author, Robert Fabyan, was a prominent member of the London oligarchy. He served his city as an alderman and sheriff, and in his role as a merchant held important positions in the Drapers' company, one of the wealthiest and most influential of London's guilds. His

---

[5]  A photograph of the binding is available on the Houghton Library's digital site 'Medieval and Renaissance Manuscripts': see https://curiosity.lib.harvard.edu/medieval-renaissance-manuscripts. See further Nicholas Pickwoad, 'Tacketed Bindings: A Hundred Years of European Bookbinding,' in David Pearson, ed., *'For the Love of the Binding': Studies in Bookbinding History Presented to Mirjam Foot* (London, 2000), pp. 119–67. Pickwoad's analysis suggests a peak in the use of tacketed bindings around 1530. I am grateful to Professor Tamara Atkin for advice on the manuscript's binding.

[6]  No full description of this manuscript has been published. Brief details of ownership are supplied in Payne, 'The Books of Robert Fabyan,' pp. 271–72.

London residence was in the parish of St Michael's Cornhill, and although his latter years were mostly spent at his out-of-town residence at Theydon Garnon in Essex, he must have retained local London connections. One volume of his own two-part holograph manuscript of the *New Chronicles* (BL MS Cotton Nero C XI) was by the later sixteenth century in the hands of the historian John Stow, some of whose godparents were residents of the parish of St Michael's Cornhill and among the individuals remembered in Fabyan's will.[7]

The two-part manuscript that is now York Minster Library MS XVI. Q. 9 and Houghton MS Eng 766 was almost certainly produced in London, perhaps commissioned by Fabyan or his family members and acquaintances or a London institution. One possibility is that it was made to be kept at the Guildhall, in the library from which Fabyan had borrowed books used in its compilation.[8] It is known that the court of Aldermen at the Guildhall had a printed copy of the *New Chronicles* in the 1530s, and before this they could well have owned a manuscript. Since Fabyan was himself an alderman in the 1490s he may have seen his *New Chronicles* (parts of which deal with London's history) as a work which had some relevance to the activities of London's administrative centre. If the volumes were in the Guildhall library they are likely to have been among the collection of books removed around 1549 on the order of the reforming Edward Seymour, duke of Somerset (Protector Somerset).[9] Other possible connections link the sixteenth-century history of the two-part manuscript to the activities of the printer Pynson, who clearly used them for the edition of the *New Chronicles* that he printed in 1516. The volumes could have remained for some time in Pynson's premises in the parish of St Dunstan-in-the-West in Fleet Street, and subsequently in those of his successors, as his business passed to Robert Redman, Redman's business to his wife Elizabeth, Elizabeth's to her second

---

[7]   Boffey, *Manuscript and Print*, p. 164. A partial transcription of Fabyan's will is in Ellis, ed., *The New Chronicles*, and a full one in Payne, 'The Books of Robert Fabyan,' pp. 257–69.

[8]   See Caroline M. Barron, *The Medieval Guildhall of London* (London, 1974); David Pearson, ed., *London, 1000 Years: Treasures from the Collections of the City of London* (London, 2011), p. 27; Nick Bateman, 'John Carpenter's Library: Corporate Charity and London's Guildhall,' in David Gaimster & Roberta Gilchrist, eds, *The Archaeology of Reformation 1480 to 1580* (London, 2018), pp. 356–70; Barrett L. Beer, 'Seymour, Edward, duke of Somerset (*c.* 1500–1552), Soldier and Royal Servant,' *ODNB*.

[9]   'These books as it is said were in the raign of Edward the 6. Sent for by Edward Duke of Somerset, Lorde Protector, with promise to be restored shortly: men laded from thence three Carries with them, but they were neuer returned'; Charles Lethbridge Kingsford, ed., John Stow, *A Survey of London*, 2 vols (Oxford 1908, reprinted 1971), i, 275.

husband William Middleton, and Middleton's to William Powell, who married his widow.[10] Since all these printers were based near St Dunstan's church such a history would have kept the two parts in the area around Fleet Street.

The 1656 purchase of Houghton MS Eng 766, the second part of this two-volume manuscript, is recorded as taking place in Bethlehem, the area of London close to Bishopsgate and the present site of Liverpool Street Station, where until 1675 Bedlam hospital (Britain's first hospital for treatment of the mentally ill) was situated.[11] The 'M[r] Bourne' from whom it was bought seems likely to have been the bookseller Thomas Bourne, who is recorded as selling from premises at or near Bethlehem hospital in 1628 and 1671, and whose business as a seller of secondhand books can be reconstructed from some inscriptions in surviving volumes.[12] The purchase price of 1s seems low but is hard to contextualise. Records of comparable sales are hard to recover and relate mainly to books sold at auction: a 1510 printed *Brut* went for 11s 6d and a printed *Polychronicon* for 17s 1d at the London auction of books from

[10] See the biographies of printers in STC iii.

[11] In 1675 the hospital moved to new premises near Moorfields. On locations for buying secondhand books in London, see Henry Woudhuysen, 'From Duck Lane to Lazarus Seaman: Buying and Selling Old Books in England during the Sixteenth and Seventeenth Centuries,' in Adam Smyth, ed., *The Oxford Handbook of the History of the Book in Early Modern England* (Oxford, 2023), pp. 493–509.

[12] The cutting on 'Neglect of Manuscripts in America' from *The Springfield Sunday Republican* identifies 'M[r] Bourne' as Major Nehemiah Bourne, a parliamentary soldier, but this seems unconvincing. Another possibility might be the Nicholas Bourne, one half of 'Butter and Bourne,' known for selling newsheets and corantos. This Bourne was a Londoner who served an apprenticeship in Cornhill and inherited his master's business there. At his death in 1660 he was buried in the parish church of St Michael's Cornhill. On Thomas Bourne, see STC iii, 27, which notes that he was involved in the printing of Church of England visitation articles for Chichester, STC 10182 (1628) and 10182.5 (1631). Further information is in Henry R. Plomer, *A Dictionary of the Booksellers and Printers Who Were at Work in England, Scotland and Ireland from 1641 to 1667* (London, 1907) p. 30; *The Obituary of Richard Smyth*, ed. Sir Henry Ellis, Camden Society 44 (London, 1849), 91; Edward Arber, *A Transcript of the Registers of the Worshipful Company of Stationers, from 1640 to 1708 AD*, Roxburghe Club, 3 vols (London, 1913–14), iii, 685. I am grateful to Professor Tamara Atkin for these references, and for the further information that Thomas Bourne's activities as a seller of secondhand books are attested by inscriptions in books in the library of Cambridge, St John's College (Qq.3.28: 'I warrant this booke to be perfect. April 8th, 1647 Thomas Bourne'), and in the Folger Library, Washington DC (Folger STC 22273 Fo 1 no 60: 'at ye returne to allow 5s 6d Tho: Bourne).

the library of the Dutch Calvinist theologian Gilbertus Voetius in 1678;[13] a parchment manuscript of the *Polychronicon* offered at the 1687 sale of the library of William Cecil, first lord Burghley (d. 1598) made £5 7s.[14] Because Houghton MS Eng 766 contains only the second part of *The New Chronicles* its contents may have resisted identification, and even in 1656 its binding and appearance may have kept its value down; it is copied in several hands, on paper, and with limited and undistinguished ornamentation.

The purchaser, Samuel Lee, was a nonconformist minister with interests in natural philosophy and other fields.[15] Like the chronicler Fabyan and the bookseller Bourne, he too was born in the city of London (*c.* 1625), in Fish St, and attended St Paul's School before leaving London for Oxford, where he became successively bursar, sub-warden and dean of Wadham College. During the Commonwealth period, Cromwell persuaded Lee back to London to become rector of St Botolph without Billingsgate, a post he held from 1655 until the Restoration and the change of religious climate in 1660. His purchase of Houghton MS Eng 766 took place during this period – according to the inscription, in 1656. Richard Smyth's *Obituary* notes that the bookseller Bourne ('my old acquaintance') was buried in the church of St Botolph without Bishopsgate, so he was perhaps known to Samuel Lee through parish networks and not simply as a dealer in books.

Lee wrote theological works while at Wadham, and he continued to publish collections of sermons and tracts on various subjects.[16] His purchase of a manuscript of the second part of the *New Chronicles* reflects what was evidently a wide range of interests that covered history and science as well as theology.[17] By the Restoration in 1660 he had left St Botolph's for Oxfordshire and, pursuing an enthusiasm for natural history, in 1666 received a license to

---

[13] Leah Orr, 'The Prices of English Books at Auction *c.* 1680,' *The Library*, 7th series, 20 (2019), 501–26 (at 517).

[14] Richard Beadle, 'Medieval English Manuscripts at Auction 1676–*c.* 1700,' *The Book Collector*, 53 (2004), 46–63.

[15] See Dewey W. Wallace Jnr, 'Lee, Samuel (1625?–1691),' *ODNB*. Edmund Calamy, *The Nonconformists' Memorial, being an Account of the Ministers who were Ejected or Silenced after the Restoration … now Abridged and Corrected by Samuel Palmer*, 3 vols (London, 1775), i, 95–96.

[16] For an account of his intellectual interests in the context of his puritan beliefs, see Theodore Hornberger, 'Samuel Lee (1625–1691), a Clerical Channel for the Flow of New Ideas to Seventeenth-Century New England,' *Osiris*, 1 (1936), 341–55.

[17] Calamy, *Nonconformists' Memorial*, p. 95: 'He was a considerable scholar … no stranger to any part of polite and useful learning.'

visit America and the Caribbean.[18] On his return to England he continued to write and publish, and to hold livings in non-conformist congregations in and around London. But James II's accession in 1685 may have prompted fears about new changes in the religious climate, and these or other factors persuaded him to leave again for America. This time he sailed with his wife and daughters, arriving in Boston on 22 August 1686. Lee's second North American visit was a longer one: he preached in various places in and around Boston, and became pastor of the congregational church of Bristol, Rhode Island.[19] The Fabyan manuscript that he had bought in London must have crossed the Atlantic with him, and when in 1690 he decided to return to England it remained in America with those of his family members who stayed there. His return journey had an unfortunate end, as the ship on which he took passage was captured by a privateer and Lee ended up in St Malo in France, where he eventually died in 1691 of a fever. By the will that he had made in 1685, his estate went at his death to his wife and daughters, with some specifications about particular bequests:

> to my daughter Rebeccah all my Manuscripts in divinity if she be not disposed in … marriage before this will take effect[;] to Anna, Lydia and Elizabeth all my manuscripts in Naturall Philosophy, Chemistry or Physick or of any the Liberall Arts and Sciences, and all the printed books in Chimicall Physick to be devided equally share and share alike the eldest choosing first excepting <onely> one manuscript book in Octavo large with black covers in the first leafe thereof is found written Experimentorum liber III which I give and bequeath to my daughter Elizabeth.[20]

---

[18] These interests are reflected in correspondence in 1690 between Lee and the English botanist Nehemiah Grew: see George Lyman Kittredge, ed., *Letters of Samuel Lee and Samuel Sewall Relating to New England and the Indians* (Cambridge, MA, 1912).

[19] 'Dr Stiles's account of the Rev. Samuel Lee of Bristol and his Church,' *Publications of the Massachusetts Historical Society*, 8 (1864–65), 219–20, notes that 'Mr Lee was much complained of for preaching in too learned a style.'

[20] The National Archives, PROB 11/409/202; partly transcribed in Henry F. Waters, *Genealogical Gleanings in England: Abstracts of Wills Relating to early American Families*, enlarged edition, 2 vols (Boston, MA, 1901), ii, 470–71. *Book Owners Online* has an entry for Lee (https://bookowners.online/Samuel_Lee_1625%3F-1691) but notes that none of his books have been identified. 'Dr Stiles's account' notes that Lee 'was sorely disappointed' in his daughters in relation to marriages that must have taken place in the years between the making of his will and his death: 'He was a Man of high Temper, & wealthy, & expected his children would intermarry with the best & most honorable Families. He was disappointed & mortified.'

In its travels to a New England environment the value and significance of Houghton MS Eng 766 must necessarily have changed. Lee had bought it in London, close to its place of production and to locales that featured importantly in its chronicle contents. For those who encountered it in North America, it preserved – in a rather unprepossessing state – a partial account of the by now fairly ancient history of the distant countries of England and France. Its fate when Lee's library was sold in 1693 by those of his daughters who remained in New England is not clear. The sale was organized through the Boston bookseller Duncan Campbell, a native of Scotland, whose catalogue is the earliest book sale catalogue to be printed in North America.[21] It describes:

> The Library of the Late Reverend and Learned Mr Samuel Lee: containing a Choice Variety of Books on all Subjects; particularly, Commentaries on the Bible; Bodies of Divinity. The Works as well of the Ancient, as of the Modern Divines; Treatises on the Mathematicks, in all parts; History; Antiquities; Natural Philosophy Physick, and Chymistry; with Grammar and School-books. With many more Choice Books not mentioned in this Catalogue.

Most of the *c.* 1200 works listed in the catalogue are indeed on divinity, but there are two-and-a-half pages of 'histories' of one sort or another, in Latin and English, folio and octavo. Listed among the Latin books are works by Walsingham and Matthew Paris, and among the English books the chronicles of Hall and Holinshed, with Foxe's *Acts and Monuments*. The English histories include what is called 'Stout's Survey of London,' surely an edition of John Stow's *Survey*; and 'Eabran's Chronicles,' perhaps the Houghton Fabyan, or a copy of one of the sixteenth-century printed editions of the *New Chronicles*. That the library included manuscripts as well as printed books is suggested by the presence of '*Histor. Angl. Scripti antiq.*' Even if the manuscript that is now Houghton Eng 766 is not specified among the named titles in the catalogue, it could well have been among the 'many more Choice Books' not listed by name.

Lee's library was substantial but not extraordinarily so in New England at this date. The statement in T. G. Wright's 1920 study of *Literary Culture*

---

[21] *The Library of the Late Reverend and Learned Mr. Samuel Lee* (Boston, MA, 1693), ESTC System No. 006467597. *Robert B. Winans, A Descriptive Checklist of Book Catalogues Separately Printed in America 1693–1800* (Worcester, MA, 1981), no. 1. On Campbell, see George Littlefield, *Early Boston Booksellers, 1642–1711* (Boston, MA, 1900), 130–36 (at 132). For some comparison of Lee's library with the collection of William Byrd II of Westover, PA (1674–1744), see Kevin J. Hates, *The Library of William Byrd of Westover* (Madison, WI, 1997), pp. 75–76.

*in Early New England* that 'Very few of the pilgrims were without books' has been endorsed and extended in numerous more recent studies of early North American book production and importation. James Raven notes that:

> In total, hundreds of treasured books accompanied the 20,000 people migrating to New England in the 1640s, and the wealthiest and best-connected among the settled soon made attempts to secure further parcels of new and valued works. In succeeding decades, diverse individual orders for print were placed with London and European friends, associates, and book-sellers.[22]

Surviving wills and inventories include some references to European and English histories. At his death in 1656 Miles Standish left 'a History of England'; a donation of books to Harvard College made by Governor John Winthrop included Polydore Vergil's *Historia Anglicana*; William Brewster and Thomas Jenner had copies of works by Camden.[23] Middle English works were not unknown: Governor Thomas Dudley (d. 1653) left a collection of books which included a 'Vision of Pierc Plowman,' perhaps one of the editions printed by Crowley.[24]

It is unclear whether Lee's Fabyan manuscript was included in the Boston sale or remained in the hands of one of his daughters, at least two of whom moved in learned New England circles. One daughter, Rebecca, married as his third wife John Saffin (1626–1710), merchant, judge and minor poet; another, Lydia (d. 1733–34), after the death of her first husband John George, became in 1715 the third wife of Cotton Mather (1663–1728), Harvard graduate

[22] T. G. Wright, *Literary Culture in New England* (New Haven, CT, 1920), p. 27; James Raven, *The Business of Books* (New Haven, CT, 2007), p. 103. See also Hugh Amory, 'British Books Abroad: The American Colonies,' in John Barnard & D. F. McKenzie, eds, *The History of the Book in Britain, Volume IV, 1557–1695* (Cambridge, 2002), pp. 744–52.

[23] Wright, *Literary Culture*, p. 2; Franklin B. Dexter, 'Early Private Libraries in New England,' *American Antiquarian Society*, April 1907, 135–47; Wright, *Literary Culture*, p. 254 (Brewster) and Samuel Eliot Morison, *The Intellectual Life of Colonial New England* 3rd edn (New York, 1965), p. 136 (Jenner).

[24] 'Gov. Thomas Dudley's Library,' *New England Historical and Genealogical Register*, 12 (1858), 355–56 (at 355). Two folio volumes of Chaucer have sometimes been associated with Daniel Russell of Charlestown (by, for example, Morison, *The Intellectual Life*, pp. 138–39, and Nancy Bradley Warren, *Chaucer and Religious Controversies in the Medieval and Early Modern Eras* [Notre Dame, IN, 2019], p. 135) but this is the result of a misreading; see Misha Teramura, 'Chaucer Folios in Colonia America: A Correction,' *The Chaucer Review*, 51 (2016), 503–14.

and at that point pastor of the Old North Church in Boston.[25] In its course through the hands of what seem to have been members of the Boston elite, the manuscript reached the library of Thomas Newton (1660–1721), who had arrived in New Hampshire in 1688 and went on to become a distinguished Massachusetts lawyer.[26] In 1724, after his death, Newton's wife gave it, 'to remember her deceased husband' (as recorded in a note in the manuscript's inner cover), to Timothy Cutler (1684–1765), previously rector of Yale College, and by 1723 (after a visit to England during which he was re-ordained in London) founding rector of Christ Church in Boston.[27] So from the hands of the puritan minister Lee, who seems to have bought it cheaply and in a relatively neglected state in London, Houghton MS Eng 766 entered the libraries of men and women with scholarly interests in history, and perhaps with enthusiasm for preserving material remains of the continent from which they or their antecedents had travelled.

After Cutler's death the manuscript passed through the hands of several further New England owners. It is likely to have been owned by the jurist and loyalist Samuel Curwen (1715–1802), since a note on the inside cover records that it was bought 'at Mr Curwen's sale Friday 23 July 1802.' (Curwen had died the previous April.)[28] It also passed through the hands of a William Appleton Jr, possibly the trader, banker and member of the House of Representatives named

---

[25]   On the marriages of Lee's daughters, see Waters, *Genealogical Gleanings*, p. 471 and Kenneth Silverman, ed., *Selected Letters of Cotton Mather* (Baton Rouge, LA, 1971), pp. 93–95. On Saffin, see John T. Shawcroft, 'John Saffin (22 November 1626–18 July 1710),' *American National Biography* online, and Albert J. Von Frank, John Saffin, Slavery and Racism in Colonial Massachusetts,' *Early American Literature*, 29 (1994), 254–72; and on Mather, see Robert Middlekauff, 'Mather, Cotton (12 February 1663–13 February 1728),' *American National Biography* online, and Virginia Bernhard, 'Cotton Mather's "Most Unhappy Wife": Reflections on the Uses of Historical Evidence,' *The New England Quarterly*, 60 (1987), 341–62. Lee's daughter Anna married Henry Wyrley of New Bristol, said to have been Lee's manservant; see 'Dr Stiles's Account.' According to Water, *Genealogical Gleanings*, p. 471, the daughter who left New England with her mother and father in 1688, Elizabeth, may have married a bishop.

[26]   Ermina Newton Leonard, *Newton Genealogy, Genealogical, Biographical, Historical, Being a Record of the Descendants of Richard Newton, of Sudbury and Marlborough, Massachusetts 1638* (De Pere, WI, 1915), 799–801.

[27]   Allen C. Guelzo, 'Cutler, Timothy (31 May 1684–17 August 1765),' *American National Biography* online.

[28]   *The Journal and Letters of Samuel Curwen: an American in England, from 1775 to 1783; with an Appendix of Biographical Sketches* (Boston, MA, 1864), and Andrew Oliver, ed., *The Journal of Samuel Curwen, Loyalist*, 2 vols (Cambridge, MA, 1972). Details of some of the sales are listed in de Ricci & Wilson, I, 954.

William Appleton (1786–1862), but perhaps more likely his son, William Appleton Junior (1825–77).[29] For these owners the interest was presumably its historical content: Curwen, who spent some years in England, may also have appreciated its local London connections. But for another in the sequence of the manuscript's nineteenth-century owners, David Pulsifer (1802–94), its attractions may also have included its material features. Pulsifer was an author and antiquarian but also a professional scribe, chirographer and bookbinder, who had developed an interest in old documents during his apprenticeship to a bookbinder in Salem; he moved to Boston in 1841 and worked as a Clerk of the Courts and Registry of Deeds, while also making formal copies of significant runs of records and writing antiquarian works.[30] He may have been responsible for making good some of the losses of leaves by the insertion of hand-made facsimiles, transcribed presumably from one of the sixteenth-century printed editions or maybe even from Sir Henry Ellis's edition of 1811.

By 1911 the manuscript was in the hands of the Boston dealer Charles Eliot Goodspeed, who had set up business in Park Street, Beacon Hill, in 1898.[31] A note kept with the manuscript suggests that in 1910 Harvard had made overtures about buying it, but by 1912 it had been sold to a private owner, the businessman Francis W. Fabyan (1871–1937). The appeal of the *New Chronicles* to this twentieth-century Fabyan must surely have been prompted in part by its author's name, but Francis Fabyan also had serious bibliographical interests, especially in books associated with Cotton and Increase Mather, and he may have known that one of Samuel Lee's daughters became Cotton Mather's

---

[29] On the elder William Appleton, see the Rev. Chandler Robbins, *Memoir of Hon William Appleton, Prepared Agreeably to a Resolution of the Massachusetts Historical Society* (Boston, MA, 1863), and Susan M. Loring, ed., *Selections from the Diaries of William Appleton 1786–1862* (Boston, MA, 1922). This elder William Appleton's father was Joseph. Neither William Sumner Appleton, numismatist (1840–1903) nor William Appleton, publisher (1814–99), both with Massachusetts connections, was the son of a William Appleton.

[30] John Ward Dean, 'David Pulsifer, A.M.,' reprinted from the *Necrology of the New-England Historic Genealogical Society* (Boston, 1896); a news item in the *Waterbury Evening Democrat*, 11 September 1890, p. 2, described him as 'a notable antiquarian … profoundly learned in all matters pertaining to the state of Massachusetts.' Pulsifer's association with the manuscript is recorded in a note that reads 'David Pulsifer 3d.' This was interpreted as 'David Pulsifer III' by de Ricci & Wilson, I, 954 – a possibility, as Pulsifer's father was another David – but it may instead indicate that Pulsifer paid 3 dollars for it.

[31] Walter Muir Whitehill, 'Charles Eliot Goodspeed,' *Proceedings of the Massachusetts Historical Society*, 3rd Series, 71 (1953–57), 362–65; and Goodspeed's own *Yankee Bookseller, Being the Reminiscences of Charles E. Goodspeed* (Boston, MA, 1937).

third wife.[32] The manuscript seems to have remained in Fabyan's library until his death in 1937; it was there when de Ricci was compiling his *Census* for publication in 1935. Finally, in 1945, when it was again in the hands of the bookseller Goodspeed, it was bought by Harvard, the purchase supported by the Friends of Harvard College Library. One of the justifications for the purchase is likely to have been the fact that the library by this point held a copy of Pynson's 1513 printed edition of *The New Chronicles* (STC 10659), acquired in 1916.

Houghton MS Eng 766 remains of interest to bibliographers and codicologists on a number of counts. Although a note in the Houghton Library's file on the manuscript reports that 'its real importance is that it served as copy for typesetting for one of England's celebrated early printers, Richard Pynson, for an edition he printed in 1516,' its extraordinary early journey to New England seems at least as remarkable a feature of its history. The reverend Samuel Lee would be pleased to learn of its present location in the Houghton Library at Harvard, a place on which he reported in 1690 to Nehemiah Grew:

> In New England there is a very pretty [] [*sic*] a handsome library & several [c]onveniences for Scholars at a place now called, Cambridge about 5 or 6 miles fro Boston & is styled, the Colledge, hath a president & some fellowes. It was given by one Mr Harvard & calld by his name.[33]

Its long residence in North America has limited scholarly access to it – it has gone unremarked in editions and most studies of Fabyan's *New Chronicles* – and stands as a pointed reminder that the location of books and documents can have a meaningful influence on scholarship. In its current material state, still in the leather wrapper that evidently served as its first binding, it is a visibly striking old book, palpably a piece of history in its own right as well as in terms of the chronicle it contains. That same material state is what is likely to keep it something of a scholarly secret: its fragility is such that digital reproductions of only the binding and fol. 30 have been made for the excellent *Digital Medieval Manuscripts at Houghton Library* pages, and to learn more you still have to go and see it for yourself.

---

[32]  See *American Rarissima from the Private Library of Francis W. Fabyan, Esq., of Boston, including a Remarkable Collection of Works by Increase and Cotton Mather … to be Sold February 17th, 1920* (New York, 1920). Francis's millionaire brother George Fabyan, a cryptographer with developed interests in the Shakespeare/Bacon controversy, established the research centre Riverbank Laboratories to investigate what were alleged to be Shakespearean ciphers. See William F. Friedman & Elizabeth Friedman, *The Shakespearean Ciphers Examined* (Cambridge, 1957).

[33]  Kittredge, ed., *Letters of Samuel Lee*, p. 145 (from BL, MS Sloane 4062, fol. 235).

# 5

# F. J. Furnivall and the Macro Manuscript[1]

~

*Michael P. Kuczynski*

Washington, DC, Folger Shakespeare Library MS V.a.354, more commonly known as the Macro Manuscript, is a nearly unique record of three fifteenth-century English morality plays: *Mankind, Wisdom,* and *The Castle of Perseverance.*[2] Most of *Mankind* and the whole of *Wisdom* are copied in the same late fifteenth-century hand, *Castle* in a different, earlier fifteenth-century one.[3] A fragment of the second of these dramas, *Wisdom,* also survives in BodL MS Digby 133, along with some biblical plays and various scientific treatises.[4]

Many scholars know Macro almost exclusively for its final leaf: the drawing of what appears to be a stage design for a medieval production of *Castle*

[1] I conducted much of the research for this essay during a short-term fellowship at the Folger Shakespeare Library, Washington, DC in Spring 2019. I am grateful to Michael Witmore, director of the Folger, for granting me unlimited access to the Macro Manuscript and to the Folger's archives. I also wish to thank Renate Mesmer, Rhea Destefano, and Adrienne Bell for their almost daily hospitality and advice, over the course of three months, in the Folger's conservation lab, where I was required to work with the manuscript due to its fragile condition. I am likewise indebted for many illuminating conversations about the Macro Manuscript to Richard Beadle, Theresa Coletti, and Gail Gibson. Finally, I am grateful to A. S. G. Edwards, Helen Spencer, and Katherine Thorn for particular help. The views expressed here and any errors, of course, are my own.

[2] It is customary now for scholars to refer to the Macro 'manuscripts' in the plural. To avoid confusion in this essay, I use the singular 'Macro Manuscript' and hereafter simply 'Macro' or 'the manuscript' when referring to the codex, and the plural 'Macro plays' or 'the plays' when referring to the dramas contained in it.

[3] On the scribe of *Mankind* and *Wisdom,* see Richard Beadle, 'Monk Thomas Hyngham's Hand in the Macro Manuscript,' in Richard Beadle & A. J. Piper, eds, *New Science Out of Old Books: Studies in Manuscripts and Early Printed Books in Honour of A. I. Doyle* (Aldershot, 1995), pp. 315–41.

[4] See Donald C. Baker & J. L. Murphy, eds, *The Digby Plays: Facsimiles of the Plays in Bodley MSS Digby 133 and e Museo 160* (Leeds, 1976) and Milla Cozart Riggio, *The Play of Wisdom: Its Texts and Contexts* (New York, 1998).

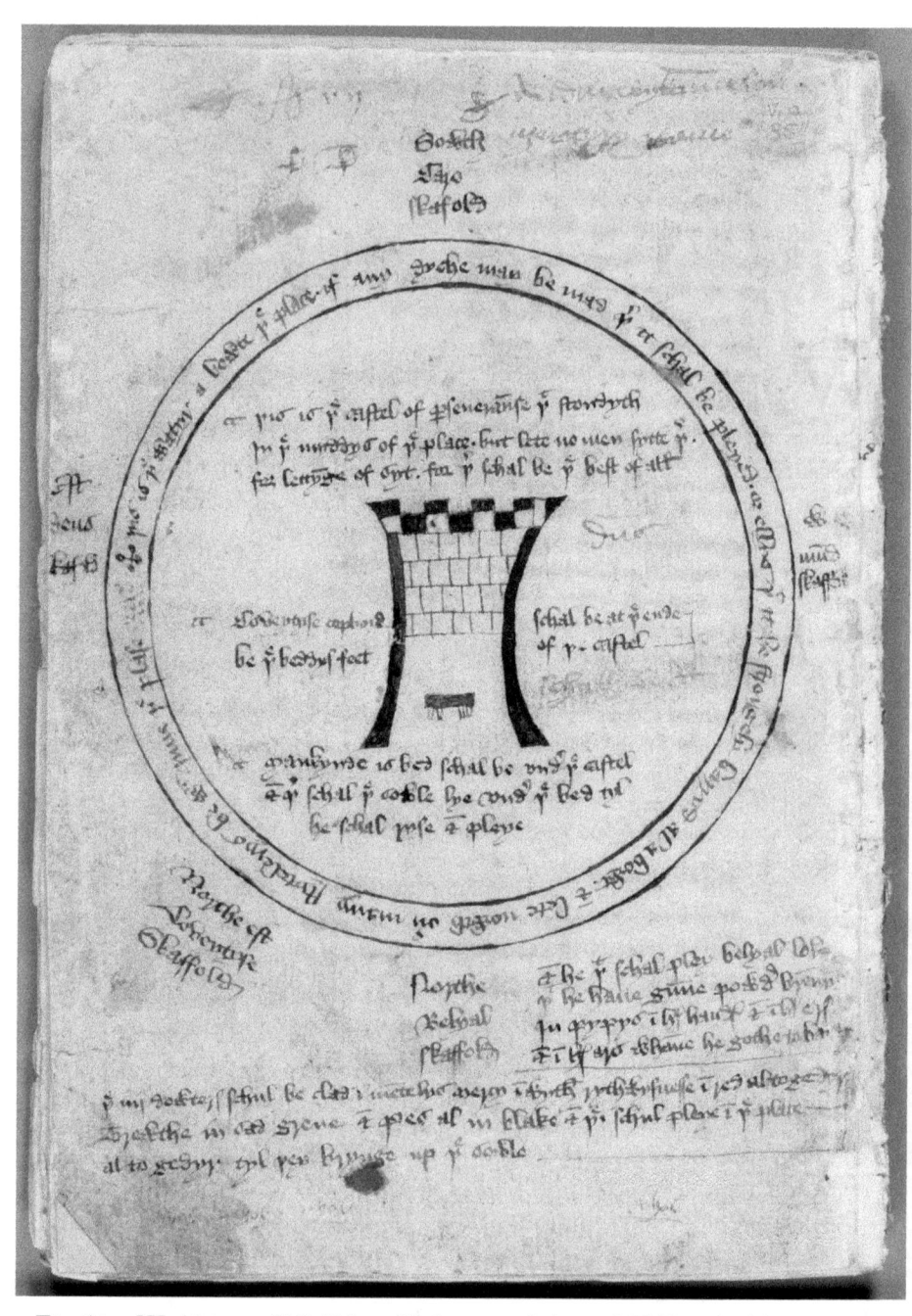

Fig. 5.1. Washington, DC, Folger Shakespeare Library, MS V.a.354, fol. 191ᵛ, stage design for *The Castle of Perseverance*. Courtesy of the Folger Shakespeare Library.

(Figure 5.1).[5] In this essay, I focus on the manuscript's curatorial history, especially its use during the Victorian period by F. J. Furnivall (1825–1910), who in 1864 founded the Early English Text Society (henceforward EETS) and in 1904, with Alfred W. Pollard, edited the Macro plays for EETS. As I hope to make clear, understanding Furnivall's involvement with Macro requires that one study this episode in its history alongside the manuscript's history at the Folger, where since 1971 Macro has been disbound and stored as individual plays in three separate wrappers.

By the time Furnivall gained access to the three morality plays that now constitute Macro they had been removed, several decades previously, from a much larger composite manuscript. Sometime in the 1830s, the Quaker banker and collector Hudson Gurney (1775–1864) had had the three morality plays bound together, having abstracted their fragile paper gatherings from a larger miscellany that included a fourteenth-century copy of Juvenal's poems, a treatise on Anglo-Saxon law dating from the eleventh century, and several booklets concerned with astrology and alchemy, mostly of the early sixteenth century. How and when these very diverse items were first brought together in a single volume is not known.[6] That miscellany – the nature of its binding is unknown – had previously belonged to the famous eighteenth-century antiquary Cox Macro (1686–1767) of Bury St Edmunds, and Gurney had Macro's name stamped and gilt on the four uniformly rebound components of the volume, just beneath his own self-styled coat-of-arms. Figure 5.2 shows the binding of the volume in which Gurney brought together the three morality plays.

In 1820, Cox Macro's heirs had sent a large quantity of his manuscripts for public auction, but all were bought privately and jointly by Dawson Turner, another English banker and collector, and Hudson Gurney, who divided the collection between them. Most of those acquired by Gurney were listed and described in Sotheby's catalogue for the sale of the Gurney collection on March 30–31, 1936 and have since been dispersed widely.[7] Another early play manuscript from the same collection, also extracted from a larger volume and rebound in dark blue Morocco like Macro, was the unique copy of *A merye enterlude entitled Respublica*, a late morality play written in 1553, which is now

---

[5]   A nearly complete digital record of the manuscript is available at https://luna. folger.edu. On the noteworthy omissions, see below.

[6]   For a meticulous historical reconstruction of the miscellany that Gurney broke up and reorganised, see Richard Beadle, 'Macro MS 5: A Historical Reconstruction,' *Transactions of the Cambridge Bibliographical Society*, 16 (2016), 35–77.

[7]   See Sotheby's, *Catalogue of a selected portion of the valuable library and collection of manuscripts, the property of Major Q. E. Gurney, D. L.*, 31 March 1936, lot 170.

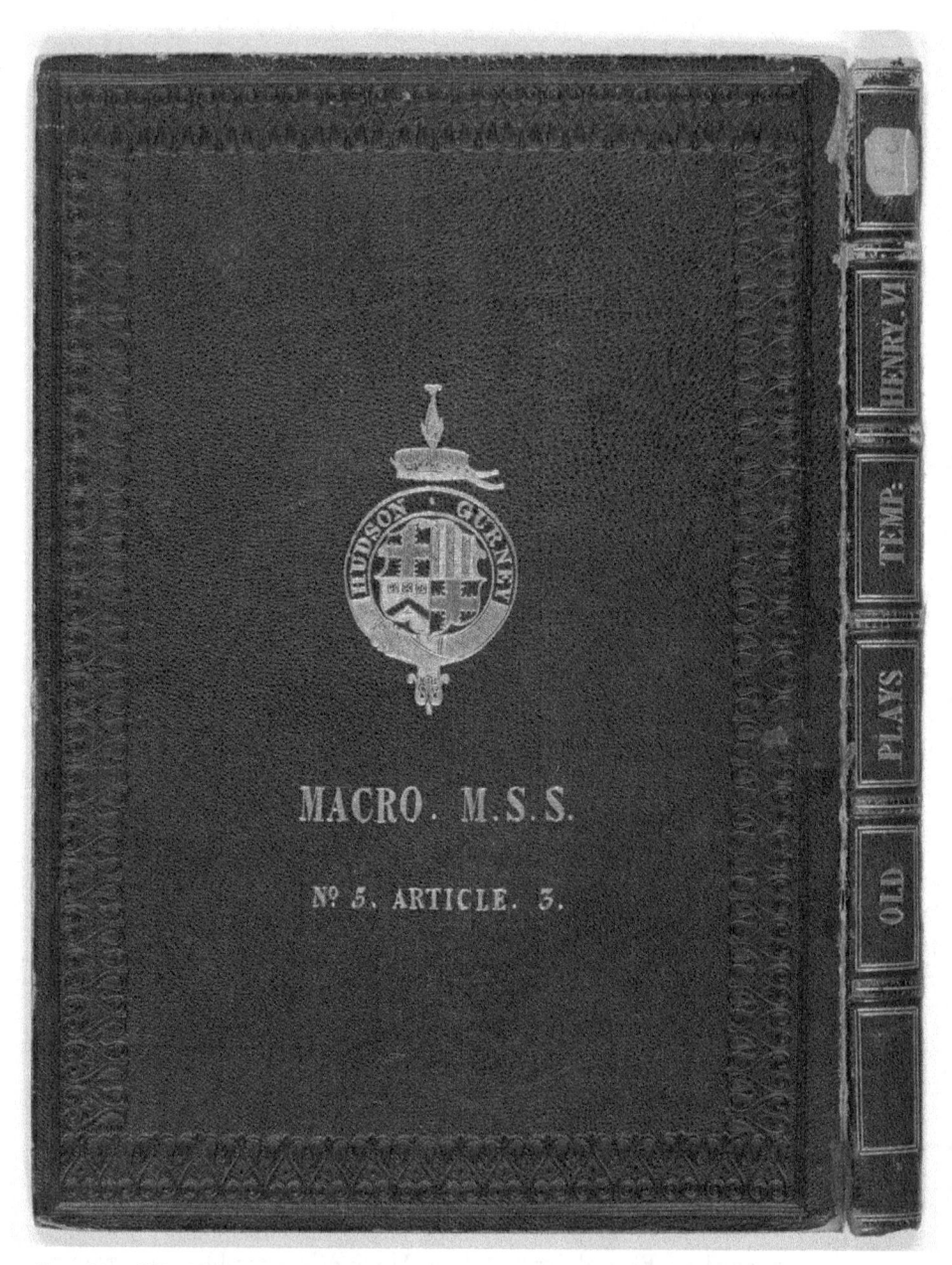

Fig. 5.2. Washington, DC, Folger Shakespeare Library, MS V.a.354, back board and spine. Courtesy of the Folger Shakespeare Library.

at the Harry Ransom Center at the University of Texas, Austin.[8] 'No. 5' on the Gurney binding of Macro refers to the number assigned to Cox Macro's miscellany, including the Juvenal and other texts, in the 1820 sale catalogue of the Macro collection.[9] 'Article 3' refers to Gurney's newly created volume, the so-called Macro Manuscript of medieval English morality plays, as it is numbered in Gurney's reorganization of the diverse components of Cox Macro's miscellany.[10]

The Folger acquired Macro in 1936, only four years after the library opened its doors. Since Mark Eccles's 1969 EETS edition of the plays, an important revision of Furnivall and Pollard's first edition for EETS, scholars have stated routinely that Bernard Quaritch booksellers, acting on behalf of the Folger, purchased Macro at the Gurney sale for £440.[11] That account is in error. While Quaritch did pay this price at auction for the manuscript, they bought it for their own stock.[12] Five months later, they sold the volume to Joseph Quincy Adams, then acting director of the Folger, for almost triple that amount, less the usual 10% discount: £1,125 or $5,689.82, according to calculations on the Quaritch invoice.[13] This sum represented more than half of the Folger Library's acquisitions budget for the year.

A long letter that Adams wrote immediately after the purchase, in August 1936, is rhapsodic.[14] Its recipient was Stanley King, then president of Amherst College: the Folger endowment was established with Standard Oil money and is based at Amherst, Henry Clay Folger's alma mater. Adams begins by explaining how he asked Quaritch for an option on the purchase until

---

[8]   A complete digital record of the manuscript is available at https://hrc.contentdm. oclc.org/digital/collection. The extraction and rebinding of *Respublica* is known to have occurred in 1836, and the similar treatment of the other Macro moralities may have taken place at about the same time; see Beadle, 'Macro MS 5', pp. 41–42.

[9]   *A Catalogue of the Ancient Manuscripts ... collected by the Rev .Dr. Cox Macro ...* [etc.] (London, 1820).

[10]  The title stamped and gilt on the spine of the Gurney volume is 'OLD PLAYS TEMP[ORE] HENRY VI.'

[11]  See Mark Eccles, ed., *The Macro Plays: The Castle of Perseverance, Wisdom, Mankind*, EETS, original series 262 (Oxford, 1969), p. vii.

[12]  See Bernard Quaritch, Catalogue 520 (1936), no. 784.

[13]  Bernard Quaritch, Ltd., invoice for 7 August 1936, order no. 1388 (Folger Library Archives). The invoice also notes that the item was 'purchased by Dr. Adams in England' and that Quaritch sent its bill for the book to the United States on 8 August 1936.

[14]  Carbon of Adams's typewritten letter, dated 29 August 1936, and the original of King's congratulatory response, dated 3 September 1936 (Folger Library Archives).

September, so that he could return to America to consult with King. Quaritch refused, indicating that the British Museum has also expressed interest in buying Macro. Following a sleepless night, Adams raced by cab across London and back to the bookseller's, agreeing to the asking price. He may have been in the dark about the considerable markup, since he effuses to King that in purchasing Macro, the Folger has 'stolen a march' on the English people.

Adams's justification for the extravagant purchase is two-fold. First, he explains, quite accurately, that Macro is really three manuscripts, not one. King accepted the argument, referring in his subsequent correspondence with Adams to the 'Macro manuscripts' and even once to the 'Macro collection.'[15] Indeed, Quaritch's invoice indicates that this may have been their plain as well as shrewd reason for tripling the book's price: there, they describe the purchased item as 'The Macro Plays. sm. 4to. Three manuscripts on paper, morocco gilt, 15th century.' More outrageously, Adams then tells King that in acquiring Macro he has secured for the Folger the equivalent, in terms of theatre history, of America's foundational documents: the Declaration of Independence and the Constitution. Beneath the bombast, he is thinking, as many early scholars of medieval drama did, of the morality play as the rude embryo whence Shakespeare's sophisticated genius evolved and of the final leaf of Macro – the stage design for *Castle* – as the record of a planned or enacted fifteenth-century performance.[16]

This is how Furnivall, too, understood the primary importance of Macro. The stage design had been fetishised a century earlier than the Folger's purchase of the manuscript – in 1825, when Thomas Sharp, with Hudson Gurney's support, published a highly accurate copperplate etching of it in his *Dissertation on the pageants or dramatic mysteries anciently performed at Coventry* – although, as Gail Gibson points out, Sharp misdescribes the drawing there as the first rather than the last leaf of *Castle*.[17] Correspondingly, Furnivall, in some 'Afterwords' (as he entitles them) to Pollard's introduction to their collaborative EETS edition,

---

[15] King uses the first phrase in his letter of 3 September 1936, the second in a letter of 13 October 1936 (Folger Library Archives).

[16] For a less literal-minded analysis of the diagram, as 'a means of expressing [*Castle*'s] meaning in map form,' see Pamela M. King, 'Morality Plays,' in R. Beadle, ed., *The Cambridge Companion to Medieval English Theatre* (Cambridge, 1994), pp. 240–64.

[17] See Thomas Sharp, *A Dissertation on the pageants or dramatic mysteries anciently performed at Coventry* (Coventry, 1825), between pp. 22 and 23. For an account of the etching and its artist, Mary Turner, wife of the collector Dawson Turner, a friend of Hudson Gurney, see Gail McMurray Gibson, 'The Macro Manuscripts and the Making of the Morality Play,' *Papers of the Bibliographical Society of America*, 113 (2019), 255–95.

declares that 'the main interest in the volume [that is, the manuscript] to me is the plan of the scene,' which he and Pollard present, in photolithographic reproduction, as the frontispiece to their edition. Significantly, they reproduce the same diagram a second time, in edited form, later in the EETS edition, facing the first page of text in *Castle*.[18]

Furnivall goes on in his 'Afterwords' to associate the *Castle* stage design with three cruder manuscript diagrams, presumably related to staging, already published by the British orientalist Edwin Norris in his two-volume 1859 edition of some Cornish biblical plays, found in BodL MS Bodley 791.[19] He then concludes from this analogy that rather than being performed on moveable pageant wagons like some biblical plays, or indeed possibly indoors, 'the early Country Moralities were played on a Green or in a Meadow, in a ring surrounded by a ditch, paling, or posts and ropes, with scaffolds for the players inside.'[20] As a youth, Furnivall was fervently religious, although he became in adulthood agnostic and irreverent about religion.[21] For him, the study of early drama is a type of social history and the morality play represents a crucial turning point in the secularising of English theatre: 'In the progress of the drama, Moralities followed Mysteries [that is, biblical plays], and were succeeded by Interludes. When folk tired of Religion on the Stage, they took to the inculcation of morality and prudence; and when this bored them, they set up Fun.'[22] In his view, the *Castle* design is therefore invaluable to historians of the English theatre, because it is uniquely descriptive of the morality plays and paradigmatic, by implication, for the historical development of the English stage.

The production of the 1904 EETS edition of the Macro plays was a complex affair. At first, Furnivall had a difficult time tracing the manuscript. He began investigating Macro's whereabouts in 1880 or so, while at work on an edition of the biblical and morality plays in Digby 133, including its

[18]  F. J. Furnivall & Alfred W. Pollard, eds, *The Macro Plays: Mankind, Wisdom, The Castle of Perseverance*, EETS extra series 91 (Oxford, 1904), p. 76.

[19]  See Edwin Norris, *The Ancient Cornish Drama*, 2 vols (Oxford, 1859), I, 219 and 479 and II, 201.

[20]  Furnivall & Pollard, *The Macro Plays*, p. xxxv.

[21]  On Furnivall's religion, see William Benzie, *Dr. F. J. Furnivall, Victorian Scholar Adventurer* (Norman, OK, 1983), pp. 41–70.

[22]  F. J. Furnivall, ed., *The Digby Mysteries* (London, 1882), p. xiii. On Furnivall's social history approach to the early drama, see Arthur F. Leach, 'Some English Plays and Players, 1220–1548,' in *An English Miscellany Presented to Dr. Furnivall in Honour of his Seventy-Fifth Birthday* (New York, 1901), pp. 205–34. Leach was an educational theorist whose approach to medieval archives was congruent with Furnivall's.

*Wisdom* fragment. He published this edition in 1882 with the New Shakspere Society, which he founded in 1873, and it was reprinted by EETS in 1896.[23] Furnivall likewise planned a solo edition of the Macro plays for the New Shakspere Society, rather than in the first instance for EETS. [24] His original Digby edition and this initial plan for editing Macro further reflects Furnivall's regard for medieval drama as an earlier, primitive stage in the development of Shakespeare's genius.[25]

Some time around 1882, however, the editing of the Macro plays became collaborative and its venue shifted to EETS. For many of his manuscript-related projects, Furnivall deputised transcription.[26] His amanuensis in this case was Eleanor Marx (1855–98), the youngest daughter of Karl and an active member of the New Shakspere Society, for which she produced English translations of German scholarship by Nicolaus Delius, founder of the German Shakespeare Society. As both a scholar and an afficionado of the theatre, Marx must have found the work of transcription appealing.[27] Pollard's description of her involvement with Macro, in his introduction to the EETS edition – 'About 1882 … Dr. Furnivall … obtained leave for a copy of the *Macro Plays* to be made by Miss Eleanor Marx' – suggests that she worked on the manuscript *in situ*, at the library of John Henry Gurney, Jr. (1848–1922), a talented ornithologist and the son of Hudson Gurney's cousin John Henry Sr., the English banker who inherited the Gurney collection.[28] In fact, this is the very arrangement – a scholarly residence at Keswick Hall, the Gurney

[23] Furnivall's idiosyncratic spelling of Shakespeare's name was based on his analysis of the surviving autograph signatures. For the New Shakspere Society edition, see n.18 above. It was reprinted as *The Digby Plays*, EETS, extra series 70 (London, 1896).

[24] See Alfred W. Pollard, ed., *English Miracle Plays, Moralities, and Moral Interludes* (Oxford, 1890), p. 199.

[25] Furnivall & Pollard, *Macro Plays*, pp. ix–x.

[26] On Furnivall's collaborative efforts at EETS, see Benzie, *Dr. F. J. Furnivall*, pp. 117–28. An excellent overview of his methods is given by Derek Pearsall, 'Frederick James Furnivall (1825–1910),' in Helen Damico, ed., *Medieval Scholarship: Biographical Studies on the Formation of a Discipline*, 3 vols (New York, 1995–2000), II, 125–38.

[27] See Rachel Holmes, *Eleanor Marx: A Life* (New York, 2014), pp. 134–37. Holmes mentions Marx's work on Furnivall's behalf in connection with her love of the theatre. On faults in the Marx transcript, see Norman Davis's review of David Bevington, ed., *The Macro Plays: The Castle of Perseverance, Wisdom, Mankind, a Facsimile Edition with Facing Transcriptions*. Folger Facsimiles Manuscript Series Volume 1 (New York, 1972) in *Notes & Queries*, n. s. 22 (1975), 78–79.

[28] Furnivall & Pollard, *Macro Plays*, p. ix.

seat in Norwich – that, Pollard says, John Henry Jr. proposed to him when he himself considered embarking on a solo edition of the Macro plays around 1890. That plan, Pollard reports, was interrupted by family illness and then superseded by the joint effort with Furnivall.[29] At an uncertain date after Marx completed her transcript, Furnivall persuaded Gurney to lend him the manuscript, presumably so that he could work further at the EETS edition at his convenience, thanking him 'for his hospitality when I went to his house to fetch it' and keeping it for 'many months.'[30] For all these courtesies, he and Pollard dedicate their edition to 'John Henry Gurney, Esq. of Keswick Hall and North Repps, Norfolk, Lover of Birds and Books.'

In another turn of the screw, Pollard further notes that Macro was 'temporarily mislaid' between 1897 and 1898, so that the Marx transcript became, for a time, the only witness (the Digby fragment of *Wisdom* excepted) to the texts of the three Macro plays. The transcript was then 'transferred to the Early English Text Society' for use in preparing the edition.[31] In the interim, Pollard also used it, with Furnivall's permission, to edit extracts from *Castle* that he includes in his anthology *English Miracle Plays, Moralities, and Moral Interludes.*[32] J. M. Manly also had to rely on the transcript during this time, in preparing a text of *Mankind* for his two-volume anthology, *Specimens of the Pre-Shakespearean Drama.*[33] Both Pollard and Manly make clear that Marx's transcript, which does not survive, was a diplomatic one that recorded the abbreviation and contraction marks in Macro – occasioning them to interpret and expand these in their edited texts.[34] Furnivall often worked this way: producing himself or deputizing a diplomatic transcript from a manuscript, contractions and all, taking it away for editing, and then correcting the proof against the original.[35] His published versions of medieval manuscripts attracted during his lifetime both praise and blame. Some scholars, such as Skeat, valued them highly as 'prints' – helpful if sometimes erratic records of individual manuscript copies of important texts. Others such as Henry

---

[29]  Furnivall & Pollard, *Macro Plays*, pp. ix–x.

[30]  Furnivall & Pollard, *Macro Plays*, p. xli.

[31]  Furnivall & Pollard, *Macro Plays*, pp. x–xi.

[32]  Pollard, *English Miracle Plays*, p. 199.

[33]  J. M. Manly, ed., *Specimens of the Pre-Shakespearean Drama*, 2 vols (London, 1897), I, 315–52.

[34]  Pollard, *English Miracle Plays*, p. 197 and Manly, *Specimens*, I, 315.

[35]  On Furnivall's working habits, see Benzie, *Dr. F. J. Furnivall*, pp. 150–54.

Bradshaw were inclined to dismiss them as variously inept copies rather than genuine editions.[36]

Because the date on which Gurney lent Furnivall the manuscript is uncertain, it is unclear whether Macro went missing while in his possession or back at Keswick Hall after he returned it. Some time after its recovery, however, Furnivall convinced Gurney to lend the manuscript out again – this time to a strange scholarly entrepreneur by the name of John Stephen Farmer (1854–1916). For a new venture, the Tudor Facsimile Text series, Farmer produced separate collotype reproductions of each of the Macro plays and *Respublica,* the later morality that Hudson Gurney also acquired from Cox Macro's library.[37] These facsimiles document the damaged physical state of Macro when it arrived at the Folger: for example, extensive paper and adhesive-tape patches in the gutters and along the edges of leaves, as well as very faint traces of pencil notes made in Macro by both Furnivall and John Payne Collier (1789–1883), the notorious Shakespearean forger and a Furnivall nemesis.[38] Furnivall championed Farmer's series. Shortly before his death in 1910, he blurbed it for a subscription announcement. His language reflects the personal difficulties he faced in gaining access to manuscripts of medieval dramatic texts and the principle of democratic appreciation of these that animated his founding of organizations such as EETS and the New Shakspere Society:

> The boon thus conferred on English scholarship is emphasized when it is borne in mind that these treasures are for the most part unique, or that at best but two or three copies are known to exist, these being enshrined in public collections like the British Museum or the Bodleian, from which they are never likely, humanly speaking, to emerge, or else forming part of some exclusive and inaccessible private library.[39]

---

[36]  See Benzie, *Dr. F. J. Furnivall,* pp. 121 and 164.

[37]  For a short account of his involvement with Furnivall and the condition of Macro at the time he used it, see John S. Farmer, *A Hand List to Old English Plays, Students' Facsimile Edition, Old English Plays Printed & MS. Rarities, Exact Collotype Reproductions in Folio & Quarto, under the General Editorship of John S. Farmer, Assisted by Craftsmen of Repute and Standing* (Amersham, 1914), p. 30. Aside from the early drama, Farmer's chief interests were slang (of which he compiled a seven-volume dictionary with W. E. Henley), spiritualism, and erotica.

[38]  On Furnivall's dispute with Collier and the consequent founding of the New Shakspere Society, see Jeffrey Kahan, *The Quest for Shakespeare: The Peculiar History and Surprising Legacy of the New Shakspere Society* (London, 2017), pp. 5–11.

[39]  Farmer, *Hand List,* p. 5.

Collier and Furnivall have not previously been identified as the authors of the pencil annotations to Macro nor have the annotations themselves been studied.[40] Collier's predate Furnivall's: these are three marginal notes in *Wisdom*. They highlight in turn references in the play to the seven sacraments (on fol. 101), to the five wits represented as virgins (on fol. 101$^v$), and to a dance (on fol. 112). Collier's involvement with the manuscript was likely more profound than this, however. It is probably he who, again in pencil, has numbered the three Macro plays in their Gurney order: 1. *Mankind*, 2. *Wisdom*, and 3. *Castle*. The numerals are very faint and situated in the extreme upper left-hand corner of the first leaf of each play, and resemble his.[41] If Collier wrote them, that would suggest that the plays had not yet been bound when Gurney lent him the manuscript for an edition of *Wisdom* that he prepared for publication in 1838 with the Abbotsford Club.[42] Indeed, it is entirely possible that Collier suggested the new order of plays to Gurney, changing up their sequence at the end of Cox Macro's eighteenth-century miscellany: *Wisdom*, *Mankind*, and *Castle*.[43] Perhaps, like Furnivall, Collier was drawn to the coarse realism of

[40] Collier may also be responsible for thirty-odd crosses and sundry marginal lines and brackets pencilled throughout the three plays, although some of these might be Furnivall's. For an interpretation of some of these marks as alerts to particulars of staging, in *Wisdom* specifically, see John Marshall, 'Marginal Staging Marks in the Macro Manuscript of *Wisdom*,' *Medieval English Theatre*, 7 (1985), 77–82. Richard Beadle points out to me that those in *Wisdom* track closely the passages in that play that Collier cites for illustrative purposes in his *History of English Dramatic Poetry to the Time of Shakespeare* (London, 1831), vol. 2, suggesting, at the very least, that Collier was responsible for the crosses and brackets there. These passim marks throughout the three Macro plays require further study.

[41] The faintness of the pencil annotations in Macro is in part the result of erosion of its fragile paper surfaces: all three plays are copied on low-grade supports. I am currently preparing a study of the manuscript's paper stocks and their watermarks, which have never been accurately documented. For a preliminary study of the watermarks, see Stephen Spector, 'Paper Evidence and the Genesis of the Macro Plays,' *Mediaevalia*, 5 (1979), 217–32.

[42] John Payne Collier, ed., *Mind, Will, and Understanding: A Morality, from the Macro MS. in the Possession of Hudson Gurney, Esq. F.S.A.* (Edinburgh, 1837). This edition reproduces only the parts of the drama not included in the fragmentary copy of *Wisdom*, as Furnivall came to name *Mind, Will, and Understanding*, in Digby 133. The Digby portion had already been published by the Abbotsford Club in Thomas Sharp, ed., *Ancient Mysteries from the Digby Manuscripts, Preserved in the Bodleian Library, Oxford* (Edinburgh, 1835).

[43] Three non-dramatic items appeared between *Mankind* and *Castle* in Cox Macro's miscellany. See Beadle, 'Macro 5,' p. 44.

*Mankind* as an anticipation of Shakespeare, and wished therefore to give that play priority in the Gurney volume.

Furnivall also made three annotations to Macro, probably all at the same time, in his distinctive but hurried, later hand.[44] His first note appears on the first endleaf at the front of the Gurney volume (Figure 5.3), above a list of the manuscript's contents, likewise in pencil, in a hand that I have been unable to identify.[45] Furnivall writes: '2[d] play has been printed by English *Text* Society' (emphasis his). This note refers to the play *Wisdom* and to EETS's reprinting of Furnivall's 1882 New Shakspere Society edition of the Digby plays in 1896, establishing thereby the *terminus a quo* for Furnivall's having written the note in Macro.

This first annotation was nearly lost to book history because of how Macro was handled at a key moment by the Folger. In 1971, due to wear-and-tear on the manuscript noticed by O. B. Hardison, a scholar of medieval drama who was then director of the library, the Folger determined to publish a photoreproduction of the Macro plays, with facing-page transcriptions, as the inaugural volume of a new facsimiles series.[46] *The Macro Plays*, edited by David Bevington, appeared in 1972.[47] Then a young professor at the University of Chicago, Bevington was a literary not a manuscript scholar. He was best known at the time for a critical monograph on the relationship between the English morality plays and drama of the Age of Shakespeare: *From Mankind to Marlowe*.[48] To facilitate photography for the facsimile, the Folger had Macro disbound.[49]

---

[44] On the 'deterioration' of Furnivall's handwriting, see Benzie, *Dr. F. J. Furnivall*, p. 262. These three marginal annotations to Macro have not hitherto been identified as Furnivall's. I made the identification by comparing their script with several postcards scrawled by Furnivall during the same period, now in the Folger's collection.

[45] The contents list notes that the second leaf of *Mankind* is lacking, as are one leaf after fol. 170 and another after fol. 182 in *Castle*. These details appear likewise in Quaritch's catalogue description, suggesting that the endleaf list may have been made by the bookseller.

[46] Hardison was director of the Folger between 1969 and 1983. His monograph, *Christian Rite and Christian Drama in the Middle Ages: Essays in the Origin and Early History of Modern Drama* (Baltimore, MD, 1965), dismantles traditional theories about medieval biblical plays as direct developments from Latin paraliturgical tropes, such as the *Quem quaeritis?*

[47] David Bevington, *The Macro Plays*.

[48] David Bevington, *From Mankind to Marlowe: Growth of Structure in the Popular Drama of Tudor England* (Cambridge, MA, 1962).

[49] The photographs were taken by a jobbing photographer, Robert Jackson, based in Washington, DC, who worked for the Folger between 1970 and 1975. Jackson used a special camera with gimbal purchased by the library that was discarded in 2015.

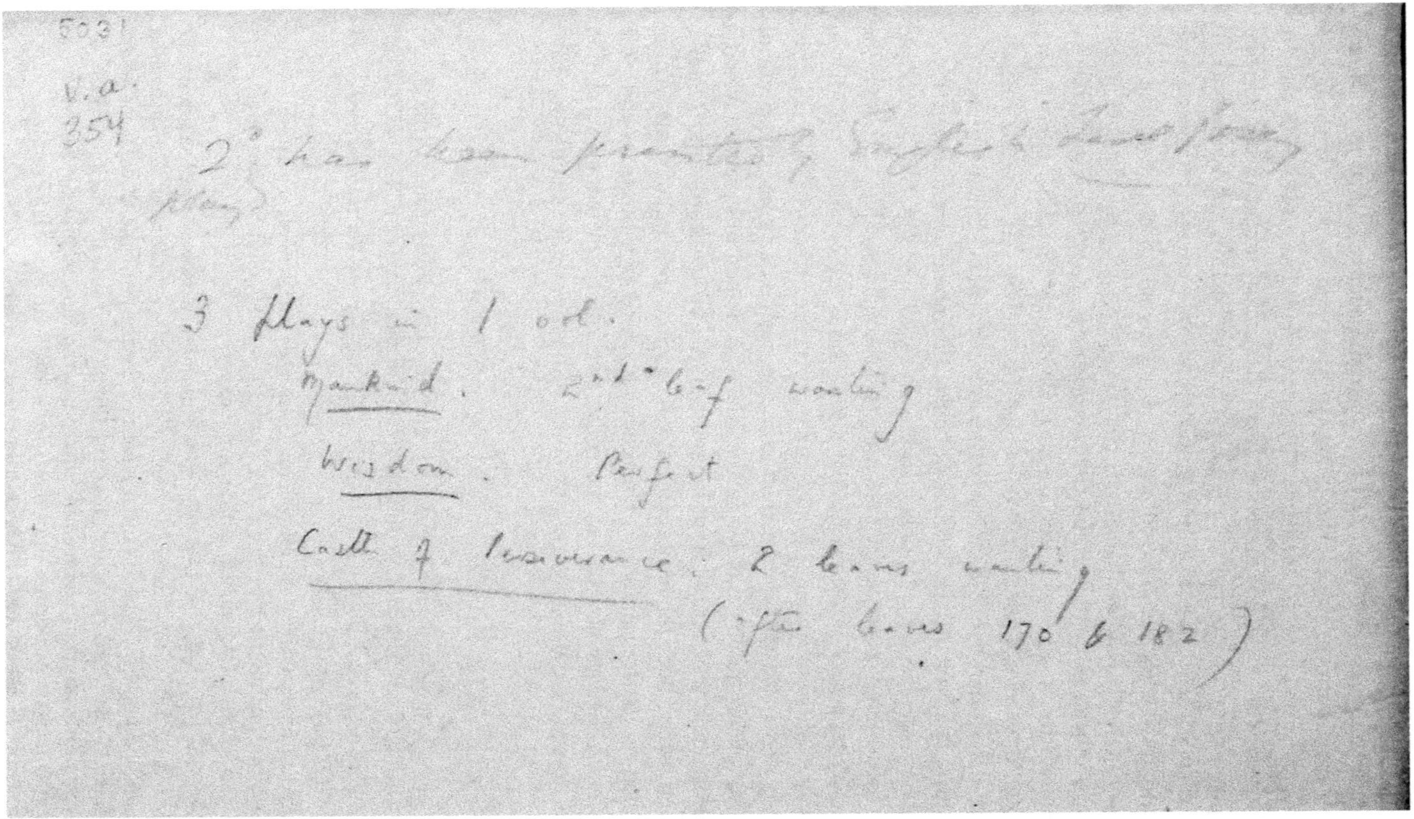

Fig. 5.3. Washington, DC, Folger Shakespeare Library, MS V.a.354, fol. i (unnumbered front endleaf), detail. Photo by Michael P. Kuczynski.

This operation was entrusted to Robert Lunow, the library's in-house binder, a proud and accomplished book artisan. Lunow trained in Germany before emigrating to the United States in 1925 and working at the Folger during the last phase of his career, between 1948 and 1971.[50] He died of cancer suddenly after taking apart Macro, hence its current disbound state, and just before the Bevington facsimile appeared. By Lunow's own report, he 'discarded' Macro's 'valueless, 19th century binding' – along, it turns out, with its front and back endleaves (four each).[51] Lunow enjoyed at the Folger a wide range of discretion in such matters, enabled at times by ambiguities in the library's official policy regarding the preservation of codicological evidence. A typewritten memo entitled 'Bindery Procedure for STC [Short Title Catalogue] Books,' under the subheading 'Instructing Mr. Lunow,' suggests giving the binder 'a free hand about technical matters,' including even the trimming of leaves and the washing of books. The memo urges further: 'Please repress (if you feel it) a tendency to preserve old bindings, old boards, old backstrips merely because they are old and reasonably sound,' although the memo writer goes on to stipulate that 'any sound boards or backstrips that in any way … show provenance can be and ought to be preserved.'[52] The Gurney binding and endleaves were rescued from the trash by a young subcurator of manuscripts at the Folger, Laetitia Yeandle, who helped to supervise Macro's disbinding and who retired from her position in 2001. According to Yeandle, she understood both the importance of the binding itself and of some writing in pencil on its front endleaf.[53] Unaccountably, although the front and back boards of Macro are now part of the Folger's nearly complete high-resolution digital record of the manuscript, made in 2007, the volume's endleaves have

---

[50] Some biographical materials on Lunow and his career are available at the United States Holocaust Museum, Washington, DC: 1 folder, Accession Number 2007.21.

[51] See Verlyn Flieger, 'The Craftsmanship of Robert Lunow,' *The Washington Post*, 13 June 1971, pp. 14–16.

[52] Dated 12 January 1959 and initialed by Giles Dawson, the Folger's curator of rare books and manuscripts between 1946 and 1967 (Folger Library Archives). It is unclear whether Dawson was author of the memo.

[53] Ms. Yeandle reported these details to me during a personal conversation on 12 April 2019. Lilly Stone (later Lievsay), another Folger subcurator, also supervised the disbinding, kept a handwritten record of the leaves of the three Macro plays (Folger Library Archives), and provided the modern pencil foliation above Cox Macro's discontinuous eighteenth-century ink through-foliation, which refers to the play texts in the positions in which they were placed in the larger miscellaneous manuscript from which Hudson Gurney extracted them.

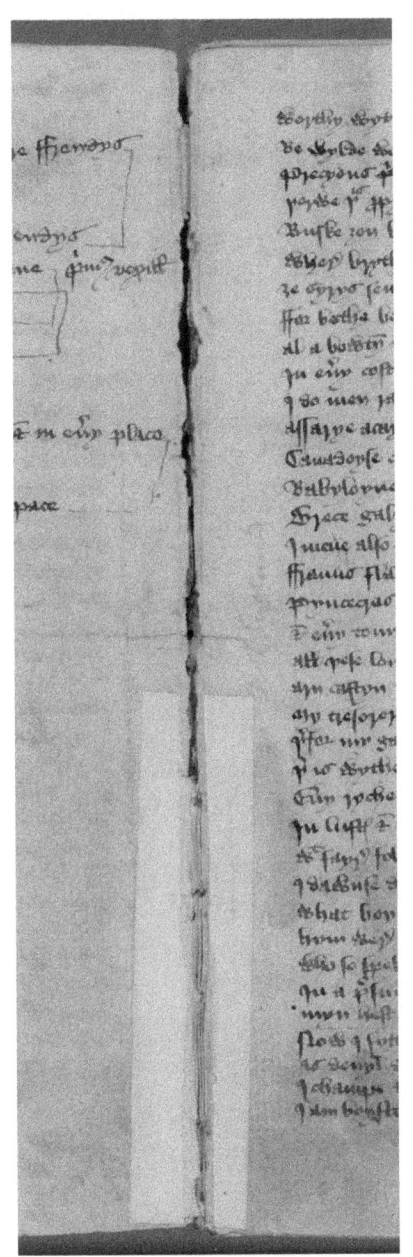

Fig. 5.4. Washington, DC, Folger Shakespeare Library, MS V.a.354, fols 155ᵛ–156 (detail). Courtesy of the Folger Shakespeare Library.

yet to be photographed and included in that record.[54]

Furnivall's other two annotations to Macro are in *Castle*. The first of these is enigmatic (Figure 5.4). It appears up the inner margin of fol. 156, next to a passage in the opening speech of the play by Mundus or the World. As Mundus introduces himself, he boasts of his general influence, providing an alphabetical catalogue of those places that his accountant, Covetousness, has helped him to buy. Assyria, Flanders, and Rome are all on the list – as is 'Bretayne' (Brittany). Furnivall scrawls next to the passage in the margin of the manuscript: 'not England.' The start of the note's initial *n* is covered slightly with a pasted paper repair to the inside margin of the leaf that may once have been conjoint with a similar repair to the inner margin of fol. 155ᵛ, the facing leaf and the end of the opening banns or proclamations to *Castle*.

It is difficult to know what to make of all this. In his side note to the text for the EETS edition, Furnivall glosses 'Bretayne' as 'Britain.'[55] Perhaps he first mistook Middle English 'Bretayne' for Modern English 'Britain' rather

---

[54] See n. 5 above. Neither the boards nor the end leaves were photographed for the Bevington facsimile.

[55] Furnivall & Pollard, *Macro Plays*, p. 82, l. 172. Pollard acknowledges Furnivall's authorship of the sidenotes in his introduction, p. xvii.

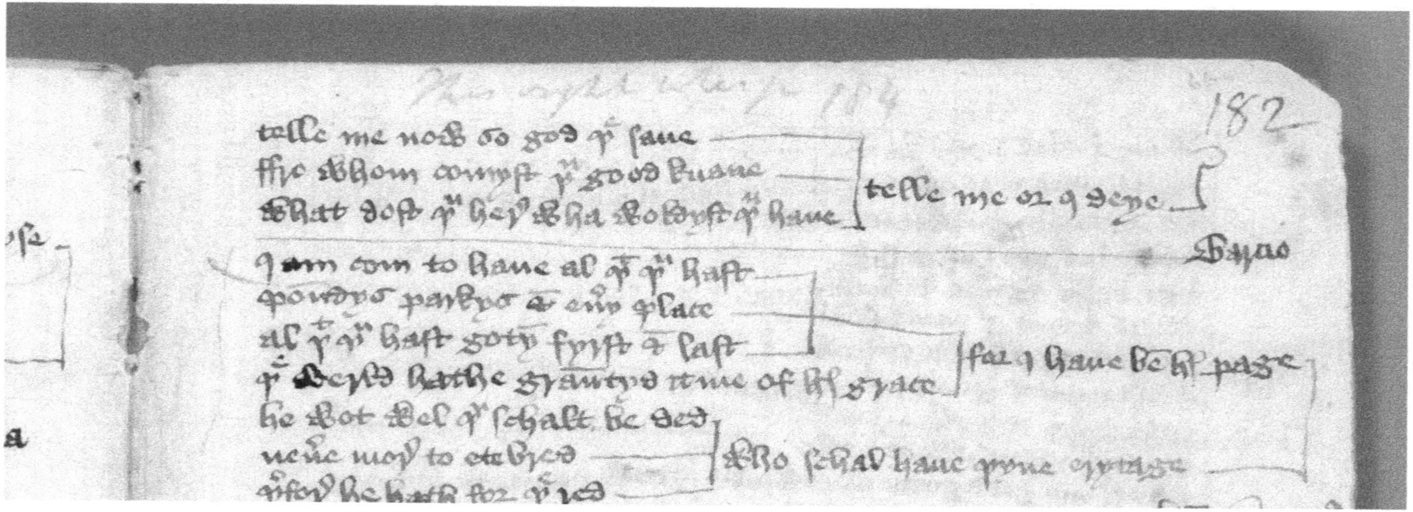

telle me now so god ye saue
ffor whom comyst ye good knaue
What dost ye hey tha koldyst of kaue

telle me or I deye

I am com to kaue al ys ye hast
powdys parkys & euy place
al ys ye hast goth ffyrst & last
ye deyd hathe grawtyd tyme of hs grace
he not wel ys schalt be ded
neue mosy to eabyed
asons he hath for ye red

Sayas

ffor I haue be hs page

who schal haue yowe cyryage

Fig. 5.5. Washington, DC, Folger Shakespeare Library, MS V.a.354, fol. 182 (detail). Courtesy of the Folger Shakespeare Library.

than 'Brittany' (see *OED Britain* n.2, II.3., citing the London *Times* for 14 July 1874), and his interest became piqued by the difference between the dramatist's choice of an Old French word rather than an Old English one; or perhaps, if he meant 'Brittany' by his side note 'Britain' (see *MED Britaine* n., sense 2), he was expressing indirectly his satisfaction at finding England exempt in *Castle* from the World's globalizing corruptions: there was always a proud, nationalistic element to Furnivall's interest in early English drama. Regardless, the pasted repair in the manuscript at this point is a more vexing problem. Since it overlaps Furnivall's handwriting, however slightly, it must have been made after he wrote his note, most likely when he had Macro on loan for his private use. This and other frequent patches in the manuscript, as I have said, are already visible in Farmer's collotypes of the three plays and receive his passing comment. Not all of the patching was necessarily done at the same time, but much of it surely was: the white wove paper frequently used for it contains a common watermark, the word 'POSTAGE,' indicating that the material was cut up roughly from standard letter-writing stationery. These repairs, in other words, do not appear to have been made by a professional.

Furnivall's third annotation to Macro is his most significant. It pertains to an important codicological problem with the manuscript of *Castle*: the displacement of two leaves in its second gathering (Figure 5.5). Across the top margin of fol. 182, Furnivall writes, 'This ought to be p. 184.' Pollard explains clearly, in his introduction to the EETS edition, that two signatures of the eight constituting the unusually large second gathering, $B_2$ and $B_4$, had become transposed, resulting in a textual confusion.[56] He then adds, very oddly, that 'a former student' noted that 'some shifting was needed,' quoting in turn his colleague Furnivall's own penciled note. Either he saw the note in Macro and failed to recognise Furnivall's hand, took report of it from someone who did not recognize it as Furnivall's, or sought for one reason or another to conceal the fact that Furnivall wrote it. The order in which Furnivall and Pollard present the text of *Castle* in their edition indicates that Furnivall resolved the codicological error in the process of examining the manuscript and editing. The oddness spreads further, however, by way of a parenthetical footnote on the page of their edition where the text of fol. 182 correctly appears: '(Old pencil note: "This ought to be p. 184.")'[57] Since Eleanor Marx made her transcript of the Macro plays before Furnivall began to edit them,

[56] This is not the only codicological conundrum in *Castle*: there are two missing leaves, noticed on Macro's front flyleaf, below Furnivall's first note, and another transposition. On these puzzles, see Bevington, *The Macro Plays*, pp. xvii–xix.

[57] Furnivall & Pollard, *Macro Plays*, p. 164.

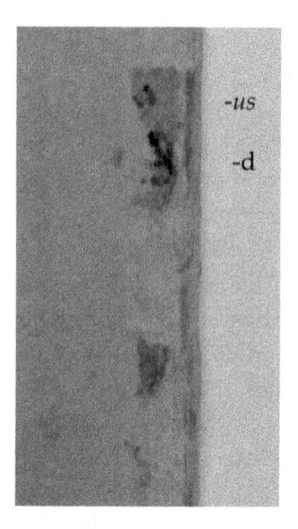

Fig. 5.6.  Washington, DC, Folger Shakespeare Library, MS V.a.354, fol. v (unnumbered back endleaf), detail flipped horizontally.  Photo by Michael P. Kuczynski.

and since Pollard indicates in his introduction to the EETS edition that he had no hand in editing the plays but only in writing the text's introduction, this parenthetical footnote must have been provided by Furnivall himself, who wrote the 'old … note' about the transposition.[58]

The first back endleaf of the Gurney volume also contains important information that might have been lost, has not previously been recorded, and arguably relates to the history of Furnivall's involvement with Macro: a small fragment of the famous last leaf of *Castle*, the stage design, came away at disbinding and remains stuck today to the inner edge of the endleaf (Figure 5.6). It contains two minor textual readings from the medieval captions to the design. These are, at the inner edge of the leaf, a suspension mark for *-us* at the end of the Latin personification Mundus in the stage direction 'Mund*us*' skaffold' ('the World's platform'); and an Anglicana *d* at the end of the word 'skaffold' itself. In the etching of the design made, probably from a tracing, for Thomas Sharp's 1825 study of the Coventry mystery plays, both details appear, presumably because Gurney had not yet sent the three plays to the binder. These details are not visible, however, in the two images of the design provided by Furnivall and Pollard for their 1904 EETS edition. In their Frontispiece, they may have been cropped by the printer. More likely, they were never recorded on the photolithographic plate because they were lost in the gutter of the Gurney

---

[58]  Neither Furnivall's second nor his third note, nor any of the confusions these raise, are registered by Eccles in his 1969 revision of the EETS edition. In his 1972 facsimile, Bevington misses Furnivall's second note entirely but does indicate his third note, although he does not identify the annotator.

binding. (The details also do not appear in the collotype reproduction of the design in Farmer's facsimile.) In the edited image of the design for the EETS edition, and as Bevington would have to do in his 1972 facsimile, Furnivall provides the losses as conjectures in square brackets.

To date, no one has noticed these minor but significant bits of damage to Macro because no one has scrutinised the first back endleaf. Other types of damage and repair throughout the now-disbound manuscript are too obvious to miss: for example, the rendering of many of its originally conjugate leaves as singletons because of tears along their folds – in *Mankind* entirely, where all the leaves are now singles, and in *Castle* somewhat less extensively. Damage to *Castle* has been aggravated by the picking away of clots of glue from the spine edge of the play's gatherings, instead of its more delicate removal by humidification. Overall, the two gatherings that constitute the play *Wisdom*, as one might expect, because these were protected by being bound between *Mankind* and *Castle,* are today the least damaged parts of Macro. Especially noteworthy are what appear to be horizontal stress tears in *Mankind,* just over halfway down the length of the leaves, where the paper may have been tugged or pulled away from the Gurney binding so that *Wisdom* and *Castle* could then be pried away from the spine more carefully. Despite his careless discarding of the Gurney binding in 1971, it must be said that Robert Lunow cut its front board away neatly, to facilitate the gentle removal of the paper gatherings of the three Macro plays. It is difficult to imagine the kind of damage *Mankind* especially sustained occurring in this kind of curatorial context.

Some of this damage almost certainly dates back further in Macro's curatorial history than the period of Gurney's ownership – although the patching with nineteenth-century letter-writing stationery does not.[59] Another possibility that must be admitted, although it cannot be proved, is that Furnivall damaged Macro when it was in his possession, perhaps by having it disbound in order to resolve the collation problem he notes across the top margin of fol. 182. Many Victorians were not as fastidious in handling medieval manuscripts as we expect ourselves to be. For them, the point of a medieval book was its utility. Furnivall's close friend, John Ruskin, a great lover of the Middle Ages, owned about ninety medieval manuscripts: he had some of these cut down to size for binding and collaged bits and pieces from others.[60] William Morris wrote instructions in the margins of some of his manuscripts for the printers at his

---

[59] Note the remark of James Cobbes (1602–85), who owned at one time both *Mankind* and *Wisdom*: 'Two olde playes or maskes but Imperfect & little worthe.' See Beadle, 'Macro 5,' p. 51.

[60] See 'Ruskin's Treatment of His Books and Manuscripts,' in James S. Dearden, *The Library of John Ruskin* (Oxford, 2012), pp. xxv–xxxi.

Kelmscott Press.[61] Ruskin and Morris, of course, were applying their energies to medieval books that they owned. Henry Bradshaw, in his role as Cambridge University librarian, broke up more than one medieval manuscript – 'with the utmost care and gentleness' – for purposes of collation.[62] Furnivall's handling of Aberystwyth, National Library of Wales, MS Hengwrt 229, the manuscript of the Chester Mystery Cycle, was more reckless. His writing, all over its surface in ink, in an effort to clarify lost readings, outraged W. W. Greg when he came to edit one of the Chester plays. He calls Furnivall's mishandling of the manuscript, which had been placed on deposit at the British Museum for J. M. Manly's use, an act of 'scholarly vandalism.'[63]

Furnivall's enthusiasm for manuscripts and people was legendary. As many of his closest friends and collaborators observed, he could become manic about both. In light of such accounts, it seems worth noting that he may have assumed a share of proprietary interest in Macro. For in 1866, at the age of forty-one, Furnivall had lost all his substantial inheritance in the collapse, due to mismanagement, of the Overend and Gurney Bank.[64] This circumstance, following fast on the death of his beloved infant daughter, Ena, must have been devastating: among other pressures, it contributed to his living close to poverty level for much of the rest of his life, alleviated only slightly by a modest government pension.[65] Like all of us, Furnivall was a person as well as a scholar. Whether he tampered with its binding or not, his involvement with the Macro Manuscript has certainly enhanced rather than diminished our interest in the volume. As I have tried to show in this essay, the complex nature of that interest is only starting to become clear.

[61] For example, his manuscript of Richard Maidstone's Middle English penitential psalms, now in the Pierpont Morgan Library along with some corrected proof sheets to the Kelmscott Press edition of these, *Psalmi penitentiales* (Hammersmith, 1894).

[62] See George Walter Prothero, *A Memoir of Henry Bradshaw* (London, 1889), pp. 336–37.

[63] W. W. Greg, ed., *The Play of Antichrist from the Chester Cycle* (Oxford, 1935), pp. xxi–xxii.

[64] For a detailed analysis of the collapse and its catastrophic effects, see Rhiannon Sowerbutts, Marco Schneebalg & Florence Hubert, 'The Demise of Overend Gurney,' *Bank of England Quarterly Bulletin*, Q2 (2016), 94–106.

[65] On the impact of Ena's death on Furnivall, see Benzie, *F. J. Furnivall*, p. 25; on his finances, see Benzie, *F. J. Furnivall*, p. 32.

# 6

## Fragmentation and Fragmentology: A Century of Ege Studies[1]

### *Lisa Fagin Davis*

The rise of antiquarianism in the late nineteenth and early twentieth centuries impacted the rare book and manuscript trade in ways that would have long-term implications for the selling and buying of manuscript fragments, especially in North America. In addition to trimmed cuttings and albums of binding fragments or miniatures, whole single leaves began to appear on the market with increasing frequency. As noted by Scott Gwara, oversize Italian choirbook leaves were already seen as frameable collectibles by the late nineteenth century, such as those donated to the Metropolitan Museum of Art by Louis L. Lorillard in 1896.[2] It was surely a natural development, then, when booksellers came to the realization that their profits would increase significantly if they broke manuscripts apart, selling 250 single leaves to 250 buyers instead of one book to one buyer. As Christopher de Hamel puts it

> This marks the crucial turning point in our story. Early nineteenth-century collectors were interested only in isolated illuminations. Miniatures were cut out and the vandalized text pages were frankly destroyed. But by the first decade of the twentieth century – not much earlier – all parts of a dismembered manuscript became collectable. When this happened, as you

[1] This essay is offered to Barbara Shailor, with immense gratitude for decades of mentorship, support, and inspiration (both intellectual and sartorial). There is no doubt in my mind that I owe my career to her, and it is a distinct honor and privilege to be part of this *Festschrift*. Portions of this essay were previously published in Lisa Fagin Davis, 'An Echo of the Remanent,' *Florilegium*, 35 (2018), 5–30 (at 109–10 and fig. 17).

[2] Scott Gwara, 'Collections, Compilations, and Convolutes of Medieval and Renaissance Manuscript Fragments in North America before ca. 1900,' *Fragmentology*, 3 (2020), 73–139.

Fig. 6.1.   Otto Frederick Ege (1888–1951).

would expect, the antiquarian booktrade obligingly changed gear. Booksellers began breaking manuscripts, to sell leaf by leaf by leaf.[3]

De Hamel identifies European dealers such as Maggs and von Scherling with this practice in the early twentieth century. The Americans had caught on by the 1920s or so and began gleefully breaking books and selling them off page by page.[4] What dealers broke, collectors bought. The United States, with its new industry-fueled wealth, was a primary beneficiary of this flooded market. From masters of industry to small-town collectors, major museums to small colleges, bibliophiles in the United States were clamoring for matted and framed leaves, in particular leaves from Gothic Books of Hours and Italian choirbooks. Today, there are tens of thousands of leaves from thousands of dismembered manuscripts in hundreds of North American collections.[5]

The most notorious of these book-breakers was Otto Frederick Ege (1888–1951), bibliophile and self-proclaimed biblioclast (Figure 6.1).[6] Ege spent most

---

[3]   Christopher de Hamel, *Cutting up Manuscripts for Pleasure and Profit*, The 1995 Sol. M. Malkin Lecture in Bibliography (Charlottesville, VA, 1996), p. 15.

[4]   de Hamel, *Cutting Up Manuscripts*, p. 16.

[5]   Melissa Conway & Lisa Fagin Davis, 'The *Directory of Institutions in the United States and Canada with Pre-1600 Manuscript Holdings*: From its Origins to the Present, and its Role in Tracking the Migration of Manuscripts in North American Repositories,' *Manuscripta*, 57 (2013), 165–81 (at 173).

[6]   For a detailed study of Ege's biblioclastic career, see Scott Gwara, *Otto Ege's Manuscripts* (Cayce, SC [2013]).

of his career as a professor of art history at the Cleveland Museum of Art and at Case Western Reserve University in Ohio. He was a collector of manuscripts – recorded in de Ricci & Wilson – but he was also a bookdealer, best known for breaking apart manuscripts and early printed books in the 1930s and 1940s and selling them leaf by leaf at a massive profit.[7] The first manuscript he bought (in 1913) was the first one he broke (sharing it with a Chicago collector).[8] He was not the first dealer to break books and scatter the leaves, but he was particularly profligate. Ege defended his 'biblioclasm' with what he considered the noble goal of putting a little bit of the Middle Ages within the economic grasp of even the humblest collector or smallest institution. In a 1938 article in a 'hobbyist' journal called *Avocations*, Ege explained:

> Book-tearers have been cursed and condemned, but have they ever been praised or justified? … Surely to allow a thousand people 'to have and to hold' an original manuscript leaf, and to get the thrill and understanding that comes only from actual and frequent contact with these art heritages, is justification enough for the scattering of fragments. Few, indeed, can hope to own a complete manuscript book; hundreds, however, may own a leaf.[9]

Ege's actions were certainly misguided, but he was correct in one important respect; small collections throughout the United States that could never have afforded to buy entire codices are the proud possessors of significant teaching collections of medieval manuscript leaves.[10] Today, several thousand leaves from several hundred manuscripts that passed through Ege's hands can be identified in at least 115 North American collections in 25 states. According to the *Directory of Collections in the United States and Canada with Pre-1600 Manuscript Holdings*, the number of fragments in North America is around 30,000; in other words, more than ten percent of the entire corpus of single leaves in the United States can be traced back to Otto Ege.[11]

Ege and his wife Louise used the leaves of several dozen manuscripts to create thematic 'portfolios' for sale. In other words, they would take one leaf of

---

[7] de Ricci & Wilson, II, 1937–48.

[8] Otto F. Ege, 'I am a Biblioclast,' *Avocations* (March 1938), 516–21 (at 519).

[9] Ege, 'I am a Biblioclast,' 518.

[10] Some of the codices dismembered by Ege or others were imperfect or damaged at the time of acquisition, a feature that Ege used to justify his biblioclasm (see Ege, 517).

[11] Conway & Davis, 'The *Directory of Institutions*,' 173. See also Melissa Conway & Lisa Fagin Davis. 'Directory of Collections in the United States and Canada with Pre-1600 Manuscript Holdings,' *Papers of the Bibliographical Society of America*, 109 (2015), 273–420.

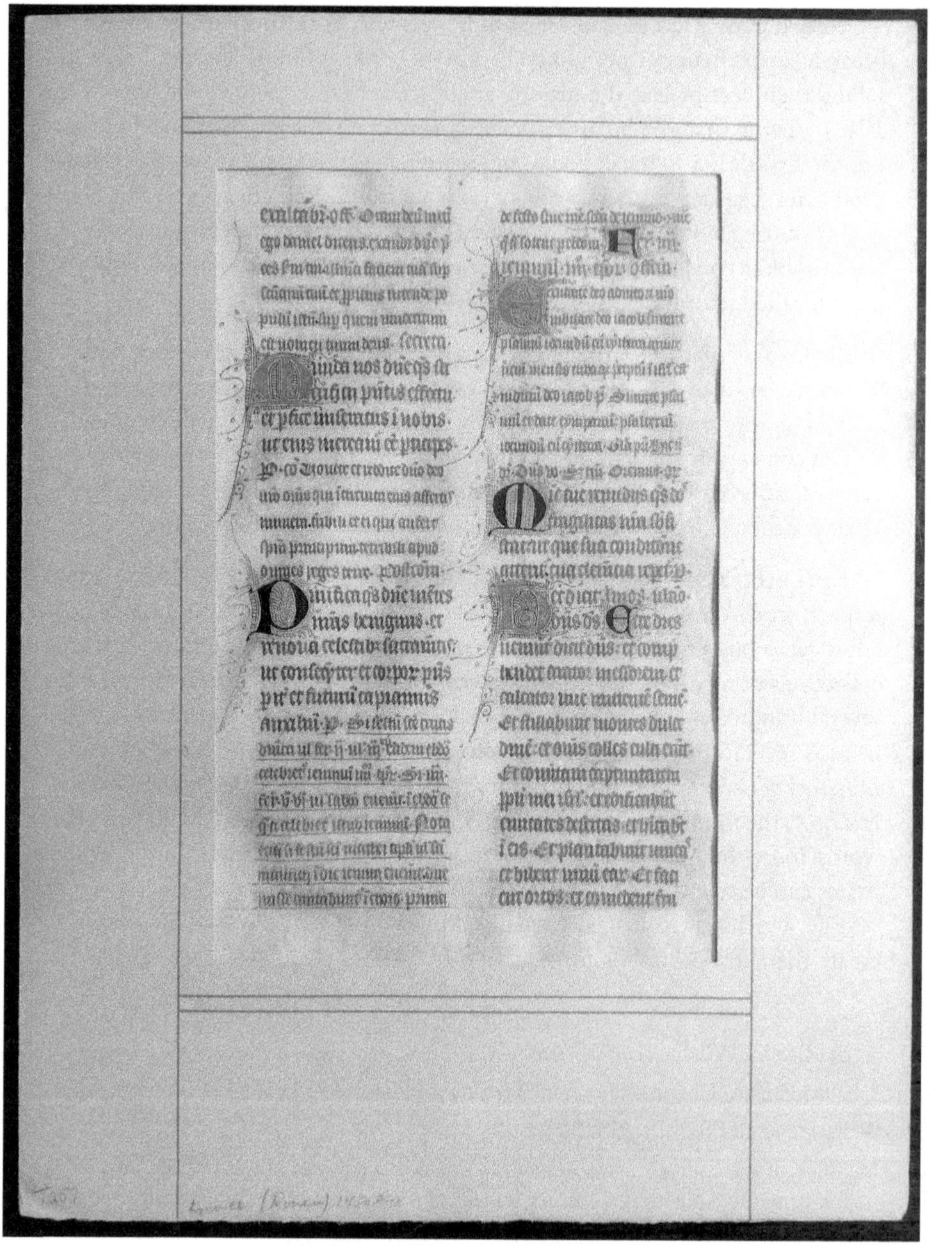

Fig. 6.2. Typical Ege matte.

this manuscript, one leaf of that one, one leaf from a third, and so on, and pile them up into a deck of manuscript leaves, each of which was from a different codex. The Eges assembled at least eight different collections of leaves in such portfolios (several created and marketed exclusively by Louise after Otto's death).[12] The most common are titled *Fifty Original Leaves from Medieval Manuscripts*; *Original Leaves from Famous Bibles*; and *Original Leaves from Famous Books*. The leaves were taped into custom mattes with a distinctive red-fillet border and the Eges' handwritten notes across the bottom, identified with Ege's letterpress label, and stored in custom buckram boxes (Figure 6.2). Because the leaves in these portfolios are always sequenced the same way, Number 5 in one portfolio comes from the same manuscript as Number 5 in every other portfolio of the same name. There were forty (perhaps forty-one) such boxes titled 'Fifty Original Leaves of Medieval Manuscripts,' of which thirty-one have been located.[13] In those thirty-one boxes are thirty-one leaves from each of those fifty manuscripts. Dozens of instantiations of the other Ege portfolios are known as well, housing hundreds of leaves from even more manuscripts and printed books. The Ege portfolios therefore represent a coherent – and intrinsically American – corpus of leaves that can be affiliated with a discreet number of manuscripts, leading to the realistic possibility of the recovery and study of at least a portion of many of these codices.

What might that recovery process look like? The obvious first step is to identify and record leaves of Ege-sourced manuscripts. Scholars have been tracking leaves from the most well-known Ege-sourced manuscripts (such as the Beauvais Missal) for decades, publishing lists of the locations of known leaves. One of the earliest such lists was included in Judith Oliver's 1985 catalogue, *Manuscripts Sacred and Secular*, where the entry for Boston University School of Theology's Beauvais Missal leaf records the location of nine additional leaves.[14]

[12] Gwara, *Otto Ege's Manuscripts*, Appendices I–VIII. John P. Chalmers, 'A Checklist of Leaf Books,' in Christopher de Hamel & Joel Silver, eds, *Disbound and Dispersed: The Leaf Book Reconsidered* (Chicago, IL, 2005), 102–37, one of the first formal explorations of this phenomenon, records only two of these in its checklist of leaf portfolios: *Fifteen Original Oriental Manuscript Leaves of six centuries* and *Fifty Original Leaves from medieval manuscripts*; see 114, nos. 50 and 51).

[13] To the twenty-nine sets recorded in Gwara, *Otto Ege's Manuscripts*, pp. 106–07 may be added Set 3 (the Ege family's personal portfolio) acquired from Otto and Louise Ege's grandchildren by the Beinecke Library in 2015 and Set 1 found in a basement in Ohio in 2020, auctioned at Christie's London on 8 December 2020, lot 9 (for £50,000), and acquired by the Houghton Library, now Cambridge, MA, Harvard University, MS Typ 1294.

[14] Judith Oliver, ed., *Manuscripts Sacred and Secular* (Boston, MA, 1985), pp. 39–40. For other early lists, see Julia Boffey & A. S. G. Edwards, *Medieval Manuscripts in the Norlin Library and the Department of Fine Arts at the University of Colorado at*

It was not until 1995, however, that Ege's biblioclasm was canonized as part of the larger narrative of manuscript fragmentation, in Christopher de Hamel's seminal lecture, 'Cutting Up Manuscripts for Pleasure and Profit' (delivered at Rare Book School in 1995 and published as a pamphlet in 1996). In this essential lecture, de Hamel laid out the three primary stages of biblioclasm (binding use, cuttings, and the American leaf trade) and made the case for Ege's importance in the formation of North American manuscript collections. Roger Wieck's essay 'Folia Fugitiva: The Pursuit of the Illuminated Manuscript Leaf' was published that same year.[15] Both of these historiographic essays situate Ege alongside figures such as James Granger (1723–76), Luigi Celotti (1759–1843) and John Ruskin (1823–1900), and as important characters in the timeline of manuscript fragmentation, but without focusing on Ege specifically. Even so, both de Hamel and Wieck assert that Ege deserves more attention and study: Wieck notes that 'Another personality, too often ignored in the world of single leaves – and who perhaps represents a uniquely American approach to the field – is Otto F. Ege.'[16] For his part, de Hamel argues that Ege is 'one of the most remarkable and fascinating of all American book-collectors, [having] probably destroyed more medieval manuscripts than any single person since the Reformation.'[17]

These essays initiated a flurry of publications, symposia, and exhibitions in the early 2000s, helping to establish Ege Studies as a sub-discipline of fragment study. This activity was also inspired, at least in part, by the symposium, 'Interpreting and Collecting Fragments of Medieval Books' at Oxford in 2000 and its associated proceedings. While most of the presentations at

---

*Boulder: A Summary Catalogue* (Fairview, NC, 2002), pp. 45–46; Christopher de Hamel, *Gilding the Lilly: A Hundred Medieval and Illuminated Manuscripts in the Lilly Library* (Bloomington, IN, 2010), 76–77; Claire Jenson, 'Imagining Priest, Church, and Synagogue in the eucharistic Liturgy: a reconstructive study of Robert of Hangest's Missal' (unpublished BA thesis, Oberlin College, 2012), 59–62; Barbara A. Shailor, 'Otto Ege: His Manuscript Fragment Collection and the Opportunities Presented by Electronic Technology,' *Journal of the Rutgers University Libraries*, 60 (2003), 1–22 (at 8–9); and Alison Stones, 'Les manuscrits du cardinal Jean Cholet et l'enluminure beauvaissienne vers la fin du xiiieme siecles,' in Alain Erlande-Brandenburg, ed., *L'art gothique dans l'Oise et ses environs, XIIème–XIVème siècle: architecture civile et religieuse, peinture murale, sculpture et arts précieux, etc.: colloque international organisé à Beauvais les 10 et 11 octobre 1998 par le G.E.M.O.B., Groupe d'etude des monuments et oeuvres d'art de l'Oise et du Beauvaisis*, (Beauvais, 2001), pp. 239–68 (at 245 n. 38).

15   Roger S. Wieck, 'Folia Fugitiva: The Pursuit of the Illuminated Manuscript Leaf,' *Journal of the Walters Art Gallery*, 54 (1996), 233–54.

16   Wieck, 'Folia Fugitiva,' 248.

17   de Hamel, *Cutting Up Manuscripts*, p. 16.

the symposium and in the proceedings focused on binding fragments and illuminated cuttings, one laid the groundwork for the entire concept of fragmentological reconstructions: Albinia de la Mare's 'A Livy copied by Giacomo Curlo dismembered by Otto Ege.'[18] In this important essay, de la Mare traces the journey of Curlo's Livy from its humanistic origins through later owners and dismemberment at Ege's hands, including an appendix listing the identified leaves by content and current location.[19] To my knowledge, this is the first study to tell the entire story of a single Ege-sourced manuscript in depth. De la Mare's essay would serve as a model for other scholars and set the stage for the next two decades of Ege Studies.

In the early 2000s, Ege Studies began to move to the fore of manuscript studies in America, beginning with Barbara A. Shailor's 2003 article 'Otto Ege: His Manuscript Fragment Collection and the Opportunities Presented by Electronic Technology,' in which she considers Ege's biblioclasm in the context of his time: 'We can reflect that Ege's end purpose was, on a philosophical level, prompted by a generous spirit to share his enthusiasm for the world of early books and manuscripts, but by today's standards he certainly went about achieving his goal with questionable means!'[20] She enumerates the implications of Ege's biblioclasm beyond the loss of the coherent codex: 1) the leaves are irrevocably scattered; 2) the bindings are lost or destroyed; and 3) colophons and provenance clues may be lost as well. With great prescience, Shailor here calls for the establishment of an 'Otto Ege Database' that would allow scholars to digitally rebuild dismembered manuscripts. 'Although it may be forever impossible to re-create an Otto Ege volume in its entirety – complete with the heft of the volume (large choir books could weigh fifty pounds or more), the velvety feel of a well-prepared piece of parchment, or the impressions on a stamped binding – the advent of electronic technology holds remarkable promise for re-assembling the fragments.'[21]

Shailor's call to action inspired the 2005 public symposium 'Remaking the Book: Digitally Reconstructing the Otto Ege Manuscript Portfolios' at the University of Saskatchewan, hosted by Saskatchewan professor Peter Stoicheff and accompanied by an exhibition of the University's *Fifty Original Leaves* portfolio. The attendees included prominent manuscript scholars such as Shailor, Consuelo Dutschke, and Anthony S. G. Edwards. A series of lectures introduced

---

[18]  In Linda Brownrigg & Margaret M. Smith, eds, *Interpreting and Collecting Fragments of Medieval Books* (Los Altos Hills, CA, 2000), pp. 57–88.

[19]  Leaves from this manuscript are now known as Handlist 39; see Gwara, *Otto Ege's Manuscripts*, p. 131.

[20]  Shailor, 'Otto Ege,' 10.

[21]  Shailor, 17.

the history of fragmenting, the impact of Otto Ege on the American leaf trade, and the potential of the Ege portfolios for study and research, culminating in a public keynote presented by Shailor titled 'Scattered Leaves: The Otto Ege Medieval Manuscript Collection.' In a closed session on the second day of the symposium, the participants discussed 'future plans for digitally reconstructing parts of the Otto Ege medieval manuscript portfolio.'[22]

The Saskatchewan symposium motivated other scholars to investigate the Ege material in their own collections, such as Denison University professor Fred Porcheddu, who wrote about his institution's 'Fifty Original Leaves' portfolio in 2007.[23] In this essay, Porcheddu expressed dismay at the destruction of unique manuscripts but also acknowledged the value of the Ege portfolios for teaching, especially at small universities like Denison that do not have the acquisition budget that might allow for the purchase of a collection of medieval codices: 'At a small college like my own Denison University, for example, which is devoted to undergraduate liberal arts education and which is not otherwise well-stocked with pre-modern materials, both introductory survey courses and more advanced medieval and early modern seminars benefit immeasurably from the discussion that such fragmentary resources inspire.'[24] Porcheddu was somewhat pragmatic about the ethics of Ege's career: 'Ege's biblioclasty, however ethically problematic it may be, has resulted in the presence of a considerable number of manuscript and printed leaves being dispersed around the world.'[25]

In 2008, Edwards, Shailor, and Porcheddu participated in the first conference session devoted to Ege's career, at the Thirty-Fifth Saint Louis Conference on Manuscript Studies. The session was titled 'Otto Ege and the Fortunes of Fragments' and the proceedings were published in *Manuscripta* in 2009. In his essay Edwards lays out the inherent complexity of addressing the ethical concerns of Ege's biblioclasm, noting on the one hand that 'The deliberate fragmentation of so many manuscripts at a single stroke is an action without precedent in the history of manuscript collecting,' while also acknowledging that 'Ege the

---

[22] The website promoting the symposium and accompanying exhibition is now defunct, but screenshots are available at: <https://wayback.archive-it.org/14753/20201021201523/http://library2.usask.ca/ege/> [accessed 3 June 2023]. The portfolio belonging to the University of Colorado at Boulder was also published online quite early, by 2000, in fact, on a site that is still live but has not been updated in many years: <http://www.umilta.net/ege.html> [accessed 3 June 2023].

[23] Frederick Porcheddu, 'Otto F. Ege: Teacher, Collector, and Biblioclast,' *Art Documentation: Bulletin of the Art Libraries Society of North America*, 26 (2007), 4–15.

[24] Porcheddu, 'Otto F. Ege,' 8.

[25] Porcheddu, 'Otto F. Ege,' 8.

collector was also Ege the destroyer, but a destroyer who created new possibilities for the wider appreciation of medieval manuscript culture.'[26] Shailor explored for the first time the distinctions in origin and purpose of the Ege portfolios vs. 'rogue' leaves that had been sold singly.[27] She also posited (following de Hamel) a business relationship between Ege and fellow bookdealer Philip Duschnes, a relationship that has since been confirmed and is currently being studied in more detail by others, including myself.[28] Finally, she laid out the importance of consistency in cataloguing the leaves and preserving Ege's original data (even when incorrect), sequencing, and numbering system for the sake of improved discoverability, standards that have since been quite rightly adopted by many holding institutions.[29]

As explained in his *Manuscripta* essay, Porcheddu was at the time in the midst of developing the website 'The Otto F. Ege Collection' at Denison, a first attempt at implementing Shailor's 'Ege Database.'[30] The website (https://ege.demison. edu) went live in 2008 and served as a repository for images of several 'Fifty Original Leaves' sets, discoverable in browse lists by location (all fifty leaves from a particular portfolio) or leaf number (leaves from the same source manuscript across portfolios). It was the latter organizational schema that began to fulfill the vision of the 2005 Saskatoon symposium: a databank of images of leaves from the same source manuscript that would allow researchers to begin to piece these broken books back together. In a 2009 article, Peter Stoicheff explained the motivation behind the project: '...one of Ege's original medieval books [might] tell us something more than the leaf itself.'[31] Given the limitations of the time, however, there was no interoperability to the Denison website besides the option to download images into a silo. Even so, the website (which is still accessible on the Denison server but is only rarely updated) remains a very useful resource for Ege's biography and bibliography and for images of portfolios that may not yet have been posted on their own institutional repositories.

---

[26] A. S. G. Edwards, 'Otto Ege: The Collector as Destroyer,' *Manuscripta*, 53 (2009), 1–12 (at 5, 11). See also A. S. G. Edwards, 'Scattering the Leaves: The Melancholy Legacy of Otto F. Ege, Book Collector and Book Destroyer,' *Times Literary Supplement*, November 8, 2007, 13–14.

[27] Barbara A. Shailor, 'Otto Ege: Portfolios vs. Leaves,' *Manuscripta*, 53 (2009), 13–27.

[28] de Hamel, *Cutting Up Manuscripts*, pp. 17–18 and Shailor, 'Otto Ege: Portfolios vs. Leaves,' 23.

[29] Shailor, 'Otto Ege: Portfolios vs. Leaves,' 26.

[30] Frederick Porcheddu, 'Reassembling the Leaves: Otto Ege and the Potential of Technology,' *Manuscripta*, 53 (2009), 29–48.

[31] Peter Stoicheff, 'Putting Humpty Together Again: Otto Ege's Scattered Leaves,' *Digital Studies/le Champ Numérique*, 12 (2008), online.

All of the publications about Ege in the 2000s worked together to build a case for a concerted effort to identify Ege-sourced material in North American collections and to leverage digital technologies to rebuild those dismembered codices in virtual space. In the 2010s, this work began in earnest. In the Appendix to the first version of our *Directory of Collections in the United States and Canada with Pre-1600 Manuscript Holdings* (published online at *Bibsite* in 2010), Melissa Conway and I identified 104 Ege portfolios in eighty-four collections in twenty-six states and two Canadian provinces.[32] Between them, these 104 sets held nearly 2,000 Ege-sourced leaves from at least sixty-five dismembered manuscripts. In addition, we recorded more than a dozen 'rogue' leaves, single leaves held outside of Ege portfolios. While we were compiling our *Directory* and initial Ege census, University of South Carolina professor Scott Gwara was working on a comprehensive Ege project: a monograph-length study and handlist, and a data- and image-bank of Ege and other leaves that was to be called *ManuscriptLink*.[33] The Conway/Davis *Appendix* was never formally published, but the information we compiled was incorporated into Gwara's seminal 2013 study, *Otto Ege's Manuscripts*, which greatly expanded our initial census.

Gwara's work marked a major turning point in Ege studies. In his monograph, Gwara assigned a handlist number to each of the more than 300 manuscripts he identified as having been dismembered or distributed by Ege, totaling thousands of single leaves that entered the market in the mid-twentieth century and have since passed into collections public and private. Gwara's handlist was a critical step in the establishment and expansion of Ege Studies as a discipline and fragmentology more generally, as it allowed scholars to easily identify and reference particular leaves by their Gwara Handlist numbers instead of a more general description. For example, leaves of the Beauvais Missal may now be referenced simply as 'Handlist [HL] 15' instead of 'that late thirteenth-century missal written in two columns of twenty-one lines.' In the Handlist portion of the book, Gwara records sales of codices and shelfmarks of single leaves from particular manuscripts as well as making important correctives to Ege's own descriptions.[34] Detailed indices record measurements, contents, and layout for each ex-Ege codex, facilitating identifications and discoverability.[35] Other online resources for Ege studies include my blog, *The Manuscript Road Trip*, in

---

[32]  Melissa Conway & Lisa Fagin Davis. *Directory of Institutions in the United States and Canada with Pre-1600 Manuscript Holdings. Appendix: Otto F. Ege Leaf Sets in North American Collections (BibSite*, The Bibliographical Society of America, 2010).

[33]  The development of ManuscriptLink has since ceased.

[34]  Gwara, *Otto Ege's Manuscripts*, pp. 115–201. A second, expanded edition is forthcoming that will include new identifications and updated bibliography.

[35]  Gwara, *Otto Ege's Manuscripts*, pp. 301–53.

which I have also contributed to the identification of Ege-sourced material, and my *Ege Field Guide*, which allows users to easily examine sample images of leaves from more than one hundred Ege-sourced manuscripts in order to identify Ege material in their own collections.[36] Additional important contributions to Ege Studies have been made recently by Alison Altstatt, Eric Johnson, Elizabeth Hebbard, Peter Kidd, and others.[37]

As Shailor, Stoicheff, and others have noted, while locating Ege material in public or university libraries can be relatively straightforward, the thousands of leaves sold to private individuals – many of whom may have no idea what they are – has proven much more challenging. 'This is the window to the world that was the medieval period,' Shailor said in 2005. 'Hopefully people will realize that what has been hanging on the wall of their family room is a part of this Ege collection.'[38] Inspired by a conversation with Dr. Shailor, I traveled to Lima, Ohio in 2017 to host an 'Antique Road Show' type of event at the Lima Public Library; the librarian reached out to the town listserv and invited anyone with a manuscript page in their home to bring it to the Library to be examined and authenticated by a visiting expert. Shailor was proven correct when more than thirty locals came to the Library that day, most of them bearing Ege-sourced leaves that they inherited from older relatives who had acquired them at the Lima Public Library in the mid-twentieth-century.[39] Another effective strategy for finding Ege-sourced leaves in private hands is publicity through print and

---

[36]  See, for example, < https://manuscriptroadtrip.wordpress.com/tag/otto-f-ege/> [accessed 31 May 2023]. The Ege Field Guide may be found here: https://www. dropbox.com/sh/u2lbhr26pgz882p/AAAYahDHUEwPhQ097CFIwnK3a?dl=0 [accessed 2 June 2023].

[37]  Alison Altstatt, 'Re-Membering the Wilton Processional,' *Notes*, 72 (2016), 690–732. Eric Johnson, '"Deathless fragments within the reach of man …": Tracing four decades of manuscript fragmentation via the Lima (OH) Public Library Staff Loan Fund Association Archive,' *Manuscript Studies* (forthcoming, 2023); Elizabeth Hebbard, 'The Peripheral Manuscripts Project: Must-Sees in the Midwest,' *Manuscript Studies* (forthcoming, 2023); and numerous posts on Peter Kidd's blog Medieval Manuscripts Provenance <https://mssprovenance.blogspot. com/> [accessed 3 June 2023].

[38]  Unnati Gandhi, 'Lost, 40 boxes of ancient text. Found, 33,' *Globe and Mail*, 8 June 2005.

[39]  For more on Ege's relationship with the Lima Public Library, see <https:// manuscriptroadtrip.wordpress.com/?s=Lima> [accessed 31 May 2023]. Ohio State University curator Eric Johnson has recently discovered several account books in Lima that detail decades of the Lima Public Library's sales of Ege material. These registers will soon be digitized and posted in the Ohio State University digital repository and will also be made available as a searchable database.

social media.[40] As more surveys of collections take place – such as the ongoing discovery, cataloguing, and imaging project 'Peripheral Manuscripts' directed by Indiana University professor Elizabeth Hebbard – it is becoming more and more clear that untold numbers of unidentified Ege-sourced leaves remain to be found in the stacks of unsuspecting libraries or 'hanging on the wall of [a] family room.'[41] Identification of Ege-sourced material, however, is only the first step.

In the early years of the twenty-first century, scholars began to realize the potential of burgeoning digital technologies for the virtual reconstruction of dismembered manuscripts, in particular those manuscripts dismembered by Ege. Shailor had issued the first call to arms in 2003: 'For Otto Ege fragments now dispersed around the world, the possibilities presented by modern technology are fascinating. It is only a matter of time, financial resources, and scholarly communication and perseverance before significant portions of Ege's intriguing collection will be reassembled and made available electronically.'[42] As he was preparing to launch the Denison website in 2008, Porcheddu explained its purpose as part of a long-term vision:

> [With the Ege portfolios,] the challenge is not to present graphically a celebrated and important single artifact, but rather to use digital technology to enable 'virtual unity' of several common types of artifacts now physically located across the United States and Canada. Currently, none of the handful of Ege sites in existence stretches beyond the boundaries of a single portfolio. The next logical step will be to bring together the images of all known portfolios' leaves, allowing a viewer to have images presented singly, or in original codex foliation order, or in portfolio sequence order, or in any other order so determined.[43]

Developments in imaging services, digital storage, and interoperability in the 2010s led to parallel developments in Digital Ege Studies. Several fragment-based projects that developed during this period were hampered by excessive data models and burdensome imaging standards, mandating detailed cataloguing metadata that many collections were unable to provide and committing to store and serve high-resolution images whose file size and superfluity are unsustainable. In other words, in order for such multi-institutional projects to

---

[40]  See, for example, this piece about a leaf of the Beauvais Missal purchased for $75 at an estate sale in Waterville, Maine: Associated Press, 'He went to an estate sale for bargains. He found a valuable 700-year-old document,' National Public Radio, 23 September 2022 <https://www.npr.org/2022/09/23/1124771471/estate-sale-700-year-old-document-france> [accessed 31 May 2023].

[41]  <https://peripheralmss.org/> [accessed 3 June 2023].

[42]  Shailor, 'Otto Ege,' 22.

[43]  Porcheddu, 'Otto F. Ege,' 12.

succeed, data must be flexible and images must be interoperable, lowering the barrier to institutional participation and increasing sustainability of both data and images.

The development of the International Image Interoperability Framework (IIIF) in the mid-2010s signaled the beginning of the next phase of Digital Ege Studies. The International Image Interoperability Framework is a way of presenting digital images in an online environment that allows them to be shared via a persistent URL instead of by downloading and uploading into a silo.[44] The underlying code (the 'manifest') includes metadata that travels with the image, metadata that can be updated and expanded by the holding institution at any time. If an online image is IIIF-compliant, it can be manifested in a workspace known as a 'shared canvas' simply by pointing to the IIIF manifest URL. The image file and the associated metadata embedded in the manifest are drawn into the shared canvas when called for rather than being physically stored there. This interoperability has the advantage of enabling a user to apply annotations and sequence images without transforming the actual JPGs or manifests. An image can be stored in one place while being used in multiple workspaces. The model is completely open-access and avoids siloing and is thus in keeping with digital best practices. For fragmentological research, this means that a fragment from one collection can be mirrored into a shared-canvas viewer alongside sister fragments from other institutions, digitally reconstructing the dismembered parent manuscript with no need for rekeying data or siloing images. Interoperability is the key to Digital Fragmentology and, specifically, Digital Ege Studies.

In May of 2014, Benjamin Albritton – one of the developers of IIIF – delivered a paper at the International Congress on Medieval Studies in Kalamazoo, Michigan describing the potential of shared-canvas viewers to digitally reconstruct dismembered manuscripts, using one of the Ege manuscripts as a case study.[45] Other fragmentologists were beginning to think along the same lines; the proliferation of open-source projects like IIIF ushered in an era of parallel development, as multiple developers customize the code for their own use. Several fragmentology projects evolved in the mid-2010s that took advantage of the new standards of open-source, -access, and -data. Dr. Albritton's case study used IIIF and the Mirador shared-canvas viewer to digitally reconstruct a manuscript that had been dismembered by Otto Ege in the 1930s.[46] At the same time, Debra Cashion at Saint Louis University was

---

[44]  For technical details, see http://iiif.io, accessed May 31, 2021.

[45]  Benjamin Albritton & Bridget Whearty, 'Scattered Leaves: New Approaches to Digital Manuscript Studies,' paper delivered at International Congress on Medieval Studies, Western Michigan University, Kalamazoo, Michigan, May 8, 2014.

[46]  Albritton's proof-of-concept project is now defunct, but screencaps are available at Simeon Warner, 'IIIF Introduction and Opportunities at Cornell,' lecture

developing the Broken Books project, combining IIIF images with a fragment-centric data model to reconstruct dismembered manuscripts in a custom shared-canvas viewer.[47] My own study of the Beauvais Missal would serve as one of two case studies for the Broken Books interface. Broken Books launched in the fall of 2015 and ran until 2019. The project served as a very successful case study in the potential of combining shared-canvas viewers with a custom data model to digitally reconstruct dismembered manuscripts.[48] A third IIIF-based project grew out of a 2013 meeting in Geneva and culminated in the 2016 launch of the online resource *Fragmentarium*.[49]

*Fragmentarium* is a fragment-centric workspace that takes advantage of IIIF functionality to easily allow users to upload, catalogue, and arrange leaves to create digital reconstructions. After the cessation of the Broken Books project, I migrated the data and images of the Beauvais Missal to the *Fragmentarium* platform and used the site's IIIF functionality to sequence the known leaves into a virtual reconstruction that combines discoverable metadata with image scrolling (Figure 6.3).[50] Using this interoperable, open-data, image- and data bank, Ege's biblioclasm can be visually reversed, making Shailor's 2003 vision a reality. More than a dozen such resequencing projects are currently underway in *Fragmentarium*, most of them focused on Ege-sourced leaves.[51] There is much work still to do and many discoveries still to be made. In 2009, Edwards noted that 'The materials sold in the 1980s indicate that a family cache of some size remained over thirty years after Ege's death…Other manuscripts (fifty-seven codices and twenty-three single leaves), the property of the Ege family, remain on deposit but seemingly inaccessible, in the Cleveland Museum of Art. And it is clear that other materials, possibly quite substantial in number, remain in

---

delivered on February 5, 2015, at Cornell University <https://www.slideshare.net/simeonwarner/2015-01-cornellvrwgiiif> [accessed 3 June 2023].

[47] Debra Taylor Cashion, 'Broken Books,' *Manuscript Studies*, 1 (2017), 342–51.

[48] The Broken Books project is now defunct.

[49] <http://*Fragmentarium*.ms> [accessed 3 June 2023].

[50] Lisa Fagin Davis, 'Beauvais Missal (Virtual Reconstruction)' <https://fragmentarium.ms/overview/F-4ihz> [accessed 3 June 2023]. See also Lisa Fagin Davis, 'Reconstructing the Beauvais Missal: A Progress Report,' *Digital Philology* (forthcoming, 2024) and Davis, 'Reconstructing the Beauvais Missal' <https://brokenbooks2.omeka.net> [accessed 2 June 2023].

[51] For an up-to-date list of Ege resequencing projects, see Lisa Fagin Davis, 'Manuscript Road Trip: Fragmentology in the Wild,' *Manuscript Road Trip* (originally posted 14 July 2019, last updated 11 March 2023) <https://manuscriptroadtrip.wordpress.com/2019/07/14/manuscript-road-trip-fragmentology-in-the-wild/> [accessed 31 May 2023].

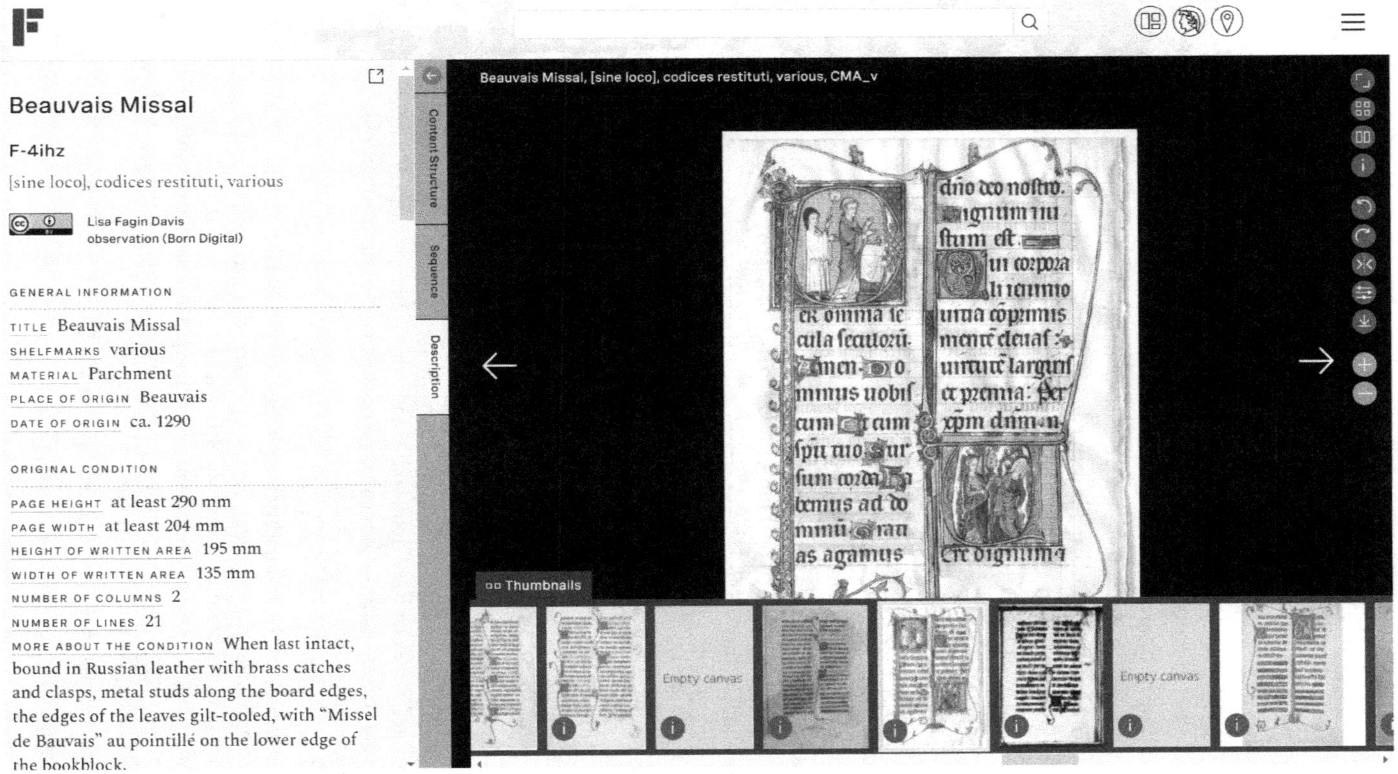

Beauvais Missal
F-4ihz
[sine loco], codices restituti, various
Lisa Fagin Davis
observation (Born Digital)
GENERAL INFORMATION
TITLE Beauvais Missal
SHELFMARKS various
MATERIAL Parchment
PLACE OF ORIGIN Beauvais
DATE OF ORIGIN ca. 1290
ORIGINAL CONDITION
PAGE HEIGHT at least 290 mm
PAGE WIDTH at least 204 mm
HEIGHT OF WRITTEN AREA 195 mm
WIDTH OF WRITTEN AREA 135 mm
NUMBER OF COLUMNS 2
NUMBER OF LINES 21
MORE ABOUT THE CONDITION When last intact, bound in Russian leather with brass catches and clasps, metal studs along the board edges, the edges of the leaves gilt-tooled, with "Missel de Bauvais" au pointillé on the lower edge of the bookblock.
Content Structure
Sequence
Description
Beauvais Missal, [sine loco], codices restituti, various, CMA_v
Thumbnails
Empty canvas
Empty canvas


Fig. 6.3. *Fragmentarium* Resequencing of the Beauvais Missal. The image of the Beauvais Missal leaf shown here is courtesy of The Cleveland Museum of Art, Gift of Mr. and Mrs. Milton Freudenheim in memory of Otto Ege 1982.141.

the possession of the Ege family, some of which, from time to time, have been donated to various institutions.'[52] Edwards' supposition was correct: in 2015, the Ege Family Collection was acquired by the Beinecke Rare Book and Manuscript Library (with Barbara Shailor's mediation) and will be ready for public study in early 2024. This extraordinary and completely unstudied treasure trove includes dozens of leaves, more than fifty codices (including those formerly on deposit at CMA, as referenced by Edwards above), several boxes of archival material, and the empty, or nearly-empty, bindings of several codices dismembered by Ege.[53] Other directions for new research include untangling and exploring the relationship between Ege and the Lima (Ohio) Public Library using new evidence recently uncovered by Eric Johnson,[54] and the discoveries resulting from Elizabeth Hebbard's detailed in-situ explorations of collections in the Midwest that are known to, or may, include Ege-sourced leaves.[55]

There is an inherent contradiction in Otto Ege's career, one that de Hamel, Edwards, Shailor, and others readily acknowledge. Ege is, de Hamel notes, 'the most endearing of arch-villains.'[56] While observing that 'Ege's evangelism and conviction of righteousness probably brought fascination and delight to many hundreds of ordinary Americans who would otherwise never have set eyes on a medieval manuscript,'[57] de Hamel takes pains to clarify his own response to Ege's biblioclasm:

> Let there be no doubt. The deliberate destruction of any unique work of art can only be regarded as unforgivable vandalism… The breaking up of a

---

[52] Edwards, 'Otto Ege: The Collector as Destroyer,' 7–8.

[53] Lisa Fagin Davis, 'Breaking and Buying with Philip and Otto,' in Laura Cleaver, Danielle Magnusson, Hannah Morcos & Angéline Rais, eds, *The Pre-Modern Manuscript Trade and its Consequences, ca. 1890–1945* (Leeds, forthcoming 2024). See also 'Beinecke Library Acquires 'treasure trove' of medieval manuscripts from Otto Ege,' Beinecke Rare Book and Manuscript Library < https://beinecke.library. yale.edu/article/beinecke-library-acquires-treasure-trove-medieval-manuscripts-otto-ege> [accessed 3 June 2023].

[54] The Lima Public Library sold leaves on Ege's behalf for decades, keeping a 30% cut for their Staff Loan Fund (which in turn helped library staffers attend graduate school and meet other needs). Johnson's recent discovery of several Lima Public Library ledgers recording hundreds of individual sales by leaf, price, and buyer will provide significant new information about the circulation of Ege-sourced leaves. As of this writing, Johnson is preparing what will be a public database of these sales, incorporating Gwara handlist numbers into the records.

[55] <https://peripheralmss.org> [accessed 3 June 2023].

[56] de Hamel, *Cutting Up Manuscripts*, p. 16.

[57] de Hamel, *Cutting Up Manuscripts*, p. 17.

medieval manuscript whether for enjoyment or for profit is, and always will be, at least for bibliographers, entirely indefensible and infinitely regrettable.[58]

In other words, Ege was a villain who destroyed hundreds of unique heritage objects. Or perhaps Ege was a socialist hero, a Robin Hood figure who made medieval manuscripts accessible and affordable for everyone. Both can be, and are, simultaneously true. This contradiction challenges us to both conduct reparative labor and advocate to ensure that the practice of biblioclasm – which is, and will likely remain, legal in most markets – is at minimum soundly discouraged. We can do this by insisting on provenance transparency before making a purchase. If a dealer does not know or will not reveal when and under what circumstances a manuscript was dismembered, we must walk away. The acquisition of Ege material or leaves from other manuscripts dismembered decades ago is less ethically precarious, but every buyer must decide for themselves where they draw that line.

Ege's stated goal of allowing the smallest collections to have access to a little bit of the Middle Ages was, by any standard, successful. Porcheddu felt that making Ege material publicly available online was 'a continuation of Professor Ege's desire to share the beauty of medieval book art with a wider audience than geography allows. Whatever one may think of his biblioclasty, we, the inheritors of his actions, can seek a virtue among the scattered leaves.'[59] Members of the general public, small colleges, museums, and public libraries across North America could, and did, buy what Ege offered. Of course, this democratization came at a horrible cost, the destruction of hundreds of unique handmade objects. One hundred years later, the practice of digital fragmentology allows scholars and teachers alike to continue the democratization of the study of medieval manuscripts, as we work to digitally reunite these scattered leaves and present the re-membered manuscripts in open-access interoperable environments. The painful damage inflicted by the knife of a century ago – the blade that cut the threads and split the bifolia – can in fact be reversed. By making images of Ege-sourced leaves discoverable and interoperable, by leveraging digital best practices to resequence these images in virtual space, and by using these resequenced manuscripts for teaching and research, we are the inheritors of the better half of Ege's legacy.

---

[58]   de Hamel, *Cutting Up Manuscripts*, p. 21.

[59]   Porcheddu, 'Otto F. Ege,' 12.

Fig. 7.1.   Mark Lansburgh.

# 7

# Mark Lansburgh: Collector and Seller of Medieval Manuscripts

~

*Consuelo Dutschke*

Mark Lansburgh's grandfather and grand-uncles came from Germany to the United States in 1854 and settled in Washington DC.[1] His parents were Mark Lansburgh, Senior (1889–1953) and Hortense Brylawski Lansburgh (1892–1957); they were married on 12 September 1917, and Mark was the youngest of their three sons, born in Washington DC on 24 May 1925. After graduation from high school, Mark enlisted in the Army Air Corps and he served in the army from 1943–45. Between 1945 and 1949, Lansburgh attended Dartmouth College, where he majored in English and graphic arts studies. After graduation Lansburgh moved to Southern California; later moves took him to Colorado, where he worked at Colorado College, and then to New Mexico.

The earliest record of Lansburgh's manuscript collecting is in Faye & Bond, pp. 24–25. The next published account of Lansburgh's collection is again in 1962 when he printed privately *An Illustrated Check List of Manuscript Leaves in the Collection of Mark Lansburgh* (Santa Barbara [CA]), described in the colophon: 'Type was set by M. Lansburgh & fifty copies were printed on handmade paper.' This consists of full-page facsimiles of thirteen manuscript pages, numbered I–XIV (the final item has two images). The rationale of this assemblage is: 'This small collection grew out of a desire to illustrate the difference between writing and calligraphy.' Production standards are high and the 'Introduction' by E. A. Lowe gives it scholarly substance. In the meantime, it is clear that from the early sixties Lansburgh began a process of dispersal that continued over some decades.

Lansburgh's sales were coupled with donations to his alma mater, Dartmouth College; he gave to his university some thirty medieval and Renaissance manuscripts, leaves or documents. Other manuscripts or leaves

---

[1] This is a necessarily summary account of Lansburgh's life; I plan to give a fuller account elsewhere.

from his collection continue to circulate through the trade, some complete manuscripts having been broken up, either by Lansburgh or dealers.

Lansburgh gives some account of his library in three articles, the first being his 'Medieval and Renaissance Manuscripts and Graphic Arts at the Colorado College,' *Colorado College Magazine*, 2.3 (1967), 9–20; it is of particular interest in that its publication date, 1967, is an attestation of Lansburgh's move to Colorado. One year later he published 'The Illuminated Manuscript Collection at Colorado College,' *Art Journal*, 28 (1968) 61–70, where he lists twenty-four items. Similarly, Lansburgh's third article, entitled 'The Drawing Collection at the Colorado College,' *Art Journal* 29 (1970), 341–48, reports the existence of 'some four dozen pen and ink drawings dating from the Gothic period through the Renaissance' (341), of which twenty are illustrated in the present article.

In later years Lansburgh's interests shifted from western medieval and Renaissance manuscripts to the cultures of the Native American tribes. His home was in New Mexico when he died on 18 June 2013.

The list below is an attempt to assemble a record of the medieval and Renaissance manuscripts that passed through Lansburgh's hands. As noted above, some of these manuscripts were broken up, either by Lansburgh himself or subsequently, and it has not been possible to comprehensively document their subsequent dispersal. And while those that passed through the auction rooms were often identified as Lansburgh's, others of his may have been sold without attribution. This list should be seen as a starting point for further research into Lansburgh's collecting and subsequent dispersal of his manuscripts.

## Medieval and Renaissance Western Manuscripts owned by Mark Lansburgh[2]

Each entry gives brief information about place, date, content, provenance and location (where known); this last is given in bold at the end of each entry. The following abbreviations are used:

| | |
|---|---|
| Dartmouth | Dartmouth College, Hanover, New Hampshire |
| Lansburgh, *Check List* | *An Illustrated Check List of Manuscript Leaves in the Collection of Mark Lansburgh.* With an introductory essay by E. A. Lowe and descriptive notes by M. Lansburgh (Santa Barbara [CA], 1962). |

---

[2]  I am grateful to Jay Satterfield for his ever-gracious help with the Dartmouth manuscripts.

| Lansburgh, *Colorado College Magazine* | Mark Lansburgh, 'Medieval and Renaissance Manuscripts and Graphic Arts at the Colorado College,' *The Colorado College Magazine* vol. 2.3 (1967) 9–20. |
|---|---|
| Lansburgh, 'Illuminated MSS' | Mark Lansburgh, 'The Illuminated Manuscript Collection at Colorado College,' *Art Journal*, 28 (1968), 61–70. |
| Lansburgh, 'Drawing Collection' | Mark Lansburgh, 'The Drawing Collection at The Colorado College,' *Art Journal*, 29 (1970), 341–48.[3] |
| McCarthy | Gaudenz Freuler, Peter Kidd, *The McCarthy Collection*, 3 vols (London, 2018–21), cited by volume and page(s). |

1.  ACCOUNTS, both domestic and household, of the Court of Star Chamber, Hilary Term, 1563. Gift of Mark Lansburgh, 1983. **Dartmouth, Rauner Special Collections, Lansburgh 17.**

2.  ANTIPHONAL; Italy, Benevento, s. ix ex; single leaf; text from Genesis IV:9, for Sunday in Sexagesima. Gift of Mark Lansburgh, 1974. **Dartmouth, Rauner Special Collections, Lansburgh 10.**

3.  ANTIPHONAL; France, possibly Lorraine, s. xii second half; bifolium; summer histories, Judith-Kings. Gift of Mark Lansburgh, 1993. **Dartmouth, Rauner Special Collections, Lansburgh 38.**

4.  ANTIPHONAL, Cistercian; northern France, s. xii second half; one cutting of an initial I with a saint, apparently female; acquired by Mark Lansburgh by 1962 with a group of other fragments from Eric Millar (1887–1966); Lansburgh, *Check List*, no. IX; acquired by Bob McCarthy in 1997 from Sam Fogg. McCarthy 3: 164–65. **McCarthy, BM 1146.**

5.  ANTIPHONAL; Flanders, between end of s. xiii and beginning of s. xiv; single leaf plus thirteen initials, border pieces and penwork initials; Lansburgh, *Check List*, no. IX; Lansburgh, 'Illuminated MSS' 62.

6.  ANTIPHONAL; Italy, s. xiv second half; Ascension of Christ; signed by Niccolò da Bologna; single leaf; part of the same book as no. 7 below; bought by Lansburgh, Sotheby's, 11 July 1966, lot 190; Lansburgh, 'Illuminated MSS,' 64. Sold by Lansburgh and entered the collection of Bernard Breslauer (1918–2004). Gift in 1975 from Anna Bing Arnold to the Los Angeles County Museum of Art. **Los Angeles, CA, County Museum of Art, M.75.3.**

---

[3]  At times Lansburgh refers to the same leaf in more than one of his publications; normally, only the first citation is given here.

7.   ANTIPHONAL; Italy, s. xiv second half; The Three Marys at the Tomb, single leaf, part of the same book as the preceding entry; Sotheby's, 11 July 1966, lot 191; Bernard Breslauer; sold by Breslauer's heirs at Christie's, 11 December 2002, lot 7 to Sam Fogg, from whom it was acquired by Bob McCarthy in May 2003. McCarthy, 1: 121–23. **McCarthy, BM 1418.**

8.   ANTIPHONAL, Cistercian; Spain, s. xiii first half; Lansburgh, *Colorado College Magazine*, 14; acquired by Bob McCarthy from Sam Fogg in May 2004; McCarthy, 2: 30–31. **McCarthy, BM 1537.**

9.   ANTIPHONAL; Switzerland, *c.* 1375; single leaf for the dedication of a church; sold Christie's, 20 November 2013, lot 36 (£2,000 to phone bidder) where provenance is given as 'MARK LANSBURGH.'

10.   ATHANASIUS, LIFE OF ANTHONY ABBOT; southern Italy, between s. xi ex and s. xii in; single leaf; Beneventan script; Lansburgh, *Check List*, no. V; Sotheby's, 11 July 1966, lot 189 (four other leaves in this lot untraced). **Berkeley, CA, University of California, Bancroft Library, BANC MS UCB 130:ff1000:07.**

11.   AZNAR GARCIA; 15 December 1065; charter; Christie's, 20 November 2013, lot 15, where provenance is given as 'MARK LANSBURGH, Colorado, by 1990' (unsold).

12.   BEDE, EXPOSITIO IN LUCAE EVANGELIUM; England or an Anglo-Saxon centre in Germany, between end of s. viii and beginning of s. ix; single leaf; Faye & Bond, p. 24, no. 2; *Check List*, no. II; acquired by Edwin J. Beinecke from E. P. Goldschmidt in 1964. **Beinecke, MS 441.**

13.   BIBLE, OT, END OF LEVITICUS–BEGINNING OF NUMBERS; northern France, s. xiii second or third quarter; 'Atlantic Bible' leaf acquired from Laurence Witten, Catalogue 12, *Early English Manuscripts and Illuminated Leaves*, (1980), no. 41 by the University of Colorado, Boulder. Julia Boffey & A. S. G. Edwards, *Medieval Manuscripts in the Norlin Library & the Department of Fine Arts at the University of Colorado at Boulder: a summary catalogue* (Fairview, N.C., 2002), p. 25. **Boulder, CO, University of Colorado, Norlin Library, MS 314.**

14.   BIBLE, OT, END OF DEUTERONOMY–BEGINNING OF PROLOGUE TO JOSHUA, JUDGES AND RUTH; northern France, s. xiii second or third quarter; single leaf; sold by Martin Schøyen, Sotheby's, 10 July 2012, lot 54; McCarthy, 3: 93–95. **McCarthy, BM 2379.**

15. BIBLE, OT, I and II SAMUEL, in Greek; Greek Near East, between 300 and 325 A.D.; two leaves; Mark Lansburgh with his initials 'ML' on the verso; gift of Edwin J. Beinecke, 1965. **Beinecke, MS 544.**

16. BIBLE, OT, PSALTER; England, s. xii, 83 fols; acquired by Lansburgh in 1960 from Duschnes, New York. Faye & Bond, p. 24, no. 4.

17. BIBLE, OT, PSALTER; Italy, s. xii; four leaves; glossed; Lansburgh, *Check List*, no. VI. Sotheby's, 6 July 2006, lot 7.

18. BIBLE, OT, PSALTER; France, s. xii; single leaf; text in gothic script, marginal notes for liturgical use in bâtarde; Lansburgh, *Check List*, no. VIII; Lansburgh, 'Illuminated MSS,' cover and 63.

19. BIBLE, OT, PSALTER or breviary; single leaf; Sotheby's, 11 July 1966, lot 192.

20. BIBLE, OT, Proverbs 29:15–30:20; single leaf, Italy, Montecassino, s. xii–xiii; Beneventan script. Sold by Lansburgh in 1963; Bernard Quaritch, Catalogue 1128 (1990), no. 19; Bloomsbury, 7 December 2021, lot 9.

21. BIBLE, OT, SAPIENTIAL BOOKS (Parabolae; Ecclesiastes; Canticum canticorum); France, probably the abbey of St Victor, s. xii ¾ with ownership attributed to Thomas Becket; 115 fols; acquired by Lansburgh in August 1958 from Bernard Quaritch; Faye & Bond, p. 24, no. 3; Lansburgh, *Check List*, no. VII; Sotheby's, 10 December 1980, lot 86 ('The Property of Mark Lansburgh'); unsold. **Stuart Rose, Ohio.**

22. BIBLE, OT, JEREMIAH; Germany or Switzerland, s. xii med; bifolium; Mark Lansburgh; Bernard Rosenthal; Bernard Quaritch, Catalogue 1147 (1991), no. 38; Martin Schøyen, his MS 640; Bernard Quaritch, Catalogue 1451, *Medieval and Renaissance Manuscripts* (2023), no. 10.

23. BIBLE, OT, JOEL; Italy, probably Rome, s. xi med or ¾; single leaf from an 'Atlantic Bible;' Christie's, 10 July 2019, lot 436.

24. BIBLE, NT, GOSPEL OF MATTHEW; Germany, upper Rhine, s. xiv; Carthusian (?); Lansburgh, 'Drawing Collection,' 342, fig. 6.

25. BIBLE, NT, GOSPEL OF MARK; northern Italy, end of s. vii or beginning of s. viii; bifolium; Faye & Bond, p. 24, no. 1. Lansburgh, *Check List*, no. I; acquired by Edwin J. Beinecke from E. P. Goldschmidt in 1964. **Beinecke, MS 440.**

26. BIBLE, NT, GOSPEL OF LUKE 11:29–46; France or Germany, s. ix; single leaf recovered from a binding; Sotheby's, 22 June 1999, lot

17 ('from the collection of Mark Lansburgh'). Julia Boffey & A. S. G. Edwards, *Medieval Manuscripts in the Norlin Library & the Department of Fine Arts at the University of Colorado at Boulder: a summary catalogue* (Fairview N.C., 2002), p. 34. **Boulder, CO, University of Colorado, Norlin Library, MS 355**.

27.    BIBLE, sketch in ink by Hans Brosamer for the woodcut for the title page of the bible printed in Frankfurt, 1551; single leaf. Lansburgh, 'Drawing Collection,' 346, fig. 17.

28.    BOOK OF HOURS; England (East Anglia?), s. xiv ex; three leaves, including two full-page miniatures, from the so-called Knyvett Hours: St Andrew, St Martin and a text page; evidence of ownership by Mark Lansburgh provided by Los Angeles County Museum of Art. **Los Angeles, CA, County Museum of Art, M.74.100.1–3**.[4]

29.    BOOK OF HOURS; France, Paris, *c.* 1402; 218 fols in 4 volumes (52, 54, 48 and 64 fols, respectively); acquired by Mark Lansburgh in 1964 from Lathrop Harper, Catalogue 10 [1960] no. 1; Lansburgh, 'Illuminated MSS,' 62 and 66; House of El Dieff, Catalogue Seventy-One (1971).

30.    BOOK OF HOURS; Paris (*c.* 1417); three leaves from the 'De Levis Hours,' (Beinecke, MS 400); Lansburgh, 'Illuminated MSS,' 64 and fig. 6; Sotheby's, 22 June 1982, lot 75.

31.    BOOK OF HOURS; France, Tours, *c.* 1470; by Jean Colombe, full-page miniature of Christ before Pilate, cut from a book of hours; single leaf; Lansburgh, 'Illuminated MSS,' 64, fig. 7; Sotheby's, 14 July 1981, lot 44 ('The Property of Mark Lansburgh'), with colour plate, to H. P. Kraus.

32.    BOOK OF HOURS; France, s. xv ex; single leaf; Christ before Pilate, full-page miniature attributed to Jean Fouquet (*c.* 1420–81); Lansburgh, 'Illuminated MSS,' 66 and fig. 7.

33.    BOOK OF HOURS; France, s. xv ex; penitential psalms; copied in batârde script; narrow miniature of fully clothed standing David, attributed to Jean Colombe; Lansburgh, 'Illuminated MSS,' 64 and fig. 8.

34.    BOOK OF HOURS, USE OF ROME; Italy, Naples, s. xv 4/4; 160 fols; 2 large miniatures; 12 historiated initials in two sizes; Sotheby's, 11 July 1966, lot 242 ('The Property of Mark Lansburgh'); Christie's (Rome), 15 December 2005, lot 272.

---

[4]    For other leaves from this manuscript see the article by A. S. G. Edwards elsewhere in this volume, pp. 158–60.

35.   BOOK OF HOURS, USE OF UTRECHT; Netherlands, s. xv 2/4 (*c.* 1435); 256 fols; two full-page miniatures; five large initials; Lansburgh, 'Drawing Collection,' 343, fig. 10; Sotheby's, 22 June 1982, lot 77 ('The Property of Mark Lansburgh Esq.').

36.   BREVIARY, DOMINICAN USE; France, *c.* 1340–50; single leaf, the Vision of Ezekiel, for the fourth Sunday in October and the first Sunday in November; on the back pastedown, the bookplate of the 'Mark Lansburgh Collection' showing Lansburgh's eagle lectern; McCarthy, 3: 292–95. **McCarthy, BM 1144.**

37.   BREVIARY, DOMINICAN USE; France, *c.* 1340–50; single leaf, Hosea kneeling before God, for the 4th Sunday in Advent; Rendell, Catalogue 146 (1979), no. 66 and plate; Christie's (South Kensington), 23 November 2009, lot 115; in 2021 in a **private collection in Belgium** (see McCarthy, 3: 293).

38.   BREVIARY or Office Book; Italy, Benevento, s. xii ex; fragment of single leaf; in Beneventan script; for Epiphany; Christie's, 20 November 2013, lot 24, where provenance is given as 'MARK LANSBURGH'; sold to Richard Linenthal (£2,200). David Gura, *A Descriptive Catalogue of the Medieval and Renaissance Manuscripts of the University of Notre Dame and Saint Mary's College* (Notre Dame, IN, 2016) 437–38. **Notre Dame, IN, University of Notre Dame, Hesburgh Library, Frag. I.27.**

39.   BREVIARY; Italy, Ferrara, 1460 (?); two leaves; from the Llangattock Breviary; feast of St Dominic; Quinquagesima Sunday. Gift of Mark Lansburgh. **Dartmouth, Rauner Special Collections, Lansburgh 53.**

40.   BRIEF: 26 April 1536; Andreas Gritti (1455–1538), Doge of Venice, to Marcantonio Cornelius, Podestà of Verona, written by Ludovico degli Arrighi. Sotheby's, 22 June 1999, lot 36 (unsold). Gift of Mark Lansburgh, 2005. **Dartmouth, Rauner Special Collections, Lansburgh 52.**

41.   CHARLES V, Holy Roman Emperor; 1529–30; Caroli Cesaris augustissimi ad Hispanos de suo discessu oratio. Gift of Mark Lansburgh. **Dartmouth, Rauner Special Collections, Lansburgh 11.**

42.   CHARLES V, Holy Roman Emperor; 14 May 1542; grant to Nicolas de Almaçán of Arequipa, Peru; written in Spanish; includes a supposed portrait of Pizarro. Gift of Mark Lansburgh, 1983. **Dartmouth, Rauner Special Collections, Lansburgh 15.**

43.   CHOIRBOOK (?); Italy, s. xiv (?); Pentecost; single leaf; Lansburgh, 'Illuminated MSS,' 64.

44. CHOIRBOOK; Italy, s. xv: Cosmas and Damian; painted by Francesco d'Antonio del Chierico; cutting from an antiphonal made for the Augustinian abbey at Fiesole; Sotheby's, 18 June 1962, lot 107 and pl. 5 to Maggs; acquired from Maggs by Lansburgh; Lansburgh, 'Illuminated MSS,' 66; Blumka Gallery, New York; acquired in 1979 by Bernard Breslauer.

45. CHRYSOSTOM, JOHANNES end of *In Epistolae Pauli I ad Timotheum*, and the beginning of *II ad Timotheum*, in Greek; eastern Mediterranean, s. xi or s. xii; single leaf; belonged to Niccolò Niccoli (*c.* 1364/5–1437); the blue half-circle book stamp of Mark Lansburgh on the leaf; Lansburgh, 'Illuminated MSS,' 62; Martin Schøyen, MS 1571/1; his sale, Sotheby's, 10 July 2012, lot 4; Aguttes (Neuilly-sur-Seine), 16 November 2022, lot 16.

46. CICERO, DE IMPERIO GN. POMPEII SIVE PRO LEGE MANILIA; Italy, s. xv med; single leaf; in humanistic script; Lansburgh, *Check List*, no. XI. **Dartmouth, Rauner Special Collections, Lansburgh MS 22.**

47. CICERO, DE OFFICIIS; Italy, Padua or Rome, s. xv ex/xvi in; in the hand of Bartolomeo Sanvito (1433–1511); single leaf; Lansburgh, 'Illuminated MSS,' 63.

48. COLLECTARIUM; Germany, s. xv in; 150 fols; Lansburgh, 'Illuminated MSS,' 68, fig. 12; Les Enluminures, Catalogue 2 (1993), no. 27.

49. CRACKENTHORPE ARCHIVE; England, 12th–19th centuries; 19 bound volumes and 122 items; New York, Parke-Bernet, 22 March 1966, lot 170, unsold; Rendell Catalogue 146 (1979) item 15. **Private collection in England.**

50. CUTTING; Germany, Upper Rhenish school; historiated initial D with drawing of a cowled monk; Lansburgh, 'Illuminated MSS,' 68.

51. CUTTING: Italy, s. xv med; St John the Baptist with the Lamb; Lansburgh, 'Illuminated MSS,' 66.

52. CUTTING: Italy, Rome, s. xvi med; drawing of the stoning of St Stephen attributed to Apollonius de Bonfratelli; Lansburgh, 'Illuminated MSS,' 66, fig. 10.

53. CALENDAR or abstract of the journals of the House of Commons from the sixth year of the reign of Edward, 1546 to 1710; 2 volumes. Gift of Mark Lansburgh. **Dartmouth, Rauner Special Collections, Lansburgh 7.**

54. CALENDAR of the journals of the House of Lords from the beginning of the reign of King Henry VIII to [1739]; manuscript copies, made by the clerks, for the printing ordered in 1742. In addition to the Calendar, each volume has, at end, lists of Peers introduced, brief index of matters covered, Writs of Error, etc. Gift of Mark Lansburgh. **Dartmouth, Rauner Special Collections, Lansburgh 5.**

55. COLLECTIVE INDULGENCE; southern France, Avignon, s. xiv second quarter; four cuttings of border illuminations; all belonged to Mark Lansburgh and were eventually acquired by Bob McCarthy. McCarthy, 3: 266–67. **McCarthy, BM 1061B, BM 1061C, BM 1349, BM 1061A.**

56. DEED INDENTURE; 12 November 1537; between Henry VIII (1491–1547) and Sir Thomas Cheyne (d. 1558) for exchange of properties. Gift of Mark Lansburgh, 1983. **Dartmouth, Rauner Special Collections, Lansburgh 13.**

57. DRAWINGS; Italy, Tuscany, s. xiv second half; on a bifolium with images on facing pages: Drawings of man and ox; of Moses (his name on a banderole across his chest) and a crowned queen; drawings in the margins of a legal text; Lansburgh, 'Illuminated MSS.' **Princeton, NJ, Princeton University, Firestone Library, Special Collections C0931 No. 268e South Wall 1.**

58. DRAWINGS; Italy, s. xv; of a boar, a goat and a partial dragon from originals by Pisanello; Lansburgh, 'Illuminated MSS,' 70.

59. DRAWINGS; Italy, s. xvi; of a bust in profile of Savonarola, copied from a lost original by Leonardo da Vinci; Lansburgh, 'Drawing Collection,' 343, fig. 14.

60. DRAWINGS; Italy, s. xvi; of a group of figures by Giulio Clovio of Moses raising the serpent; Lansburgh, 'Drawing Collection,' 346, fig. 16.

61. DRAWINGS; Germany, s. xv med; a Hell Mouth, spewing forth elaborate foliage containing images of wild men, wild women and animals; pattern for a bride's chest; Lansburgh, 'Drawing Collection,' 343, fig. 11.

62. EADMER, *Vita Beati Bregwini*; England, s. xii; fragment. **Gift of Mark Lansburgh to Christopher de Hamel, March 1999.**

63. FELIPE II, KING OF SPAIN; deed of sale, 16 December 1574, of the land Aldeaseca de la Frontera. Gift of Mark Lansburgh to **Santa Barbara, CA, University of California, Special Collections, SC 556.**

64.    GRADUAL copied and illustrated by Ludovico Gadio (or de Gacis); Italy, Cremona, 10 April 1489 for the Franciscan convent in Belluno; 220 fols; bought by Lansburgh in 1959 from H. P. Kraus, Catalogue 88 [1958], no. 46; Faye & Bond, p. 25 no. 5; Lansburgh, *Check List*, no. X; Sotheby's, 11 December 1961, lot 156 (unsold), and Sotheby's, 10 June 1963, lot 151 (£2,700 to Charles Traylen); the book was subsequently broken up, and the leaves offered individually by Inman's Book Shop, New York, Catalogue 110 (1969). Of the 13 leaves with historiated initials, present locations are known for four (plus the final leaf); locations were known in 1976 and 1978 for four other leaves; the 1994 auction record and the 1995 sale record are known for a ninth leaf. Specifically, for known present locations: one leaf, St Andrew, sold by Lansburgh, his MS 5, Sotheby's, 10 June 1963, lot 151 to Traylen; Christie's, 7 July 2010, lot 26 (unsold); now New York, **Morgan Library & Museum, M.1181**; one leaf, SS Peter and Paul, now Washington, DC, **National Gallery of Art, Rosenwald Collection, 1980.45.614**; one leaf, St Lawrence, now **Ann Arbor, MI, University of Michigan Museum, 1986/2.8**; one bifolium, St Francis, sold Christie's, 6 July 2011, lot 6, from the Arcana Collection Part III; now **Morgan Library & Museum, M.1177**. The final leaf with the very extensive colophon by Ludovico de Gacis, now Washington, DC, **National Gallery of Art, 1995.51.1.a–b**. Four more leaves with historiated initials have been noticed in circulation, although their present locations are not known: in 1976, one leaf with the Transfiguration (6 August) owned by Frell Albright (but not now at the University of Houston with his other manuscripts). In 1978, five leaves including three with historiated initials owned by Mr. and Mrs. S. Eberly Thompson (but not now at Mount Angel Abbey, Oregon with their other manuscripts): Philip and James (3 May), John the Baptist (24 June), Nativity of the Virgin (8 September; fol. 50) One more leaf, Anthony of Padua (13 June), with a historiated initial noticed in sales, although its present location is not known: at Christie's, 28 June 1994, lot 21 and then Bruce Ferrini, Catalogue 3 (1995), no. 4.

65.    GRANT OF RIGHTS; 24 April 1592, to Johannes Paulus Nussio in several parishes of the Patriarchate of Aquileia, by the patriarch Giovanni Grimani. Gift of Mark Lansburgh, 1989. **Dartmouth, Rauner Special Collections, Lansburgh 24**.

66.    GUI, Bernard, *Arbor genealogiae regum Francorum*; southern France (Toulouse?), *c.* 1330; three leaves; each leaf acquired separately by Bob

McCarthy. McCarthy 3: 244–48. **McCarthy, BM 1560, BM 1809, BM 1865A.**

67. HENRY VII; letter to Juana la Loca (1479–1555), written by Petrus Carmelianus (1451–1527); Lansburgh, 'Illuminated MSS,' 62.

68. HENRY VIII; in Latin, sale of lands that had belonged to the Carmelites of Appleby-in-Westmoreland, written between the suppression of the friaries (July 1538 to March 1539) and the last year of Henry's reign (ending on 28 January 1547); Lansburgh, *Colorado College Magazine*, 11.

69. INDENTURE OF A RECEIPT; England, 27 February 1540; inventory of ceremonial plate and jewels collected from religious houses by the King's Commissioners; bookplate of the Mark Lansburgh Collection; purchased by Yale Beinecke Library from Bernard Quaritch in 2001. **Beinecke, MS Osborn fa 37.**

70. LECTIONARY; France, Paris, s. xv ex; 130 fols; written for the Dominican convent in Rue St Jacques, Paris; 14 large miniatures; Faye & Bond, p. 25, no. 6; H. P. Kraus, Catalogue 188, *100 Distinguished Manuscripts* [1991], no. 23.

71. LECTIONARY; southern Germany, s. xi probably first half; one leaf; Fifth Sunday after Easter through the vigil of the Ascension; from Mark Lansburgh sold in 1963 through Bernard Rosenthal to Quaritch, Catalogue 1147 (1991), no. 27; Martin Schøyen, MS 628; his sale, Bloomsbury, 8 July 2020, lot 33.

72. LECTIONARY; Germany, s. xv; single leaf; initial B with figures on the initial and a profile head of a man sticking out his tongue facing into the margin; Lansburgh, *Colorado College Magazine*, 14.

73. LETTER; 1 October 1490, from Ferrara, from Niccolò da Correggio (1450–1508) describing ambassadorial duties. Gift of Mark Lansburgh, 1989. **Dartmouth, Rauner Special Collections, Lansburgh 32.**

74. LETTER; 7 May 1498, to Ludovico Sforza, Duke of Milan (1452–98) from Ercole I d'Este, Duke of Ferrara, Modena and Reggio (1431–1505). Gift of Mark Lansburgh, 1989. **Dartmouth, Rauner Special Collections, Lansburgh 31.**

75. LETTER; 15 May 1521, concerning Giulio de' Medici (in 1523, pope Clement VII) and affairs of the archdiocese of Florence; copied by Ludovico degli Arrighi. Gift of Mark Lansburgh, 1989. **Dartmouth, Rauner Special Collections, Lansburgh 33.**

76. LETTER; 28 July 1562, by Francisco Ferdinando Avalos, Marchese of Pescara asking that Daniel da Saxavalle be paid the monies owed to him. Gift of Mark Lansburgh, 1989. **Dartmouth, Rauner Special Collections, Lansburgh 34**.

77. LETTER; 27 January [*c.* 1590], from Elizabeth Carew, at Chipping Ongar, Essex, to her father, Sir Nicholas Carew, in London. Gift of Mark Lansburgh, 1989. **Dartmouth, Rauner Special Collections, Lansburgh 29.**

78. LIBER GLOSSARUM; northern France, Aix-la-Chapelle (today: Germany, Aachen), *c.* 825; single leaf; formerly Phillipps MS 36181; Lansburgh, *Check List*, no. III. Gift of Mark Lansburgh, 1971. **Dartmouth, Rauner Special Collections, Lansburgh 3.**

79. MARTYROLOGY; Italy, s. xi first half; contains part of the Life of Saint Palatia, martyred in Ancona, Italy during the reign of Diocletian; written in an Ottonian hand; single leaf. Gift of Mark Lansburgh, 1989. **Dartmouth, Rauner Special Collections, Lansburgh 35.**

80. A MEMORIALL of a discours used by the late wourthy Emperour Charles the fythe, upon the Resignement of government, and States, to Phillippe his sonne, now Kinge of Spaine, *c.* 1556. Copy of the English translation of the memorial prepared by Charles V (1500–58) for Philip II of Spain (1527–98). Gift of Mark Lansburgh, 1983. **Dartmouth, Rauner Special Collections, Lansburgh 18.**

81. MISSAL; Italy, s. xi ex; two leaves; texts from early Lent with neumes; note possibly by Domenico Maria Manni (1690–1788); part of Sotheby's, 6 July 2006, lot 8. David Gura, *A Descriptive Catalogue of the Medieval and Renaissance Manuscripts of the University of Notre Dame and Saint Mary's College* (Notre Dame, IN, 2016) 437–38. **Notre Dame, IN, University of Notre Dame, Hesburgh Library Frag.I.28.**

82. MISSAL; Italy, Arezzo, s. xii first half; two leaves from the requiem mass for children and bishops; single-line staff with neumes. Gift of Mark Lansburgh, 1993. **Dartmouth, Rauner Special Collections, Lansburgh 37.**

83. MISSAL; Italy, Florence, s. xv second half; 111 fols; 18 full-page miniatures; New York, Parke-Bernet Galleries, 22 March 1966, lot 198.

84. MISSAL; Germany, Augsburg, 1485; single leaf; Pentecost; James H. Marrow, 'Unpublished leaves from the Missal of Johannes von Giltlingen,' *Harvard Library Bulletin*, 21 (2011), 125–42; see also the blog by Peter

Kidd, 'Medieval Manuscripts Provenance,' entry for 5 July 2020, 'Another Leaf of the Missal of Johannes von Giltlingen (Augsburg, *c.* 1485)'. **Private German collection.**

85. NEUDORFFER, Johann der Jüngerer and Antonius, writing manual; southern Germany, 1598; 26 fols; Lansburgh, *Check List*, nos. XIII, XIV; Lansburgh, 'Illuminated MSS,' p. 61.

86. NOTARIAL DOCUMENT; 30 March 1392, written in Pordenone, Italy about repayment of a debt. Gift of Mark Lansburgh, 1985. **Dartmouth, Rauner Special Collections, Lansburgh 392230.**

87. ORIGEN, *In Leviticum homiliae*; southern Germany, s. xii first half; single leaf; Lansburgh, 'Drawing Collection,' 342, fig. 2. Sotheby's, 6 July 2006, lot 5.

88. PAPAL BRIEF; 4 November 1513, from Leo X (1475–1521) to Ioanin Francisco de Rugerio confirming a grant of land in Bologna; copied by Ludovico degli Arrighi. Gift of Mark Lansburgh, 1989. **Dartmouth, Rauner Special Collections Library, Lansburgh 26.**

89. PAPAL BULL; 1 January 1627, Rome, by Urban VIII (1568–1644); with pendant bull. Gift of Mark Lansburgh. **Dartmouth, Rauner Special Collections, Lansburgh 627101.**

90. PAPAL LETTER; 6 June 1520, Rome, by Leo X; addressed to cardinal Albrecht of Brandenburg, archbishop and elector of Mainz, appointing Marino Caracciolo as nuncio; copied by Ludovico degli Arrighi; Lansburgh, *Check List*, no. XII. **Beinecke, Takamiya MS 76.**

91. PASSIO of SS. Alexander and Theodore; Germany, s. xii; single leaf; Lansburgh, 'Drawing Collection,' 342, fig. 3.

92. POLE, Reginald, cardinal (1500–58); Italy, 1538 (?); pleas to the papacy for the overthrow of Henry VIII, in the hand of Ludovico Beccatelli (1501–72); Lansburgh, 'Illuminated MSS,' 62–63.

93. POLISH DOCUMENT; 4 January 1341, Stara, Bohemia, appointing Ernest of Pardubice as executor; in Latin; with 6 pendant seals. Gift of Mark Lansburgh. **Dartmouth, Rauner Special Collections, Lansburgh 1a.**

94. POLISH CHARTER; 21 March 1352; archepiscopal grant of the church of Kostolac (Serbia) to the Augustinian house of Mount Saint Mary in Glatz (Klodzko), Poland; with 2 pendant seals. Gift of Mark Lansburgh. **Dartmouth, Rauner Special Collections, Lansburgh 1b.**

95.    POLISH CONFIRMATION; 26 January 1354; via the papal bull of Innocent IV; confirming the archdiocesan grant of the church of Kostolac (Serbia) by Ernest (or Arnošt; 1297–1364) of Pardubice to the Augustinian house of Mount Saint Mary in Glatz (Klodzko), Poland, 21 March 1352; with pendant lead seal. **Dartmouth, Rauner Special Collections, Lansburgh 1c.**

96.    PONTIFICAL; France, Châlons, s. xvi in; for Gilles de Luxembourg; formerly belonged to Mark Lansburgh, according to Joseph Pope, in whose collection this was MS 39; Pope later sold the manuscript to Sam Fogg.

97.    PONTIFICAL; Germany, s. xii first half; bifolium; sold by Lansburgh at Sotheby's, 22 June 1999, lot 20.

98.    PRAYERBOOK; Germany, s. xvi in (*c.* 1520); in German; seated Virgin and Child before a kneeling Benedictine monk; Lansburgh, 'Illuminated MSS,' 68 and fig. 11. **New York, Morgan Library & Museum, M.1047.**

99.    PRIVILEGES; 22 June 1466, issued by Bianca Maria Sforza, Milan, to the town of Fontanella (prov. Cremona) confirming tax exemptions; Sotheby's, 22 June 1982, lot 76 ('The Property of Mark Lansburgh Esq.').

100.   RICORDI dell'imperatore Carlo Quinto per suo figliuolo fatti in Augusta l'anno di nostra salute 1548; contemporary Italian copies of two instructions of the Holy Roman Emperor, Charles V (1500–58) to his son Philip II of Spain; 170 fols. Gift of Mark Lansburgh, 1983. **Dartmouth, Rauner Special Collections, Lansburgh 19.**

101.   SACRAMENTARY; France, s. ix ¾; three leaves, containing portions of the services for the infirm, procedures for making and applying holy water and oil, and masses for several saints; sold by Lansburgh, Sotheby's, 22 June 1999, lot 18 ('now in the collection of Mark Lansburgh'; bought in). Gift of Mark Lansburgh, 2000. **Dartmouth, Rauner Special Collections, Lansburgh 40.**

102.   SACRAMENTARY; Italy, Benevento, before or *c.* 1100; openings of two readings on 1 Peter V:6 and on Mark II:13; written in Beneventan minuscule; Lansburgh, 'Drawing Collection,' 341 and fig. 1. **Dartmouth, Rauner Special Collections, Lansburgh 9.**

103.   SALLUST, *De coniuratione Catilinae, De bello jugurthino*; Italy, Florence, 1465; 90 fols; miniatures by Attavante degli Attavanti; Sam Fogg, Catalogue 15, *Text Manuscripts of the Middle Ages and Renaissance* (1992), no. 30.

104. SKETCH; s. xii; youth in a classical toga; single leaf; Lansburgh, 'Illuminated MSS,' 70.

105. SKETCH in pen and wash by Antonio Tempesta for the title page of a work on hunting; signed and dated 1598; single leaf; Lansburgh, 'Drawing Collection,' 346, fig. 18.

106. STATUTA ANGLIE; single leaf with historiated initial of Henry VII (or VIII?); Sotheby's, 10 July 1967, lot 34; Rendell, Catalogue 149 (1980) no. 158; Sotheby's, 7 December 1992, lot 25.

107. TABLE OF WEIGHTS; England, Winchester, s. xvi; single leaf; Lansburgh bookplate on former binding; sold by Sam Fogg to Lawrence J. Schoenberg, February 1998; gift of Lawrence J. Schoenberg and Barbara Brizdle, 2011 to **Philadelphia, PA, University of Pennsylvania, Rare Book and Manuscript Library, MS LJS 238**.

108. THEOLOGICAL COMMENTARY; northern Spain, s. x first half; bifolium; Lansburgh, *Check List*, no. IV; written in Visigothic script; acquired from E. P. Goldschmidt in 1964 by Edwin J. and Frederick W. Beinecke. **Beinecke, MS 447**.

109. TUDOR DOCUMENTS, 1550–1602; collection of miscellaneous Tudor documents, many of which are from the Phillipps Collection, including several leaves of Edward VI's journal, 1550–51, an agreement of lord Henry Seymour, documents relating to Jane Seymour, and records of penance and compurgation in the diocesan court of Ely with a transcription by Dick Hoefnagel. Gift of Mark Lansburgh, 1983. **Dartmouth, Rauner Special Collections, Lansburgh 16**.

# 8

# MEDIEVAL MANUSCRIPTS OWNED BY
# EDWARD DUFF BALKEN OF PITTSBURGH

~

*William P. Stoneman*

Barbara Shailor's catalogue descriptions of medieval and Renaissance manuscripts in Yale's Beinecke Library have become models for their thoughtful arrangement of pertinent information and the accuracy of that information. Given the enormous range of Beinecke manuscripts she graciously acknowledges the contributions of other scholars. Even when she cannot fully decipher or interpret the evidence, her descriptions allow those using her work to benefit from her observations. For example, in her description of Beinecke MS 126 she describes its early provenance as unknown but goes on to record the presence of the bookplate of Edward Duff Balken and then an 'unidentified note from a sale catalogue (no. 41) pasted inside front cover.'[1] The manuscript was presented to Yale in 1950 by Henry Fletcher.[2]

In an article on the role of the Italian-American bookseller Giuseppe Martini (1870–1944) in building American collections I briefly used Balken as one of the examples of American collectors who used Martini to build their collections and which later moved into institutions.[3] My example then was a manuscript of Gregory the Great which passed from Martini to Balken through Maggs Bros. to Phyllis Walter Goodhart Gordon (1913–94) and her father, Howard Lehman Goodhart (1884–1951) and was their gift to Bryn Mawr College Library, PA, where it is now MS 11.[4] Martini material had

---

[1]   *Catalogue of Medieval and Renaissance Manuscripts in the Beinecke Library, Volume I: Manuscripts 1–250.* (Binghamton, NY, 1984), pp. 173–74.

[2]   This manuscript is EDB 14 in the list below.

[3]   William P. Stoneman, 'The Role of Giuseppe Martini in Building the Medieval and Renaissance Manuscript Collections now in North American Libraries,' in Edoardo Barbieri, ed., *Da Lucca a New York a Lugano: Giuseppe Martini Libraio tra Otto e Novecento.* Biblioteca di Bibliografia: Documents and Studies in Book and Library History CCVI (Florence, 2017), pp. 65–80 at 79–80.

[4]   This manuscript is EDB 25 in the list below.

often been on the market in London or on the Continent before it appeared in his catalogues, especially during the decade he was based in New York (1912–22) and he was an important source for other well-known American collectors such as George A. Plimpton (1855–1936), Henry Walters (1848–1931), Grenville Kane (1854–1943), William King Richardson (1859–1951), and James K. Moffitt (1874–1955), for example.

In this contribution to honor Barbara, I would like to begin with Beinecke MS 126 to explore further the collection of Edward Duff Balken (1874–1960) of Pittsburgh, PA, an important American collector of medieval manuscripts who deserves to be better known, but because his collection was dispersed before the publication of de Ricci & Wilson, nor was he included by name in any auction sale or bookseller's catalogue, nor were any of his manuscripts bequeathed to an institution, manuscripts from his collection are now widely scattered and not always easy to identify.

Balken was a member of the Princeton University Class of 1897, the same class as two other well-known book collectors, Sir Alfred Chester Beatty (1875–1968) and Robert Garrett (1875–1961). Balken was a member of the Grolier Club from 1911–39, but he is not included in any of the standard reference works on American book collecting.

Balken developed a major folk art collection which is now at the Princeton University Art Museum and this collection clearly overtook his collection of medieval manuscripts. Beatrix T. Mumford has observed that 'any list of important collectors of [American] folk art must include Edward Duff Balken.'[5] Balken was born into a wealthy Pittsburgh family; after graduating from Princeton, he took part in archaeological expeditions to Greece and the Near East, travelled in Europe in 1901 and 1902, worked briefly in Pittsburgh and retired at the age of thirty-two.[6] In 1916 he became the curator of the newly founded Department of Prints at Pittsburgh's Carnegie Institute. A year after the unexpected death of his wife from complications due to acute appendicitis he made his first major

---

[5]    Beatrix T. Mumford, 'Uncommon Art of the Common People: A Review of Trends in the Collecting and Exhibiting of American Folk Art,' in Ian M. G. Quimby & Scott T. Swank, eds, *Perspectives on American Folk Art* (Winterthur, 1980), pp. 13–53 at 46.

[6]    The best source for information on Balken is Charlotte Emans Moore, 'Another Generation's Folk Art: Edward Duff Balken and His Collection of American Provincial Paintings and Drawings,' in *Record of the Art Museum Princeton University*, 57 (1998), 10–28; subsequently published in *A Window into Collecting American Folk Art: The Edwards Duff Balken Collection at Princeton* (Princeton, NJ, 1999), pp. 11–28.

acquisition of American folk art in 1920.[7] His American folk art collection was first publicly exhibited in Pittsburgh in 1947 and later in Princeton in 1958 to celebrate his gift of the collection. Balken also donated prints to the Carnegie Institute, and manuscripts and early printed books, including 6 incunables, to the Princeton University Library.

Balken is not as well known as other American collectors of medieval manuscripts because he appears to have sold his collection privately to the London booksellers Maggs Bros., who dispersed it without mentioning his name. Buyers certainly could not avoid knowing the previous owner of their manuscripts when they opened them on receipt from Maggs because Balken's bookplate is large and prominent on the front pastedown or flyleaf.[8] Balken manuscripts first began to appear in Maggs' mammoth Catalogue 542 (1930): *The Art of Writing 2800 B.C. to 1930 A.D. Illustrated in a Collection of Original Documents written on Vellum, Paper, Papyrus, Silk, Linen, Bamboo, or inscribed on Clay, Marble, Steatite, Jasper, Haematite, Matrix of Emerald and Chalcedony exhibiting Forty Styles of Scripts in the Languages of Europe, Asia and Africa*. At least seventeen of the manuscripts from Balken's collection, MSS EDB 4, 5, 7, 8, 11, 13, 14, 16, 20, 21, 22, 23, 25, 26, 27, A and B, were included in that Catalogue.

Knowing Martini's role in building Balken's collection and Maggs' role in dispersing it, one has every reason to suspect that the note from the unidentified sale catalogue no. 41 in Beinecke MS 126 might well be from a Martini or Maggs catalogue. It is, in fact, from Maggs Catalogue 542. The manuscript was also in three Martini catalogues that appeared between 1913 and 1917. Recently the Beinecke Library has acquired another Balken manuscript, now Beinecke MS 1104, which was formerly Cologny-Genève, Fondation Martin Bodmer MS Bodmer 179. It is EDB 13 in the list that follows and was in Maggs Catalogue 342, no. 36.

I have assembled the following list of medieval manuscripts owned by Edward Duff Balken. My hope is that this provisional list will spark interest in Balken and his collection and spur others to assist in its completion. The EDB numbers appear in pencil in the upper left corner of Balken's bookplate and my working assumption is that they were added there by Maggs in order to keep track of the collection. Thus far I can document that Balken owned at

---

[7]  Moore, p. 16.

[8]  Balken appears to have had two bookplates. The first depicts a reader reading in an armchair before a roaring fire; it was designed by Edwin Davis French, dated 1902 and appears in two states. I have not seen it used in any of his medieval manuscripts. A second bookplate depicts a shelf of books and is dated 1903.

least twenty-seven medieval manuscripts, including two untraced manuscripts (A and B) that are at the end of the list below.

While this evidence is incomplete, one can begin to see patterns. Balken could certainly have bought from other dealers, but he would appear to have been a good client of Giuseppe Martini. Martini's base in New York appears to have been key for his other customers[9] and Balken's regular trips to New York for the Carnegie Institute may have facilitated his purchases. For example, Balken bought four manuscripts from Martini's Catalogue 13 (1917), MSS EDB 11, 12, 14 and A. Another, EDB 25, was acquired from Martini Catalogue 18 (1922). It is also worth noting, for example, that Martini had MS EDB 14 in stock for a while and when he lowered the price, Balken acquired it. One can also see that some of the Balken manuscripts remained in Maggs' stock for over seven years, for example, MSS EDB 8, 20, 27, and again required a price reduction before they found buyers.

### Edward Duff Balken's Medieval Manuscripts[10]

The following abbreviations are used:

Lyell Catalogue       A. C. de la Mare, *Catalogue of the Medieval Manuscripts Bequeathed to the Bodleian Library Oxford by James P. R. Lyell* (Oxford, 1971).

Ullman              Berthold L. Ullman, 'Latin Manuscripts in American Libraries,' *Philological Quarterly*, 5 (1926), 152–56.

**EDB 4** Breviary (Use of Rome). Maggs Bros., Catalogue 542 (1930), no. 214 and pl. (£52/10); Catalogue 687 (1940), no. 206; to Charles E. Roseman, Jr., of Cleveland Heights, Ohio; his sale, Sotheby's, 6 December 2005, lot 45; Les Enluminures, *Text Manuscripts* (2006), no. 181 ($23,200); acquired from Les

---

[9]  The acquisitions from Martini by Plimpton, Kane, and Richardson also seem to have occurred mainly during the period Martini was based in New York; see Stoneman, pp. 71–73.

[10]  This list could not have been compiled without the generous assistance of the following individuals and I remain grateful to them: Pablo Alvarez (University of Michigan), Regan Brumagen (Corning Museum of Glass), Andrew Dunning (Bodleian Library), Roland Folter, John D. Gordan III, Marianne H. Hansen (Bryn Mawr College), Laura Light (Les Enluminures), Eric Pumroy, Agnieszka Rec (Beinecke Library), Stephen Tabor (Huntington Library), and Michiel Verweij (Bibliothèque royale de Belgique). Most of the information in this list has been derived from records in the Schoenberg Database of Manuscripts (https://sdbm.library.upenn.edu/) and as the Database continues to grow so will our understanding of Balken's collection.

Enluminures in January 2015. **Ann Arbor, MI, University of Michigan Library, MS 292.**

**EDB 5:** Diurnal. de Ricci & Wilson, II, 1680–81 (no. 22); Faye & Bond, p. 398. Leander van Ess (1772–1847); his *Catalogue* (1823), no. 157; Phillipps 542; his sale, Sotheby's, 6 June 1910, lot 265; to Tregaskis; Edward Duff Balken of Pittsburgh, PA; his bookplate and his MS 5; Maggs Bros., Catalogue 542 (1930), no. 206 and pl. (£63); Phyllis W. Goodhart & her father Howard L. Goodhart of New York, MS 22; by descent to Phyllis Goodhart Gordan & her husband John Dozier Gordan, Jr.; her bequest in 1994 to Bryn Mawr College Library. **Bryn Mawr, PA, Bryn Mawr College Library, MS Gordan 22.**

**EDB 7:** Dutch Psalter and Book of Hours. Faye & Bond, p. 262; C. Boot, 'Medieval Netherlandic Manuscripts in the Libraries in the State of Massachusetts,' *Archief en bibliotheekwezen in Belgie,* 50 (1979), 310–71, at 313–20; R. Wieck, *Late Medieval and Renaissance Manuscripts 1350–1525 in the Houghton Library* (Cambridge, MA, 1983), p. 124; J. H. Marrow, 'Text and Image in Two Fifteenth-Century Dutch Psalters from Delft,' in E. Cockx-Indestege et al., eds, *Spiritualia Neerlandica. Opstellen voor Dr. Albert Ampe S.J. hem door vakgenoten en vrienden aangeboden uit waardering voor zijn wetenschappelijk werk,* (Antwerp, 1990), pp. 341–52; James H. Marrow, 'Psalter, Masters of the Delft Half-length Figures,' *Beyond Words: Illuminated Manuscripts in Boston Collections* (Boston, MA, 2016), pp. 129–30. Edward Duff Balken of Pittsburgh, PA; his bookplate and his MS 7; Maggs Bros, Catalogue 542 (1930), no. 101 and pl. (reproducing fol. 67ᵛ) (£500); Catalogue 555 (1931), no. 187; Catalogue 687 (1940), no. 224; Philip Hofer (1898–1984); acquired as Francis Hofer from Maggs in June 1944; his bequest to Houghton Library. **Cambridge, MA, Harvard University, Houghton Library, MS Typ 132.**

**EDB 8:** Glossed Gospel of Mark. Lyell Catalogue, xxviii (no. 24); *Bulletin de la Bibliothèque royale de Belgique,* 7 (1958), 64; *Quinze années d'acquisitions, 1954–1968: de la pose de la première pierre à l'inauguration officielle de la Bibliothèque: exposition, Bruxelles, Bibliothèque royale Albert Ier, du 18 février au 30 mars 1969* (Brussels, 1969), no. 12. Lambinus de Brugis; his gift to Cistercians of Ourscamp; *ex-libris* inscription added to last leaf: 'Marcus glosatus quem dedit Lambinus de Brugis ecclesie sancte Marie Ursicampi. Si quis abstulerit vel alienaverit quoque modo: anathema sit. Amen.' Phillipps MS 283; his sale, Sotheby's, 10 June 1896, lot 501; Charles Butler (1821–1910) of Warren Wood, Hatfield, Hertfordshire and Connaught Place, London, Sotheby's, 18 March 1912, lot 2316 (£13); to J. & J. Leighton, *Catalogue of MSS* (1912), no. 35 for £23; sold 2 April 1918 to Giuseppe Martini, booksellers (£23); Edward Duff Balken of Pittsburgh, PA; his bookplate and MS 8; Maggs Bros, Catalogue 542 (1930), no. 39 (£350); Catalogue 666 (1938), no. 42 (£150); Catalogue 675 (1939), no. 123 (£150); to J. P. R. Lyell (1871–1948) in 1940. Bernard Quaritch, Catalogue 699 (1952), no. 24 (£250); Catalogue 731 (1954), no. 49 ($700); Catalogue 775 (1958), no. 1708 ($700); Maggs Bros; sold by Maggs in 1958. **Brussels, Bibliothèque Royale, MS IV. 18.**

**EDB 11:** St Bernard, *Sermones*. Elisabeth Pellegrin, *Manuscrits Latins de la Bodermiana* (Cologny-Genève, 1982), p. 458 (MSS vendus no. 4). Dean and Chapter of Chichester Cathedral Library; its 18th-century bookplate; P. M. Barnard, Tunbridge Wells, Catalogue 27 (1907), no. 7 (£2/12); James Park of New York, NY; his sale, Anderson Galleries, New York, 14 March 1910, lot 548; Giuseppe Martini, booksellers, New York, Catalogue 13 (1917), no. 5 for $45; Edward Duff Balken of Pittsburgh, PA; his bookplate and MS 11; Maggs Bros., Catalogue 542 (1930), no. 51A and pl. (£150); Dr. Martin Bodmer (1899–1971); his sale to H. P. Kraus, New York; his Catalogue 126 (1971), no. 2 ($125). **Durham, NC, Duke University Library, MS 129.**

**EDB 12** Cicero, *De natura deorum et de divinatione*. Ullman, 153; de Ricci & Wilson, II, 1976. Thomas Crofts sale, Paterson, 7 April 1783, lot 8233; Anthony Askew (1722–72) sale, Sotheby's, 7 March 1785, lot 443, to Lowes; Jonathan Toup sale, Sotheby's, 10 May 1786, lot 1244, to Michael Wodhull (1740–1816), by descent to J. E. Severne; his sale, Sotheby's, 11 January 1886, lot 724 (£18/5) to Bernard Quaritch, Rough List 75 (1886), no. 92 (£25); Catalogue 369 (1886), no. 35755; Catalogue 135 (September 1893), no. 246 (£24); Catalogue 138 (December 1893), no. 101 (£24); Catalogue 211 (1902), no. 152; Sotheby's, 24 June 1907, lot 719 to Quaritch; Sotheby's, 9 December 1909, lot 387 (£5/15) to Bull, Auvache & Wilson, booksellers, London, Catalogue 1 (May 1912), no. 2 (£12 guineas); Giuseppe Martini, booksellers, New York, Catalogue 13 (1917), no. 8 ($150); Edward Duff Balken of Pittsburgh, PA; his bookplate and MS 12; Maggs Bros., Catalogue 542 (1930), no. 141 and pl. (£175). **Toledo, OH, Toledo Museum of Art, MS 33 (1930.202).**

**EDB 13:** St Jerome, *Contra Jovinianum*, Bede, *Commentarius in acta apostolorum*. Ullman, 154; Elisabeth Pellegrin, *Manuscrits Latins de la Bodermiana* (Cologny-Genève, 1982), pp. 427–29. Cistercian abbey of Loos near Lille, diocese of Tournai; Luigi Celotti (1759–1843); his sale, Sotheby's, 26 February 1821, lot. 211; Rev. Henry Drury (1778–1841) of Harrow; his sale, Evans, London, 19 February 1827, lot 2034 (£2/2/6); to John Henry Bohn (1757–1843), bookseller, London; Sotheby's, 30 June 1913, lot 85; to F. S. Ellis, booksellers, London; Catalogue 150 (1913), no. 65; Edward Duff Balken of Pittsburgh, PA; his bookplate and MS 13; Maggs Bros., Catalogue 542 (1930), no. 36 and pl. (£250); Catalogue 555 (1931), no. 114; Dr. Martin Bodmer (1899–1971); his bequest to his family; their sale, Sotheby's, 5 July 2005, lot 81. **Beinecke, MS 1104.**

**EDB 14:** Bible: Book of Numbers. Faye & Bond, p. 32; Barbara A. Shailor, *Catalogue of Medieval and Renaissance Manuscripts in the Beinecke Library, Volume I: Manuscripts 1–250* (Binghamton, NY, 1984), pp. 173–74. Giuseppe Martini, booksellers, New York; Catalogue 10 (1913), no. 1 for $160; Catalogue 12 (1915), no. 4 ($85); Catalogue 13 (1917), no. 6 ($85); to Edward Duff Balken of Pittsburgh, PA; his bookplate and his MS 14; Maggs Bros., Catalogue 542 (1930), no. 41 (£175); Henry Fletcher (1898–1952); his gift in 1950 to Yale University. **Beinecke, MS 126.**

**EDB 16:** Cicero, *Opera*. Ullman, 53; de Ricci & Wilson, II, 1676 (no. 4). Benedictines of St Justina in Padua; Payne & Foss, booksellers, London; *Catalogue* (1845), no. 51; *Catalogue* (1848), no. 5536; *Catalogue* (1850), no. 94; John T. Payne; his sale, Sotheby's, 30 April 1857, lot 93; Puttick & Simpson, 23 December 1857, lot 198; Guglielmo Libri; his sale, Sotheby's, 28 March 1859, lot 242; Phillipps 16285; his sale, Sotheby's, 21 March 1895, lot 175; to Maggs Bros.; Catalogue 157 (20 September 1898), no. 634 (£10 guineas); Sotheby's, 25 July 1899, lot 1087 for £2 guineas, to Maggs Bros.; Giuseppe Martini, booksellers, New York; Edward Duff Balken of Pittsburgh, PA; his bookplate and MS 16; Maggs Bros., Catalogue 542 (1930), no. 122 and pl. (£175); Phyllis W. & her father Howard L. Goodhart of New York. MS 4; Phyllis Goodhart Gordan & her husband John Dozier Gordan, Jr.; her bequest in 1994 to Bryn Mawr College Library. **Bryn Mawr, PA, Bryn Mawr College Library, MS Gordan 4.**

**EDB 20:** Isidore, *Etymologiae*. Ullman, 154; Faye & Bond, p. 316. Cistercian abbey of Royaumont; Charles Chardin, Catalogue (1911), no. 204; his sale, Paris, 9 February 1824, lot 1102; Phillipps MS 2812; his sale, Sotheby's, 5 June 1899, lot 765 for £7; to J. & J. Leighton, booksellers, London, Catalogue (1912), no. 182 (£35); their Ledger 1916–18 (2 April 1918), no. 182 for £35; to Giuseppe Martini, bookseller, New York; Edward Duff Balken of Pittsburgh, PA; his bookplate and his MS 20; Maggs Bros., Catalogue 542 (1930), no. 75 and pl. (£475); Catalogue 582 (1933), no. 2; Catalogue 645 (1937), no. 25 (£350); Hamill & Barker, booksellers, Chicago, 1951. **Corning, NY, Corning Museum of Glass Library, MS 3.**

**EDB 21:** St Prosper, *De vita contemplativa* and other works. Faye & Bond, p. 179; Christopher de Hamel, *Gilding the Lilly: A Hundred Medieval and Illuminated Manuscripts in the Lilly Library* (Bloomington, IN, 2010), pp. 42–43, no. 18.

Cistercian Abbey of Pontigny, near Auxerre; François-Nicolas Comynet (1791–1848); acquired from the municipality of Auxerre in 1825; sent to Sylvestre, booksellers, Paris; Abbé Joseph-Félix Allard; acquired probably from Sylvestre, and sold perhaps through Teschener, booksellers; Phillipps 3735; his sale, Sotheby's, 23 March 1895, lot 918; Harold Baillie Weaver (d. 1926), Christie's, London, 29 March 1898, lot 483; J. & J. Leighton, booksellers, London; their Stock Ledger 1899–1900 (January 1899) (£20); to Laurence W. Hodson (1864–1933); his sale, Sotheby's, 5 December 1906, lot 504 (£16); to J. & J. Leighton, booksellers, London; Maggs Bros., Catalogue 226 (February 1907), no. 518; Catalogue 232 (November 1907), no. 1204 (£35); Catalogue 246 (1909), no. 820 (£35); Catalogue 259 (1910), no. 380 (£35); Catalogue 287 (1912), no. 1183 (£350); Sotheby's, July 1913, lot 1077; Maggs Bros., Catalogue 380 (1919), no. 1699 (£33); Edward Duff Balken of Pittsburgh, PA; his bookplate and his MS 21; Maggs Bros., Catalogue 542 (1930), no. 46 and pl. (£215); Giuseppe Martini, booksellers, New York, Catalogue 28 (1938), no. 17 (£75); Catalogue 30 (1942), no. 22 (CHF 1900); H. P. Kraus, New York, Catalogue 75 (1955), no. 5 ($950); to George A. Poole, Jr. (1907–90), in 1955; Lilly Library; with the Poole Collection in 1958. **Bloomington, IN, Indiana University, Lilly Library, MS Poole 18.**

**EDB 22:** Raymond of Pennafort, *Summa de penitentia*. Lyell Catalogue, pp. 283–84. Sir Edward Dering (1598–1644) (his binding); Francis Benthal of Buckford (his armorial bookplate); George Dunn (1865–1912); his sale, Sotheby's, 22 November 1917, lot 3351; Edward Duff Balken of Pittsburgh, PA; his bookplate and MS 22; Maggs Bros., Catalogue 542 (1930), no. 88 and pl. (£42); Catalogue 687 (1940), no. 161 (£50); bought by James P. R. Lyell (1871–1948) in January 1943; acquired by Bodleian Library from Lyell's executors. **BodL, MS Lyell empt. 3.**

**EDB 23:** Thomas Kempis, *De imitatione Christi*. de Ricci & Wilson, I, 993 (no. C.803.09.10); Faye & Bond, p. 243. Nathaniel Wanley, vicar of Beeby (1664); Jacques Rosenthal, booksellers, Munich, Catalogue 27 (1901), no. 62 (DEM 500); to William Amhurst Tyssen-Amherst (1835–1909), 1st baron Amherst of Hackney; his sale, Sotheby's, 17 January 1921, lot 529 for £6; to Davis & Orioli, booksellers, London, Catalogue 36 (February 1923), no. 10 (£20); Edward Duff Balken of Pittsburgh, PA; his bookplate and his MS 23; Maggs Bros., Catalogue 542 (1930), no. 144 and pl. (£135); Catalogue 555 (1931), no. 255 and pl. XCI; acquired in May 1931 from Maggs by Harvard College Library, now **Cambridge, MA, Harvard University, Houghton Library, MS Lat 241.**

**EDB 25:** Gregory the Great, *Homilies*. de Ricci & Wilson, II, 1679–80 (no. 17); Faye & Bond, p. 398 (no. 17); 434 (no. 11). Written in the first half of the 11$^{\text{th}}$ century at St Martin of Tournai; George Spencer-Churchill, marquess of Blandford and later 5$^{\text{th}}$ duke of Marlborough; his sale, Evans, London, 7 June 1819, lot 1960; Rev. Henry Drury (1778–1841) of Harrow; his sale, Evans, London, 19 February 1827, lot 2015; to Thomas Thorpe, booksellers, London; Phillipps MS 3373; his sale, Sotheby's, 19 May 1913, lot 547 (£31); J. & J. Leighton, booksellers, London; their Stock Book 1911–13 (21 May 1913, no. 9338 (£31); their sale, Sotheby's, 14 November 1918, lot 339 (£7/15); to Maggs Bros., Catalogue 380 (1919), no. 1668 (£12 guineas); Wilfred Voynich, booksellers, London; Giuseppe Martini, booksellers, New York; Catalogue 16 (1920), no. 12 ($750); Catalogue 17 (1921), no. 8 ($750); Catalogue 18 (1922), no. 8 ($750); Edward Duff Balken of Pittsburgh, PA; his bookplate and his MS 25; Maggs Bros., Catalogue 542 (1930), no. 35 and pl. (£500); Catalogue *555* (1931), no. 99; Phyllis W. & her father Howard L. Goodhart of New York, MS 17; his gift in November 1951 to Bryn Mawr College Library. **Bryn Mawr, PA, Bryn Mawr College Library, MS 11.**

**EDB 26**: Cicero, *Opera*. Berthold L. Ullman, 'Latin Manuscripts in American Libraries,' *Philological Quarterly*, 7 (1928), 6–8 at 7; Elisabeth Pellegrin, *Manuscrits Latins de la Bodermiana* (Cologny-Genève, 1982), pp. 95–97. Friedrich von Schennis (1852–1918); Karl W. Hiersemann, booksellers, Catalogue 471 (June 1919), no. 201a (DEM 4200); Edward Duff Balken of Pittsburgh, PA; his bookplate and MS 26; Maggs Bros., Catalogue 542 (1930), no. 145 and pl. (£135); Dr. Martin Bodmer (1899–1971); acquired presumably from Maggs; his bequest to Fondation Martin Bodmer. **Cologny-Genève, Fondation Martin Bodmer, MS Bodmer 50.**

**EDB 27**: Bible: St Luke. Lyell Catalogue, pp. 120–21. 19$^{\text{th}}$-century French pressmark: 'Yc.4' and a paper label with 'B.6'; Edward Duff Balken of Pittsburgh, PA; his bookplate and MS 27; Maggs Bros., Catalogue 542 (1930), no. 71 and pl. (£250); Catalogue 666 (1938), no. 43 (£63); Catalogue 675 (1939), no. 125 (£63); bought by James P. R. Lyell (1871–1948) from Maggs in December 1940; his bequest to Bodleian Library. **BodL, MS Lyell 43.**

**EDB A**: Jacobus de Voragine, *Legenda aurea*. de Ricci & Wilson, II, 1682 (no. 29). Thomas Thorpe, booksellers, London, Catalogue Supplement (1836), no. 646; Phillipps 9377; his sale, Sotheby's, 27 April 1903, lot 618; Giuseppe Martini, booksellers, New York; Catalogue 13 (1917), no. 31 for $250; Edward Duff Balken of Pittsburgh, PA; his bookplate; Maggs Bros., Catalogue 542 (1930), no. 72 and pl. (£210); Phyllis W. Goodhart, later Gordan & her father, Howard L. Goodhart, & her husband, John Dozier Gordan, Jr., of New York, MS 29; by descent to John D. Gordan, III, of New York. **Unlocated.**

**EDB B:** Conrad, Cistercian Abbot, *Sermones de sanctis*. de Ricci & Wilson, II, 1683 (no. 32); Faye & Bond, p. 398; Sigrid Krämer & Michael Bernhard, *Handschriftenerbe des deutschen Mittelalters* (München, 1989–90), II, 431. Carthusian abbey of St Barbara in Cologne, shelfmark: 0.117; Leander van Ess (1772–1847), *Catalogue* (1823), no. 214; Phillipps 598; his sale, Sotheby's, 6 June 1910, lot 206 (£2 guineas); Tregaskis, Catalogue 698 (1911), no. 519; Edward Duff Balken of Pittsburgh, PA; his bookplate; Maggs Bros., Catalogue 542 (1930), no. 109 and pl. (£52/10); Phyllis W. Goodhart, later Gordan & her father, Howard L. Goodhart, & her husband, John Dozier Gordan, Jr., of New York, MS 32; by descent to John D. Gordan, III, of New York. **Unlocated.**

# 9

## H. Harvey Frost's Collecting of Medieval and Renaissance Manuscripts and the 1931 Quaritch Illuminated Manuscripts Catalogue[1]

~

*A. S. G. Edwards*

It is necessary to preface this tribute to an old friend by mention of another. I first met Jeremy Griffiths in the late 1970s shortly after he began his DPhil at Oxford. We quickly became friends and I have many memories of extended lunches and dinners and of being driven very fast in his large and frequently changing cars. We shared a number of interests and planned various collaborative projects. But the often-shifting patterns of Jeremy's career that took him from graduate student to university lecturer, to publisher to manuscript cataloguer to book dealer to war correspondent, meant that on his untimely death on 14 August 1997 much of his research was left incomplete.

One interest that Jeremy and I shared was the famous *Catalogue of Illuminated and Other Manuscripts together with Other Works on Palaeography* issued by Quaritch in late 1931. We exchanged notes about the subsequent history of some of the manuscripts that appeared in it. At some point Jeremy had acquired H. Harvey Frost's copy of the catalogue in which he recorded details of his purchases; after his death I bought it from Bennett & Kerr. It provided the initial impetus to the present article.

The Quaritch *Catalogue* was unusual in form and in the extent of its content. In folio, in boards and with 66 pages of plates, including a colour frontispiece, it contained descriptions of 124 medieval and Renaissance manuscripts,

---

[1]  I am indebted for information to Dr Eugenio Donadoni, Richard Linenthal and Dr Catherine Reynolds. I am particularly grateful to Peter Kidd, who kindly pointed out several errors and who has drawn my attention to the current locations of several manuscripts. My thanks to Alex Day and Alfred Pasternak of Bernard Quaritch for giving me access to Quaritch's annotated file copy of the 1931 *Catalogue*.

divided into 'Religious Books' (nos. 1–95) and 'Secular Books' (nos. 96–124), 37 separate leaves or fragments and over 350 works to do with palaeography or other aspects of manuscript study. The assembling of a dealer's catalogue in England that included so many Western medieval and Renaissance manuscripts had few precedents or parallels in the history of bookselling.[2]

In spite of its remarkable scope and the fact that many of the manuscripts in it were modestly priced,[3] the *Catalogue* was a commercial failure when it was first issued. E. M. Dring, the member of the firm responsible for it, recalled much later that 'hardly anything was sold.'[4] The Depression years of the 1930s made buyers scarce. The only significant institutional buyer was Liverpool Cathedral Library, which bought six cheap items.[5] A few private collectors bought from it in a piecemeal way. Estelle Doheny (1875–1958) bought six manuscripts over a number of years.[6] J. P. R. Lyell (1871–1958) bought sixteen manuscripts between 1936 and 1944.[7] And occasionally others left the shelves.[8] But the majority of the manuscripts were still in stock in 1945, some having appeared in subsequent Quaritch catalogues, including some of the most expensive.

[2] One parallel is close in time. In 1930 Maggs Bros issued *The Art of Writing, 2800 B.C. to 1930 A.D … exhibiting forty styles of scripts in the languages of Europe, Asia and Africa*. It included 284 separate entries. While a large number were medieval or Renaissance Western manuscripts, as the title indicates its scope was much wider than the Quaritch *Catalogue*.

[3] Over a third of the items were under a hundred pounds: nos. 2, 5, 6, 20, 23, 26, 27, 29, 30, 32, 34, 38, 53, 54, 55, 62, 63, 64, 65, 66, 67, 69, 70, 74, 75, 79, 80, 85, 86, 89, 91, 93, 95, 98, 102, 105, 106, 109, 110, 114, 115, 118, 121, 124. Only eleven were a thousand pounds or more: nos. 9 (£1,200), 14 (£2,000), 72 (£1,000), 81 (£1,000), 94 (£8,500), 96 (£2,000), 97 (£1,500), 100 (£1,000), 113 (£1,500), 119 (£1,500), 120 (£3,250). Frost bought five of these: nos. 9, 94, 97, 100, 119, 120.

[4] 'Forty Years at Quaritch,' *The Book Collector*, Special Number (1997), 39.

[5] Five were seemingly bought shortly after the *Catalogue* appeared and another at some point in or after 1937. See below, Appendix, nos. 23, 34, 53, 80, 85 and 73.

[6] Nos 14 and 78 were purchased through Alice Millard in 1932; no. 52 was purchased in 1939 and nos. 81, 88 in 1940 and 97 in 1948 from Rosenbach.

[7] See below, Appendix, nos. 17, 29, 64, 66, 79, 91, 105, 106, 114, 124 all now in the Bodleian Library; he also owned six other manuscripts (nos. 22, 25, 32, 57, 97, 100, 123) that he subsequently sold; see below Appendix for details.

[8] For example, *Catalogue* no. 1, now Boston Public Library MSS 1514, was bought by the Library in November 1938 and nos. 35 and 49, now MSS 1517 and Q. med. 88, respectively, in December 1939.

There is no full account of Henry Harvey Frost's life and facts are not easy to retrieve.[9] He was born on 13 August 1873 and subsequently achieved considerable success as an industrialist. He died on 30 May 1969 aged 96.[10] He appears to have turned to collecting manuscripts immediately after the Second World War, when he was in his early seventies. His activities as a collector were curtailed by failing eyesight and he seems to have mainly sold his collection to Maggs, possibly in stages, in the early 1950s, although he seems to have started to sell off some of his acquisitions earlier.[11] His was a brief but intense interlude as a collector of manuscripts.[12]

Frost's copy of the 1931 Quaritch *Catalogue* records the beginnings of his activities in this field. In it he notes his purchase of twenty-nine manuscripts. These are all marked by an 'X' in the margin opposite each catalogue description, usually in blue crayon, occasionally in pencil, sometimes with his initials in pencil 'HHF.' Ten of the items so marked are given numbers in pencil in the margins, together with the year of purchase, invariably '1945.' Thus, number 9 in the *Catalogue*, a thirteenth-century Latin Bible, is 'No. 1'; no. 24, an early fifteenth-century Sarum Breviary is 'No. 2'; no. 28, an early sixteenth-century German manuscript, is 'No. 4'; no. 37, a thirteenth-century Flemish Book of Hours, Use of Liege, is 'No. 6'; no. 41, another Book of Hours, Use of Paris, is 'No. 8'; no. 58, a Sarum Hours, is 'No. 10'; no. 82, an English prayer roll, is 'No. 13'; no. 84, an early French Psalter is 'No. 15'; no. 87, a Sarum psalter is 'No. 14'; no. 116, *Modus tenendi parliamentum*, is 'No. 11'. Frost also underlined the opening lines of the description of each manuscript he bought, normally in blue crayon, including the price, unless he received a discount, in which case that price is noted in the margin. Occasionally, the discounts were deep. For example, for no. 9 he records that he paid £1,000 against a published

---

[9]   He does not figure in *ODNB*. The only obituary appeared in *The Book Collector*, 19 (1970), 379–80. It was written, but not signed, by the editor, Nicolas Barker, drawing (he has told me) on information provided by Brian Sawyer Cron. I am indebted to it here.

[10]  His death was reported in *The Times*, 2 June 1969; details of his will are in *The Times*, 7 August 1969.

[11]  For example, *Catalogue* nos. 100 and 123 reappear in Quaritch, *Descriptions of Three Miniatures Four Manuscripts and Ten Printed Books of the First Importance* (1948), as nos. 6 and 15. Frost marked them as acquisitions in his copy of the 1931 *Catalogue*; it seems likely that he resold them to Quaritch by 1948 rather than acquiring them then.

[12]  Frost also collected printed books, including, perhaps most notably, the First, Second and Fourth Shakespeare Folios, now all in the University of Toronto Fisher Library.

price of £1,200; for no. 24, £500 against £750; for no. 48, £650 against £750; for no. 82 £63 against £105; for no. 87, £120 against £200; for no. 116, £500 against £600. Overall, Frost records payments amounting to £23,339 for his manuscripts from the Quaritch *Catalogue*, including discounts. Nearly half of this sum comes from his purchase of the two most expensive items in it, nos. 94, *La Legende Dorée*, the French translation of the *Legenda Aurea* (£8,500) and 120, Petrarch's *Trionfi* (£3,250). Since the total printed asking prices for 122 manuscripts was £50,200/48/0 the significance of his purchases, even allowing for discounts, is clear.[13]

Frost's own annotated *Catalogue* provides the fullest details of his purchases. The Quaritch annotated *Catalogue* records only the purchase of three items, no. 39, 45, 46 on '30.viii. 46' to 'H. Frost' and no. 84 to 'H. C. FROST' but does not identify him as purchaser of other items. It also provides notes of reductions for nos. 39 (from £300 to £200), 45 (from £400 to £300) and 46 (from £100 to £80), discounts not recorded by Frost.

The gaps in his numbering sequence in the 1931 *Catalogue* suggest that Frost was buying elsewhere simultaneously and that his purchases from Quaritch were made in more than one stage. The full record of Frost's purchases is detailed below.

## H. Harvey Frost's Purchases from the 1931 Quaritch Catalogue

I have added such information as I have as to the prior and subsequent history of the manuscripts Frost bought from this catalogue, sometimes selectively. [14] Prices as they appear in the 1931 *Catalogue* are given in parentheses; where Frost has noted a different price paid in his copy of the Catalogue this is given separately in parentheses, in quotation marks. Frost's other notes, generally manuscript number and date of acquisition, are also given in parentheses in quotation marks. Present locations, where known, are given in bold.

---

[13] Two items (nos. 50 and 111) are noted in print in the *Catalogue* as 'SOLD' and no price is given. Allowing for Frost's discounts reduces the maximum amount that Quaritch would have received to £49043/48/0 on the basis of his notes on prices paid. But Quaritch's own annotated copy of the *Catalogue* shows that prices on many items were subsequently reduced and that trade buyers routinely received the customary 10% discount. I have not recorded here the discounted prices that appear in the Quaritch copy apart from those recorded by Frost for his own purchases.

[14] I have not attempted an exhaustive listing of all sale records, particularly where an item appeared in several catalogues from the same dealer.

The following abbreviations are used:

Boisouvray    *Manuscrits à Peintures offert à la Bibliothèque Nationale par le Comte Guy du Boisouvray* ([Paris],1961)

Ker, *MMBL III*    N. R. Ker, *Medieval Manuscripts in British Libraries III: Lampeter to Oxford* (Oxford, 1983)

*Lyell Catalogue*    A. C. de la Mare, *Catalogue of the Medieval Manuscripts Bequeathed to the Bodleian Library Oxford by James P. R. Lyell* (Oxford, 1971)

Thomas    M. Thomas, 'Nouvelles acquisitions latine et françaises du département des manuscrits de la Bibliothèque Nationale pendant les annees 1958–1964,' *Bibliothèque de l'Ecole des chartes*, 124 (1966)

9.    Latin Bible, 'Anglo-French', *c.* 1280 (£1,200) ('No. 1, 1945; £1,000').

24.    Sarum Breviary, England, early 15$^{th}$ c. (£700) ('No. 2, £500'); sold Sotheby's 19 May 1958, lot 97; purchased by William Foyle for £360; sold to the British Library before his sale at Christie's in July 2000. **BL, MS Add. 74755.**

25.    Sarum Breviary, England, 15$^{th}$ c. (£180). Quaritch, *Manuscripts (Mostly from the Collection of the late J. P. R. Lyell)*, Catalogue 699 (1952), no. 33; Sotheby's, 9 July 1973, lot 64.

27.    Fra Domenico Cavalcha, *Questo library di se chiana Specchio ...*, Italy, 15$^{th}$ c. (£25).

28.    Henry Suso, *Centum meditationes de passione domini*, Germany, early 16$^{th}$ c. (£110), ('No. 4, 1945; £105'); subsequently Quaritch, Catalogue 609 (1943), no. 481, Catalogue 629 (1945), no. 4.

37.    Book of Hours, Use of Liège, Flemish, 13$^{th}$ c. (£550), ('No. 6, 1945; £500'). Sotheby's, 2 December 1986, lot 54 (£99,000 to Fogg). Sam Fogg, *Medieval Manuscripts*, Catalogue 12 (1989), no. 9, sold to private buyer; reacquired by Fogg in 1995. **Toronto, Ontario, Art Gallery of Ontario.**

39.    Book of Hours, Use of Paris, France, early 15$^{th}$ c. (£300). Sotheby's, 12 December 1967, lot 22 (£700, W. F. Hammond); Christie's, 16 July 1969, lot 140 (to Charles Traylen, Guildford).

41.    Book of Hours, Use of Paris, France, mid-15$^{th}$ c. (£275), ('No. 8, 1945'). Thomas, 172–73; F. Avril & N. Reynaud, *Les manuscripts a peintures en France 1440–1520* (Paris, 1993), no. 99. **BNF, n.a. lat. 3113.**

44.     Book of Hours, Use of Rome, France, 15th c. (£275). Quaritch, *Catalogue of English and Foreign Bookbindings*, December 1921, no. 112; Albert Natural; sold Sotheby's, 23 June 1987, lot 114 (to Tenschert), and again Sotheby's 6 July 2000 (Ritman sale), lot 47; Bonhams & Butterfields, 26 June 2003, lot 3012. Sotheran's, *Illumination: The Decorated Book Through the Middle Age*s (London, 2009), no. 3.

45.     Book of Hours, Use of Rome, late 15th c. (£400).

46.     Book of Hours, Use of Rome, Flemish, *c.* 1480 (£100).

47.     Book of Hours, Use of Rome, Lyons, 1484 (£500). Subsequently in the possession of Robert Lehman, New York; see Sandra Hindman et al., *The Robert Lehman Collection IV Illuminations* (New York, 1997), pp. 38–39 ('its whereabouts are unknown'); sold Christie's, 19 November 2003, lot 25, where the Frost provenance is not noted. **New York, NY, Morgan Library & Museum, MS M.1162**.

48.     Book of Hours, Use of Rome, France, *c.* 1490 (£750) ('£650'). Thomas, 176–77. **BNF, MS n.a. 3117**.

57.     Sarum Hours, late 15th c. (£400); reacquired by Quaritch, *Manuscripts (Mostly from the Collection of the late J. P. R. Lyell)*, Catalogue 699 (1952), no. 81. Sold to Gordon H. Craine in 1955; his sale, Christie's, 6 June 2007, lot 26 (£45,600 to European trade).

58.     Sarum Hours, late 15th c. (£300), ('No. 10, 1945'): Faye & Bond, p. 216, no. 139 (cited as 'MS 1563') bought 1956 from Maggs. **Boston, MA, Boston Public Library, MS q. Med. 139**.

60.     Book of Hours, Use of 'Tullensem (?)', France, late 14th c. (£120).

77.     Office of the Virgin, Use of Rome, Italy, *c.* 1490 (£100); bought from Maggs in 1955. Faye & Bond, p. 215, no. 136 (cited as MS 1560), Jeffrey F. Hamburger, William P. Stoneman, Anne-Marie Eze, Lisa Fagin Davis & Nancy Netzer, eds, *Beyond Words: Illuminated Manuscripts in Boston Collections* (Boston, MA, 2016), no. 229. **Boston, MA, Boston Public Library, MS q. Med 136**.

82.     Prayer roll, England, *c.* 1430 (£105) ('No. 13 £63'); also in Quaritch Catalogue 609 (1943), item 500; sale at Swann Galleries in New York *c.* 1981; L. C. Witten, Catalogue 18 (1983), no. 22 ($8,500); sold to the New Haven bookseller C. A. Stonehill, thence to Toshiyuki Takamiya, Tokyo. See Raymond Clemens, Diane Ducharme, Emily Ulrich, *A Gathering*

*of Medieval Manuscripts: The Takamiya Collection at the Beinecke Library* (New Haven, CT, 2017), p. 31. **Beinecke, MS Takamiya 112.**

83.    Prayers, France, 17th c. (£225).

84.    Psalter, France, early 13th c. (£200) ('No. 15 £180').

87.    Sarum Psalter, England, *c.* 1440 (£200), ('No 14 £120'); Benjamin R. Donaldson, sold Christie's (New York), 25 September 1981, lot 6. **Tokyo, Japan, Keio University Library, MS [120X@582@1].**

94.    Jacques de Voragine, *La legende dorée*, Montpensier, 1480 (£8,500); Pierre Beres, Catalogue 60 (1963), no. x; Beres, Bulletin 20, p. 7; Hilary Elizabeth Maddocks, 'The Illuminated Manuscripts of the *Légende Dorée*,' PhD thesis, University of Melbourne, 1990, p. 17, reports this as 'untraced'.

97.    Baptista Agnese, Portolan, Italy, 16th c. (£1,500). Quaritch, *Manuscripts (Mostly from the Collection of the late J. P. R. Lyell*, Catalogue 699 (1952) no. 2, again for £1,500. Estelle Doheny sale, Christie's (New York), 8 November 1987, lot 177 (£600,000).

100.    John Lydgate, *Fall of Princes*, England; 15th c. (£1,000); subsequently Quaritch, *Manuscripts (Mostly from the Collection of the late J. P. R. Lyell)*, Catalogue 699 (1952) no. 28, in both again for £1,000; then Robert H. Taylor. Don C. Skemer, *Medieval & Renaissance Manuscripts in the Princeton University Library*, 2 vols (Princeton, NJ, 2013), I, 404–07. **Princeton, NJ, Princeton University Library, MS Taylor 2.**

115.    Pomponius Mela, *De Cosmographia*, 16th c. (£21) then Thomas E. Marston. Barbara A. Shailor, *Catalogue of Medieval and Renaissance Manuscripts in the Beinecke Rare Book and Manuscript Library Yale University, Volume III: Marston Manuscripts* (Binghamton, NY, 1992), pp. 144–47. (The Frost provenance is not noted.) **Beinecke, MS Marston 76.**

116.    *Modus tenendi parliamentum*, England, late 15th c. (£600) ('No 11 £500'); for its post-Quaritch provenance see K. L. Scott's description in James R. Tanis, ed., *Leaves of Gold: Manuscript Illumination from Philadelphia Collections* (Philadelphia, PA, 2001), p. 228. Faye & Bond, p. 450. **Philadelphia, PA, Philadelphia Free Library, MS LC.14.9.5.**

119.    Petrarch, *Trionfi*, Italy, 16th c. (£1,500). Previously Quaritch, Catalogue 371 (1922), no. 1239. Sotheby's, 23 June 1992 (collection of Philip Robinson), lot 75; Sotheby's 22 June 2004, lot 73 (£190,000). **Private collection in France.**

120.    Petrarch, *Trionfi*, Italy, *c.* 1400 (£3,250); previously Sotheby's 29 July 1929, lot 6; acquired from Harvey Frost by Maggs in 1955; Faye & Bond, p. 199 (where number is given as '571'); Dorothy Miner, 'Since de Ricci – Western Illustrated Manuscripts Acquired Since 1934. A Report in Two Parts. Part II,' *Journal of the Walters Art Gallery*, 31–32 (1968–69), 102–118 (with plates); Dennis Dutschke, *Census of Petrarch Manuscripts in the United States* (Padova, 1986), pp. 49–55. **Baltimore, MD, Walters Museum, MS W.755**.

123.    Valerius Maximus, Italy, late 14<sup>th</sup> c. (£750); previously Sotheby's, 30 January 1920, lot 121; subsequently, Quaritch, *Descriptions of Three Miniatures Four Manuscripts and Ten Printed Books of the First Importance* (1948), no. 15, and Quaritch, *Manuscripts (Mostly from the Collection of the late J. P. R. Lyell)*, Catalogue 699 (1952) no. 139, in both again for £750. Susan M. Hansen, 'Valerius Maximus, Facta et Dicta Memorabilia,' *The Indiana University Bookman*, 17 (1988), 76–80 (where the Frost provenance is not noted). **Bloomington, IN, Indiana University, Lilly Library, MS Poole 23**.

As I have said, Frost's purchases from the Quaritch *Catalogue* seem to have taken place in more than one phase, starting in 1945. It was possibly at around this time, although dates of acquisition or sources for the most part cannot be established, that he purchased a number of other manuscripts. These are noted below.

## Other manuscripts owned by H. Harvey Frost

(i)    **Cambridge, Fitzwilliam Museum, MS 1-1956**: Latin Psalter, Germany, 13<sup>th</sup> c.; Maggs Catalogue 816 (1953), item 390. Donated by T. S. Blakeney in 1956. Francis Wormald and Phyllis M. Giles, *A Descriptive Catalogue of the Additional Illuminated Manuscripts in the Fitzwilliam Museum Acquired between 1895 and 1979*, 2 vols (Cambridge, 1982), II, 514–15.

(ii)    **Tokyo, Japan, Keio University Library, MS [120X@1149@2@1]**: Cicero, *De finibus*, subsequently Brian Cron MS 20; see Richard Linenthal, 'Medieval and Renaissance Manuscripts: A Handlist of the Collection of B. S. Cron,' *The Book Collector*, 54 (2005), 557.

(iii)    **New York, NY, Morgan Library & Museum, MS G.18**: Latin Bible, England, St Augustine's Canterbury, 13<sup>th</sup> c.; sold to Frost at Sotheby's, 27 July 1948, lot 358 for £250. Faye & Bond, p. 394; William S. Glazier. N. R. Ker, *Medieval Libraries of Great Britain*, 2<sup>nd</sup> edn (London: Royal

Historical Society, 1964), p. 45; John Plummer, *The Glazier Collection of Illuminated Manuscripts* (New York, 1968), p. 23, no. 26.

(iv) **New York, NY, Morgan Library & Museum, MS G. 19**: Psalter, England, Hyde Abbey, 14th c.; purchased in 1952 from Maggs. Faye & Bond, p. 394; William S. Glazier. N. R. Ker, *Medieval Libraries of Great Britain*, 2nd edn (London, 1964), p. 104; John Plummer, *The Glazier Collection of Illuminated Manuscripts* (New York, 1968), p. 28, no. 35.

(v) **London, Victoria & Albert Museum, National Art Library, MS L/1953/1792**: The 'Eleanor of Toledo Hours'; Florence, 1541; Rowan Watson, *Western Illuminated Manuscripts: A catalogue of works in the National Art Library from the eleventh to the early twentieth century*, 3 vols (London, 2011), II, 851–57, no. 165. Watson reports (p. 852) that the manuscript was offered to the National Art Library 'through Maggs for £275 in 1952 and was presumably acquired for about this amount in 1953.'

(vi) **London, Victoria & Albert Museum, National Art Library, MS L/1952/1769**: Macrobius, *Saturnalia*; see Rowan Watson, *Western illuminated manuscripts: A catalogue of works in the National Art Library from the eleventh to the early twentieth century*, 3 vols (London, 2011), II, no. 105, pp. 559–61; Watson reports (p. 559) that it was 'bought by the V&A from Frost in 1952.'

(vii) **Cambridge, MA, Harvard University, Houghton Library, MS Typ 252**: Prayer Book, Tours, early 16th c.; Faye & Bond, p. 274, Roger Wieck, *Late Medieval and Renaissance Manuscripts 1350–1525 in the Houghton Library* (Cambridge, MA, 1983), p. 44, Jeffrey F. Hamburger, William P. Stoneman, Anne-Marie Eze, Lisa Fagin Davis & Nancy Netzer, eds, *Beyond Words: Illuminated Manuscripts in Boston Collections* (Boston, 2016), no. 113; bought by Philip Hofer from Maggs in 1952.

(viii) **Cambridge, MA, Harvard University, Houghton Library, MS Typ 260**: Psalter, Italy, 12th c.; bought by Philip Hofer from Maggs in 1952. Faye & Bond, p. 274; Jeffrey F. Hamburger, William P. Stoneman, Anne-Marie Eze, Lisa Fagin Davis & Nancy Netzer, eds, *Beyond Words: Illuminated Manuscripts in Boston Collections* (Boston, 2016), no. 28.

(ix) **Beinecke, MS Marston 55**. Nonius Marcellus, *De compendiosa doctrina*; Faye & Bond, p. 70, no. 55; then Thomas E. Marston. Barbara A. Shailor, *Catalogue of Medieval and Renaissance Manuscripts in the Beinecke Rare Book and Manuscript Library, Volume III: Marston Manuscripts* (Binghamton, NY, 1992), pp. 104–05. The manuscript has Frost's bookplate on the front pastedown, together with that of C. H. St John Hornby; bought by L. C. Witten, the New Haven dealer, in 1955 from Davis & Orioli.

(x)    **Boston, MA, Boston Public Library, MS q. Med. 132**: Psalter, Flanders, 14th c. Faye & Bond, p. 215, no. 132. Probably Maggs Catalogue 816 (1953), no. 158 (£250).

(xi)    **BNF, MS n.a. lat. 3101**: Latin Bible, Paris, 14th c.; Boisouvray, no. 3; Thomas, 162–63.

(xii)    **BNF, MS n.a. lat. 3111**: Hours, Use of Rome. Paris (?), 15th c. Boisouvray, no. 16; Thomas, 170–77.

(xiii)    **BNF, MS n.a. lat. 3114**: Hours, Use of Rome. France (Loire), 15th c. Boisouvray, no. 20; Thomas, 173–74.

(xiv)    **BNF, MS n.a. lat. 3115**: Hours, Use of Paris. 15th c. Boisouvray, no. 21; Thomas, 174–75.

(xv)    **BNF, MS n.a. lat. 3116**: Hours, Use of Rome. Bourges (?) *c.* 1500. Boisouvray, no. 27; Thomas, 175–76.

(xvi)    **BNF, MS n.a. lat. 3121**: Hours, Use of Rouen. Gand (?), late 15th c. Boisouvray, no. 25; Thomas, 179–80.

(xvii)    **BNF, MS n.a. lat 3113**: Hours of Michel Jouvenel des Ursin and Yolande de Montberon. Tours, 15th c. Boisouvray, no. 18; Thomas, 172–73.

(xviii)    **BNF, MS n.a. lat. 3117**: Hours, Use of Rome. Angers (?), *c.* 1480. Boisouvray, no. 23; Thomas, 176.

(xix)    **Brussels, Belgium, Bibliothèque Royale, MS IV. 35**: Hours, Use of Rome. This manuscript is part of a dismembered volume, which included Brussels, Royal Library of Belgium, MS IV 375 and Chicago, IL, Newberry Library, MS 39. Jan Deschamps, *Middelnederlandse handschriften* (Brussels, 1970), no. 70, pp. 205–06.

(xx)    **C. King**: Hours of the Virgin, Use of Paris; formerly John Ruskin; last sold at auction, Sotheby's, 13 July 1977, lot 73, as 'The Property of Mrs Sven Ericsson'; for full details of provenance see James S. Dearden, *The Library of John Ruskin* (Oxford, 2010), pp. 172–73.

(xxi)    **Hours of the Virgin, (Molé Hours), Use of Troyes**; sold Sotheby's, 13 July 1977, lot 76 as 'The Property of Mrs Sven Ericsson' to Laurence Witten; William H. Schab Gallery, bought by Alexandre P. Rosenberg on 27 March 1979; Christie's, New York, 23 April 2021, lot 9 from the collection of Elaine and Alexandre Rosenberg (MS 5); currently (2023) on offer online for $3,630,000 by Les Enluminures.

(xxii)  **Plutarch,** *Vies de Romulus et Caton d'Utique*: sold Sotheby's, 7 December 2010, *Medieval Manuscripts from the Collection of Frederick, 2nd Lord Hesketh*, lot 3; sold for £505,250. Subsequently Sotheby's (Paris), *La Bibliothèque de Pierre Bergé*, 14 December 2018, lot 836; sold for €671,780.

(xxiii)  **Hours, Use of Paris (?)**: bought by Frost, Sotheby's, 12 July 1948, lot 58; sold Christie's, 25 November 1992, lot 26, for £154,000 to a private European collector.

(xxiv)  **Book of Hours, Use of Rome**; sold, from the collection of Sir James Caird, who acquired it *c.* 1953 at Christie's, 25 November 1992, lot 27 (£93,500); now owned by the same private European collector as xxiii above.

(xxv)  **Ovid,** *Heroides*, France, early 16th c. Sold to Maggs by Frost in the early 1950s; subsequently in the collection of William Stuart Spalding (d. 1961) and his wife Angele Louise Maggi (d. 2005); Sotheby's, 6 December 2005, lot 38.

(xxvi)  **BNF, n.a. fr. 28800**: *Les Douze Cesars en Mignature*, France, *c.* 1510. Quaritch, *A Catalogue of Books and Manuscripts issued to Celebrate the One Hundredth Anniversary of the Firm of Bernard Quaritch 1847–1947*. Subsequently acquired by Frost; see Desmond Flower, *A Thousand Years of French Books: Catalogue of an Exhibition of Manuscripts, First Editions and Bindings* (Cambridge, 1948), p. 15, no. 15; Sotheby's, 2 December 1992, lot 41; Jorn Gunther, *Timeless Treasures: A Selection of Illuminated Manuscripts, Miniatures and Early Printed Books*, Brochure No. 14 (2013), no. 22.

(xxvii)  **BNF, MS Néerl. 129**, Suffering and Miracles of St Catherine: J. Deschamps, *Middelnederlandse Handschriften uit Europese en Amerikaanse Bibliothekene* (Brussels, 1972), no. 72.

(xxviii)  **Processional of Isabeau de la Tour**; southern France, early s. xvi: Sotheby's, 6 December 1983, lot 78: £20,000 to John Howell (previously bought privately from Frost by Maggs)

(xxix)  **Book of Hours, Use of Paris**: property of Sir James Caird, who acquired it *c.* 1953; sold Christie's, 25 November 1992, lot 25; £82,500 to Heribert Tenschert; his *Leuchtendes Mittelalter 5, Psalter und Stundenbuch in Frankreich vom 13. bis zum 16. Jahrhundert: mit Miniaturen von den Meistern der Historienbibel des Duc de Berry*, Katalog No. 30 (1993), no. 12.

(xxx)    **Latin Bible**, Paris, 13<sup>th</sup> c., with Frost's bookplate; Foyle sale, Christie's, 11 July 2000, lot 19 (£75,000), to French trade.

(xxxi)    **Book of Hours, Use of Sarum**, Paris, 1532: with Frost's bookplate; bought from Harry Levinson in 1954; Christie's (New York), The Cornelius J. Hauck Collection, 27 June 2006, lot 134, where the Quaritch provenance is not noted (sold for $262,400).

(xxxii)    **Anthoine de Villars, Heures Royalles**, on paper, Paris 1690. See Desmond Flower, *A Thousand Years of French Books: Catalogue of an Exhibition of Manuscripts, First Editions and Bindings* (Cambridge, 1948), p. 16, no. 17.[15]

The manuscripts Frost owned seem all to have been bought between 1945 and the very beginning of the 1950s. To have assembled a collection of nearly sixty manuscripts, some of very considerable quality, in little more than five years is an achievement that warrants recording.

---

[15]   Frost also contributed a printed book to this exhibition; see Flower, no. 225.

## Appendix

Current or Latest Locations for Other Manuscripts in the 1931 Quaritch Catalogue (excluding fragments).

Unattributed quotations below come from Quaritch's annotated copy of the *Catalogue*; prices are those recorded in this copy, sometimes different from those given in the published catalogue.

1.    *Ars moriendi*, France, 15$^{th}$ c. (£180). Faye & Bond, p. 208, no. 87; acquired November 1938. **Boston, MA, Boston Public Library, MS 1514.**

2.    Athanasius, Italy. 15$^{th}$ c. (£63). Bought by Quaritch in Mostyn sale, Sotheby's 13 July 1920, lot 6. **Cambridge, MA, Harvard University, Houghton Library MS Typ. 289.**

3.    Augustine, *Opera varia*, Germany, 11$^{th}$ c. (£225). Faye & Bond, p. 431, no. 2. Frederick B. Artz, Oberlin College, Ohio.

4.    St Basil, *Contra ebrios*, Italy, 15$^{th}$ c. (£105). Sold to Tamarro de Marinis 13 November 1939; Diana Norman, 'The Patronage of Cardinal Oliviero Carafa,' unpublished PhD thesis, Open University, 1989, p. 105, fn. 44: 'present whereabouts unknown'

5.    Bernard of Clairvaux, *De precepto et dispensacione*, 12$^{th}$ c. (£25). Sold 21 December 1940 to Bodleian Library. **BodL, MS Lat. th. f. 15.**

6.    Latin Bible, England, 11$^{th}$ c. (£80). Sold 15 January 1943 to lord Kenyon.

7.    Latin Bible, England (Waltham Abbey), 13$^{th}$ c. (£210). Sold to E. G. Millar, 15 March 1933; sold by Millar, Sotheby's, 18 June 1962, lot 112 (£1,500 to Francis Edwards); Sotheby's, 12 December 1967, lot 52 to Dawson's of Pall Mall. **London, Passmore Edwards Museum, MS LD PEM AD/AY0001.**

8.    Latin Bible, Anglo-Norman, late 13$^{th}$ c. (£400). Sold 14 July 1942 to 'G. Baker.'

10.   Latin Bible, France, 13$^{th}$ c. (£200). Sold 23 November 1940 to 'Miss Warrington.' According to Quaritch's annotated *Catalogue* 'Retd for a better one;' sold 10 April 1943 to lord Kenyon; according to annotated *Catalogue* 'Bought back & sold to Bradfer-Lawrence 1951;' Les Enluminures, Catalogue 1 (10 December 1998), no. 1 (£111,250); Christie's, 20 November 2002, lot 17.

11.   Latin Bible, France, late 13$^{th}$ c. (£325).

12.     Latin Bible, France, 13<sup>th</sup> c. (£350); from Mostyn sale, 13 July 1920, lot 6 (to Quaritch). Sold to a private collector in March 1943: Sotheby's, 2 December 1997, lot 54 (collection of Neil Phillips), where *Catalogue* number is given as '2'.

13.     Latin Bible, Italy and France, 13<sup>th</sup> c. (£150). Sold 11 March 1943 to 'Goldstern.'

14.     Latin Bible, Italy, 13<sup>th</sup> c. Sold 15 October 1932 to Alice Millard for Estelle Doheny (£2,000); Doheny sale, Christie's, 2 December 1987, lot 150 (£176,000 to Tenschert); J. R. Ritman sale, Sotheby's, 17 June 2003, lot 8.

15.     Latin Bible, Italy, 13<sup>th</sup> c. (£280). Sold 15 January 1943 to lord Kenyon; his sale, Sotheby's 26 January 1959, lot 61 (£540 to Nixon); Sotheby's, 12 December 1967, lot 25.

16.     Latin Bible, Italy, 13<sup>th</sup> c. (£200). Dawson's of Los Angeles; Marguerite Smith, Librarian, Zion Research Foundation; Endowment for Biblical Research (Boston) MS 1; see Judith H. Oliver, *Manuscripts Sacred and Secular* (Boston, 1985), pp. 27–31; de-accessioned 1998; Sam Fogg, *Illuminated Manuscripts* (London, 1999), no. 6. **Private collector in Toronto.**

17.     Wycliffite New Testament, 15<sup>th</sup> c. (£450). Bought by J. P. R. Lyell, October 1943; *Lyell Catalogue*, 56–58. **BodL, MS Lyell 26.**

18.     St Luke Gospel, Normandy, 12<sup>th</sup> c. (£120). Princeton, NJ, Princeton University, Scheide Library M 10.

19.     St Bonaventure, Psalter, early 17<sup>th</sup> c (£180). Sold to H. P. Kraus, 31 March 1943.

20.     Breviary, 'secundum consuetudinem Monachorum congregationis de observantia Sanctae Justinae,' 15<sup>th</sup> c. (£50). To J. P. R. Lyell, 25 July 1939; Quaritch, *Manuscripts (Mostly from the Collection of the late J. P. R. Lyell),* Catalogue 699 (1952), no. 32 (£70).

21.     Breviary, Use of Paris, late 15<sup>th</sup> c. (£110). Sold 17 July 1941 to 'Miss Burgess.'

22.     Breviary, Use of Rome, France, 15<sup>th</sup> c. (£140). Sold to J. P. R. Lyell (1933) and subsequently resold; Bradfer-Lawrence MS 27; sold Sotheby's, 6 July 2006, lot 51. **Private collection in Canada.**

23. Breviary, England, 14th c (£45); Ker, *MMBL III*, 197–98. **Liverpool Cathedral, MS 37.**

26. Breviary, late 14th c. (£21).

29. *Passio Sancti Eustachii*, Haimo on the Apocalypse; Germany, 12th c. (£75). To Lyell July 1942; *Lyell Catalogue*, 201–02. **BodL, MS Lyell 65.**

30. *Gebete der Passion*, Germany, c. 1500. (£65). Sold 7 April 1943 to 'G. Street.'

31. Gregory the Great, *Homilies*, etc., England, 13th c. (£450). Formerly in the collection of John Ruskin: for details of earlier provenance see James S. Dearden, 'John Ruskin, the Collector', *The Library*, 5th series 21 (1966), 133–34 (no. 14); Christie's 22 June 1988, lot 212; Sotheby's 6 July 2000 (Ritman sale), lot 4 (£80,000 to Quaritch). **York, Minster Library, MS Add. 770.**

32. Henricus der Dissen, *Viridiarum in psalmos*, Germany, 15th c. J. P. R. Lyell, 25 July 1939 (£15 guineas); J. A. Abbey, J. A. 5095; Sotheby's, 19 June 1967, lot 1818A (£750 to Breslauer).

33. St Jerome, *Vite di sancti Padri*, Italy, 15th c. (£500). Sold March 1940 to 'J. K. Moffitt.'

34. Breviary; Germany, 14th c. (£20); Ker, *MMBL III*, 182–84; **Liverpool Cathedral, MS 22.**

35. Hours, Use of Britanny, 15th c. (£225). Bought December 1939. Faye & Bond, p. 209, no. 90. **Boston, MA, Boston Public Library, MS 1517.**

36. Hours, Use of York (Bolton Hours), England, 15th c. (£550); N. R. Ker and A. J. Piper, *Medieval Manuscripts in British Libraries IV: Paisley to York* (Oxford, 1992), 786–91. **York, Minster Library, MS Add. 2.**

38. Hours, Use of Paris, c. 1300. (£65). Sold 23 October 1939 to 'Miss J. Burgess.'

40. Hours, Use of Paris, mid 15th c. (£250). Sold March 1940 to J. K. Moffitt.

42. Hours, Use of Paris, 15th c. (£300). To William Foyle, 12 October 1943 (£2,000); Foyle sale, Christie's, 11 July 2000, lot 44; Christie's, 11 July 2002, lot 31, to European trade.

43. Hours, Use of Rome, Italy, 15th c. (£700); Berkeley, CA, University of California, Berkeley, MS 030.

49.    Hours, Use of Rome, late 15th c. (£500). Bought December 1939. **Boston, MA, Boston Public Library MS q. Med. 88.**

50.    Hours, Use of Rome, *c.* 1500. Purchased by Philip Hofer, 17 May 1931 for £750. See Harvard College Library, *Illuminated & Calligraphic Manuscripts* (Cambridge, MA: Harvard College, 1955), p. 31, no. 111, where the date of acquisition is erroneously given as '1929.' **Cambridge, MA, Harvard University, Houghton Library MS Typ. 251H.**

51.    Hours, Use of Rome, France, early 16th c. (£250). Sold 22 June 1938 to Heilbron; Sotheby's, 11 December 1984, lot 69; Sotheby's, 20 June 1995, lot 93 (unsold).

52.    Hours, Use of Rome, Italy, early 17th c. (£850). Estelle Doheny sale, Christie's 2 December 1987, lot 179 (£82,500 to Kraus; the Quaritch provenance is not noted). **Baltimore, MD, Walters Art Museum, MS W.494.**

53.    Sarum hours, 14th/15th c. (£60); Ker, *MMBL III*: 194–97; **Liverpool Cathedral, MS 36.**

54.    Sarum hours, England, 15th c. (£84). Christie's, 11 July 2018, lot 47.

55.    Sarum hours, England, 15th c. (£60).

56.    Sarum Hours (Knyvett Hours), 14th c. (£350). Sold to H. P. Kraus in 1941 when it had 129 leaves and 32 full-page miniatures. Kraus sold it to Rudolf Wien who had broken it up by early 1948 when the first separate leaves appeared at auction: see (i) below. Kraus subsequently reacquired 5 leaves that appear in his *The Eightieth Catalogue* (1956), nos. 16a–e. These are the subsequent histories of individual leaves, with information on individual miniatures recorded:[1]

(i)    1 leaf, Sotheby's, 9 February 1948, lot 215 (St Bartholomew); subsequently J. Pope-Hennessy; his sale Christie's, New York, 10 January 1996, lot 4);

(ii)   1 leaf, Sotheby's, 23 June 1986, lot 50;

(iii)  1 leaf (St Saturninus). Bought from Wien by Eric Korner (his no. 20); his sale, Sotheby's 19 June 1990, lot 32 (to Fogg, £9,500 hammer); subsequently Bernard Breslauer; see W. Voelkle and R. Wieck, *The Bernard H. Breslauer Collection of Manuscript Illuminations* (New York,

---

[1]    I am indebted to the online description of Morgan Library MS M.1213 for some of the information here.

1992), no. 17; see Peter Kidd, *The McCarthy Collection, Volume II: Spanish, English, Flemish and Central Europeam Miniatures* (London, 2019), 18c. **MacCarthy BM 1434**;

(iv)    1 leaf (All Saints), Christie's 25 June 1997, lot 3; Kidd, *The McCarthy Collection*, 18b. **McCarthy BM 1106**;

(v)    3 leaves: (St Andrew, and St Martin + a text leaf). Bought from Warren Howell in 1974 (previously owned by Mark Lansburgh). **Los Angeles County Museum of Art, acc. 74.100.1–3**;

(vi)    1 leaf (St Bartholomew), Sotheby's, 9 February 1948, lot 215, to Sir John Pope-Hennessy; his sale, Christie's, 10 January 1996, lot 4 (to Fogg); Kidd, *The McCarthy Collection*, 18a. **MacCarthy BM 1055**;

(vii)    1 leaf (St George), bought from Wien by Eric Korner in 1952 [along with St Saturninus]; his sale, Sotheby's 19 June 1990, lot 32; resold in second Korner sale, Sotheby's 7 July 2009, lot 107 (to Fogg £22,000); subsequently stolen;

(viii)    1 leaf (St Christopher), Sotheby's, 18 June 2002, lot 20 (fol. 34); Sotheby's, 2 July 2013, lot 29; Kidd, *The McCarthy Collection*, 18d. **MacCarthy BM 2413**;

(ix)    2 leaves (St James and St Matthew): Sarasota, FLA, John & Mabel Ringling Museum, nos. 730–31;

(x)    1 leaf (St Nicholas), H. P. Kraus, *The Eightieth Catalogue* (1956), 16a; Sotheby's, 21 June 1994, lot 25; Bruce Ferrini, Catalogue 3 (1995), no. 18; on deposit Denver Art Museum (Berger Collection); Sotheby's, 23 May 2017, lot 18 (£13,000, Les Enluminures);

(xi)    1 leaf (St Barnabas?) Bruce Ferrini, Catalogue 3 (1995), no. 19; on deposit Denver Art Museum, Berger Collection; Sotheby's, 23 May 2017, lot 19 (£10,000 desk);

(xii)    1 leaf (St Catherine): 'bought by Martin Nachman, probably in the early 1950s; inherited by his daughter-in-law, Marian Nachman' according to the Morgan online records. (Gift of an anonymous donor). **New York, NY, Morgan Library & Museum, MS M.1213**;

(xiii)    1 leaf (St Thomas), H. P. Kraus, *The Eightieth Catalogue* (1956), 16b ($185). Sold to Bruce Ferrini (now New York, private collection);

(xiv)    1 leaf (St Helena), H. P. Kraus, *The Eightieth Catalogue* (1956), 16c ($185); in possession of Sam Fogg, December 2021;

(xv)     1 leaf (St Lazarus), H. P. Kraus, *The Eightieth Catalogue* (1956), 16d ($185); New York, private collection;

(xvi)    1 leaf (St Edmund) H. P. Kraus, *The Eightieth Catalogue* (1956), 16e ($185); New York, private collection;

(xvii)   1 leaf (Thomas Becket); owned by University of South Carolina English professor George C. Brauer (d. 1993); now University of South Carolina Early MS 248;[2]

(xviii)  7 leaves (calendar), Lark Mason Associates, New Braunfels, TX, 12 October 2021, lot 6091729;

(xix)    1 leaf (St Stephen), *Les Enluminures*, Catalogue 5 (1996), no. 38.

59.      Hours, 'Use of Traiectensem (?),' 15th c. (£150); Eduardo Sandoz; Bruce Ferrini, Catalogue 1 (1987), no. 65; Sotheby's 21 June 1988, lot 103; Christie's, 7 July 2010, lot 38 (£140,000, to Dr Jörn Günter Rare Books; offered in 2012 for €390,000).

61.      Hours of the Cross, Flemish, *c.* 1500. (£140). Sold 19 November 1931 to 'Miss Clarke.'

62.      Innocent III, Bull, 1202. (£18 guineas). Sold 5 August 1939 to 'Sir F. Radcliffe.'

63.      Innocent IV, Bull, 1248 (£15 guineas).

64.      Johannes Halgrinus de Abbatsvilla, *Sermones dominicales*, England, 13th c. (£45). Bought by J. P. R. Lyell, May 1942; *Lyell Catalogue*, 13–14. **BodL, MS Lyell 6.**

65.      Lactantius, *Institutes*, France, 1537 (£75). **Harvard University, Houghton Library MS Typ. 12.**

66.      Office of the Dead &c, England, 15th c. (£45). Bought by J. P. R. Lyell, July 1939; *Lyell Catalogue*, 52–54. **BodL, MS Lyell 24.**

67.      *Memoria Sancti Christophori*, French, mid 15th c. (£30). Sold 17 July 1941 to 'Miss Burgess.'

68.      Missal. Use of Cluny, France, 15th c. (£450). Sold 15 March 1941 to H. P. Kraus; Sotheby's, 11 July 1966, lot 264.

---

2    See Scott Gwara's 'Review of Sales,' *Manuscripts on my Mind*, no. 22 September 2017, p. 7.

69.    Missal, Dominican Order, Bohemia (?), 14th c. (£15). Sold 20 May 1936 to 'Rev. Fox Bartrop.'

70.    Missal, Use of Lyons. (£95). 'Turned out'. Sold Sotheby's, 3 April 1939, lot 108 (reacquired by Quaritch, £48).

71.    Missal, Use of Paris, France, 14th c. (£275). Quaritch, Catalogue 613 (1943), no. 20.

72.    Missal, Use of Rome, Italy, 15th c. (£1,000); previously Sotheby's 4 May 1926, lot 162. Purchased by Viscount Lee of Fareham, June 1946 for £750. Francis Wormald & Phyllis M. Giles, *A Descriptive Catalogue of the Additional Illuminated Manuscripts in the Fitzwilliam Museum Acquired between 1895 and 1979*, 2 vols (Cambridge, 1982), II, 504–06. **Cambridge, Fitzwilliam Museum 6-1954.**

73.    Office, England, 15th c. (£250); subsequently in Quaritch Catalogue 532 (1937), no 403; see Ker, *MMBL III*, 165–66. **Liverpool Cathedral, MS 6.**

74.    Office, Use of Rome, Italy, 15th c. (£30). Sold Sotheby's 24 June 1980, lot 96 for £1,800. Broken up after October 1988; 52 leaves in Richard & Mary Rouse Collection at UCLA; R. H. and M. A. Rouse, *Medieval and Renaissance Manuscripts of the UCLA Library Special Collections I The Richard and Mary Rouse Collection* (Tempe, AZ, 2017), pp. 89–90. **Los Angeles, CA, UCLA Rouse MS 40.**

75.    Office BVM, Italy, *c.* 1480 (£90). Sold 3 August 1943 to '[Heinrich] Eisemann.'

76.    Office BVM, Italy, 15th c. (£100); Peter Kidd *Books of Hours Livres d'Heures* (AVOA, 2015), no. 3 (offered at £54,000)

78.    St Paul, Epistles, France, 16th c. Alice Millard ,for Estelle Doheny (£275); previously Holford sale, Sotheby's 29 July 1929, lot 5; Doheny sale, Christie's, 2 December 1987, lot 173 (£29,700 to Kraus); Ritman sale, Sotheby's 6 July 2000, lot 55.

79.    Petrus de Herenthals, *Expositio psalterii*; Richardus Ullerston, *Expositio psalmorum*; England, 15th c. (£90). Bought by J. P. R. Lyell, July 1942; *Lyell Catalogue*, 44–45. **BodL, MS Lyell 20.**

80.    Pontifical, 13th/14th c. (£60); Ker, *MMBL III*, 200–05. **Liverpool Cathedral, MS 39.**

81.   Pontifical, Italy, 14<sup>th</sup> c. (£1,000). Sold in 1940; Estelle Doheny sale, Christie's 2 December 1987, lot 156 (£99,000). Comites Latentes (Geneva).

85.   Psalter, England (?), 13<sup>th</sup>/14<sup>th</sup> c. (£42); Ker, *MMBL III*, 185–87. **Liverpool Cathedral, MS 27**.

86.   Psalter, Germany, 14<sup>th</sup> c. (£84). Sold 4 September 1943 to '[Heinrich] Eisemann.'

88.   Psalter, Sarum, England, 15<sup>th</sup> c. (£500); Estelle Doheny, Christie's, 2 December 1987, lot 162, where the Quaritch provenance is not noted; (£57,200 to Quaritch). **Museum of the Bible, Washington, DC, MS 000372**.

89.   Psalter, Italy, 15<sup>th</sup> c. (£80); owned in the 1920s by Chester Beatty; sold in 1944 to Brian Cron for £60: his first purchase; reacquired after his death in 2002 by Quaritch; see Richard Linenthal, 'Medieval and Renaissance Manuscripts: A Handlist of the Collection of B. S. Cron,' *The Book Collector*, 54 (2005), 557–58. **Tokyo, Japan, Senshu University**.

90.   Rabanus Maurus, *Commentary on the Book of Numbers*, France, 12<sup>th</sup> c. (£130). *Olim* Phillipps 3724; inherited by Julia Burgess in 1935, and subsequently acquired by University of Oregon Libraries. **University of Oregon, Burgess Collection MS 9**.

91.   Monastic Rules &c; England, 15th c. (£70). Bought by J. P. R. Lyell October 1936; *Lyell Catalogue*, 43–44. **BodL, MS Lyell 19**.

92.   Thomas Aquinas, *Quaestiones de potentia dei*, Germany, 15<sup>th</sup> c. (£100). Gift of Neil Ker. **BodL, MS Lat. th. c. 34**.

93.   *Vigiliae mortuorum*, Italy 15<sup>th</sup> c. (£80). Faye & Bond, p. 267. **Cambridge, MA, Harvard University, Houghton Library, MS Typ. 180**.

95.   *Wycliffite Ten Commandments*, England, 15<sup>th</sup> c. (£80); **Cambridge, MA, Harvard University, Houghton Library, MS Eng 738**.

96.   Baptista Agnese, Portolan, Italy, 1559 (£2,000). Subsequently Quaritch, Catalogue 613 (1943), no. 1.

98.   Alanus de Insulis, *Anticlaudianus*; Bernardus Sylvestris, *Megacosmos*; Symmachus, *Liber Epistolarum* (£50). Sold 26 September 1931 to E. P. Goldschmidt and subsequently broken up.

99.   *Album amicorum,* of Philip Hainhofer, 17th c. (£550). Christie's (New York), The Cornelius J. Hauck Collection, 27 June 2006, lot 263, where the Quaritch provenance is not noted (sold for $2,368,000).

101.  Bracton, *De legibus et consuetudinibus Angliae,* England, 13th c. (£450). Previously Sotheby's 30 March 1931. **New York, Columbia Law Library, MS B72.**

102.  Britton, Treatise on English Law, early 14th c. (£30). Sotheby's 3 April 1939, lot 45. Faye & Bond, p. 40. **New York, P. D. & J. D. Gordan MS 70.**

103.  Richard de Bury, *Philobiblon,* Netherlands, 15th c. (£105). Subsequently H. P. Kraus, Catalogue 60 (1952), no. 11.

104.  Cassiodorus, *Epistolae,* Italy, 16th c. (£600). Previously Yates Thompson, sold Sotheby's 3 June 1919, lot 19; subsequently J. A. Abbey MS J. A. 2579, his sale, Sotheby's, 1 December 1970, lot 2895; J. J. G. Alexander & A. C. de la Mare, *The Italian Manuscripts in the Library of Major J. R. Abbey* (London, 1969), pp. 161–63. **Geneva, Fondation Bodmer, Cod. Bodmer 46.**

105.  Cicero, *Orationes,* Italy, 15th c. (£60). Bought by J. P. R. Lyell, August 1944; *Lyell Catalogue,* 251–53. **BodL, MS Lyell 83.**

106.  *Collectanea de forestis,* England 15th c. (£50). Bought by J. P. R. Lyell, April 1943. *Lyell Catalogue,* 75–80. **BodL, MS Lyell 32.**

107.  Bastiano Foresi, *Triumpho delle virtu,* Italy, 15th c. (£200). Bought in 1940 by William King Richardson. **Cambridge, MA, Harvard University, Houghton Library, MS Richardson 46.**

108.  *Guy of Warwick,* England, 14th c. (£850). Formerly in the collection of Norman Holmes Pearson, his MS 270. **Beinecke, MS 591.**

109.  Ranulf Higden, *Polychronicon,* England, 14th c. (£75). Previously Ecton Hall sale, Sotheby's 24–25 July 1924, lot 110 (£30 to Quaritch); subsequently Quaritch, Catalogue 613 (1943), no. 12.[3]

110.  Hugutio of Pisa, *Verborum derivationes,* France, 13th c. (£40); Quaritch, Catalogue 520 (1936), no. 766; sold to Bodleian Library, 21 December 1940 (£20). **BodL, MS Lat. misc. d. 70.**

---

[3]  It is not mentioned in James Freeman's valuable doctoral thesis, 'The Manuscript Dissemination and Readership of the 'Polychronicon' of Ranulph Higden, *c.* 1330 – *c.* 1500,' Cambridge University, 2013. I am indebted to Dr Freeman for confirming that this manuscript cannot currently be traced.

111.   Esther Inglis, *Les six vingts et six quatrains de Guy de Faur*, England, 17th c.; see A. H. Scott-Elliott & Elspeth Yeo, 'Calligraphic Manuscripts of Esther Inglis (1571–1624): A Catalogue,' *Papers of the Bibliographical Society of America*, 84 (1990), 1–86 (73, no. 84). **Cambridge, MA, Harvard University, Houghton Library, MS Typ. 347.**

112.   *Lancelot du lac*, France, 14th c. (£600). Previously Guy Folliot sale, Sotheby's 12 May 1930; sold in 1939. P. Saenger, *Catalogue of the Pre-1500 Western Manuscript Books at the Newberry Library* (Chicago, IL, 1989), p. 37. **Chicago, IL, Newberry Library, MS f. 21.**

113.   *Roman de la Rose*, France, 15th c. (£1,500). Bought by Carleton R. Richmond (1887–1975); see Walters Art Gallery, *Illuminated Books of the Middle Ages and Renaissance* (Baltimore, MA, 1949), p. 30, no. 76 (where the Quaritch provenance is not noted); sold Ader-Tajan-Picard (Paris), 16 December 1988, lot 152.

114.   Martinus Polonus and prose *Brut*, England, 14th c. (£70). Bought by J. P. R. July 1939; *Lyell Catalogue*, 39–42. **BodL, MS Lyell 17.**

117.   *Testament de Amyra Sultan Nichemedy*, South Netherlands, *c.* 1482 (£500); previously W. H. Ingilby, his sale Sotheby's 21 October 1920, lot 5; Don C. Skemer, *Medieval & Renaissance Manuscripts in the Princeton University Library*, 2 vols (Princeton, NJ, 2013), I, 383–85. **Princeton, NJ, Princeton University Library, MS Garrett 168.**

118.   Bartholomaeus Paiellus, *Prefatio in laudes et res gestas divi Venetorum principis...*; Italy, 15th c. (£25); *Les Enluminures*, online catalogue 2006, no. 242.

121.   Poggio Bracciolini, *Oratio in facta laudem illustrissime*; Italy, 15th c. (£25). **Bryn Mawr, PA, Bryn Mawr College Library, Phyllis Gordan MS 40 (formerly 149).**

122.   Portolan, Italy, *c.* 1560 (£120).

124.   Maffeo Vegio, *Laudensis de verborum significantione...*; Italy, 15th c. (£42); to J. P. R. Lyell, May 1942; *Lyell Catalogue*, 223–24. **BodL, MS Lyell 74.**

# Index of Manuscripts

~

Sale catalogues are recorded here when they provide the last recorded location for a manuscript.

# General Index

This is essentially an index of proper names, place names and titles. Categories of books, such as Bible, Book of Hours or Breviary have not been included.

# Tabula Gratulatoria

~

Benjamin L. Albritton
Jesús Alturo i Perucho
Marlene Arnese
Sébastien Barret
Terry Belanger
Emily R. Blair
Harry W. Blair
Julia Boffey
Timothy Bolton
Elizabeth A. R. Brown
Debra Taylor Cashion
Orietta Da Rold
Jack L. Davis
Lisa Fagin Davis
Christopher de Hamel
Albert Derolez
M. J. Driscoll
Martha Westcott Driver
Consuelo W. Dutschke
A. S. G. Edwards
Mirella Ferrari
Lucy Freeman Sandler
Joan M. Friedman
David Ganz and Susan Rankin
Basie Bales Gitlin
Barbara Haggh-Huglo
Jeffrey F. Hamburger
Katherine Storm Hindley
Farley P. Katz
Peter Kidd
Kevin Kiernan
William M. Klimon
Marie Elena Korey

Andrew Kraebel
Kenneth Kreitner
Michael P. Kuczynski
Wolfram Latsch
Richard Linenthal
Sandy Malcolm
Irene Malfatto
James H. Marrow
Outi Merisalo
David L. Vander Meulen
Andrew T. Nadell
George Ong
Eef Overgaauw
Caroline Palmer
Laura Pani
Ronald Patkus
Eleanore E. Ramsey
Lynn Ransom
Caroline Schimmel
William Schipper
David Solo
Joe Stadolnik
William P. Stoneman
Alison Stones
Thomas Sullivan
Jean-François Vilain
Linda Ehrsam Voigts
Teresa Webber
Roger S. Wieck
Anders Winroth
N. Kıvılcım Yavuz
Justin Zaremby

Rare Book School at University of Virginia
Senate House Library Palaeography Room